Identity and Digital Communication

This comprehensive text explores the relationship between identity, subjectivity and digital communication, providing a strong starting point for understanding how fast-changing communication technologies, platforms, applications and practices have an impact on how we perceive ourselves, others, relationships and bodies.

Drawing on critical studies of identity, behaviour and representation, *Identity and Digital Communication* demonstrates how identity is shaped and understood in the context of significant and ongoing shifts in online communication. Chapters cover a range of topics including advances in social networking, the development of deepfake videos, intimacies of everyday communication, the emergence of cultures based on algorithms, the authenticities of TikTok and online communication's setting as a site for hostility and hate speech. Throughout the text, author Rob Cover shows how the formation and curation of self-identity is increasingly performed and engaged with through digital cultural practices, affirming that these practices must be understood if we are to make sense of identity in the 2020s and beyond.

Featuring critical accounts, everyday examples and analysis of key platforms such as TikTok, this textbook is an essential primer for scholars and students in media studies, psychology, cultural studies, sociology, anthropology, computer science, as well as health practitioners, mental health advocates and community members.

Rob Cover is Professor of Digital Communication at RMIT University, Melbourne, Australia.

Identity and Digital Communication

Concepts, Theories, Practices

Rob Cover

Routledge
Taylor & Francis Group

LONDON AND NEW YORK

First published 2023
by Routledge
4 Park Square, Milton Park, Abingdon, Oxon OX14 4RN

and by Routledge
605 Third Avenue, New York, NY 10158

Routledge is an imprint of the Taylor & Francis Group, an informa business

British Library Cataloguing-in-Publication Data
A catalogue record for this book is available from the British Library

Library of Congress Cataloging-in-Publication Data
Names: Cover, Rob, author.
Title: Identity and digital communication : concepts, theories, practices / Rob Cover.
Description: Milton Park, Abingdon, Oxon ; New York, NY : Routledge, 2023. |
Includes bibliographical references and index. |
Identifiers: LCCN 2022042318 (print) | LCCN 2022042319 (ebook) |
ISBN 9781032283968 (hardback) | ISBN 9781032283951 (paperback) |
ISBN 9781003296652 (ebook)
Subjects: LCSH: Online identities. | Internet–Social aspects. |
Digital communications. | Online social networks.
Classification: LCC HM851 .C695 2023 (print) |
LCC HM851 (ebook) | DDC 302.30285–dc23/eng/20220914
LC record available at https://lccn.loc.gov/2022042318
LC ebook record available at https://lccn.loc.gov/2022042319

ISBN: 978-1-032-28396-8 (hbk)
ISBN: 978-1-032-28395-1 (pbk)
ISBN: 978-1-003-29665-2 (ebk)

DOI: 10.4324/9781003296652

Typeset in Bembo
by Newgen Publishing UK

For Jeff Williams, who shares with me our various, entangled journeys and practices of performing identities (online and elsewhere).

Contents

Acknowledgements

The thinking, research, investigation and engagement that helps build any book is grounded in conversations with many people, occurring in both online and offline settings.

I would like to thank my colleagues, peers and students at RMIT University, including particularly Noor Aiman Rizal, Josie Gleave, Star Welis, Leesa Corbo, Lisa Waller, Lukas Parker and Linda Brennan.

Thinking about digital communication, identity and belonging has benefitted enormously from feedback from colleagues in the *Digital Ethnography Research Centre* at RMIT University, particularly Tania Lewis, Annette Markham, Ingrid Richardson, Anna Hickey-Moody, Sophie Hartley and James Meese, and from members of the *Cultural Studies Association of Australasia*, particularly Holly Randell-Moon, Ashleigh Haw, Debbie Rodan, Tinonee Pym, Amy Dobson and Panizza Allmark.

Finally, I thank the people I spend time with in online settings such as Quora, Facebook, Instagram and elsewhere (particularly during the COVID years) for providing so much insight into the affordances of digital communication in shaping who we are and what we might be.

1 Identities

Subjectivity and selfhood in a digital world

1.1 Introduction

Identity is one of the most complex facets of everyday life. It is a topic about which each of us is sometimes certain and self-assured and at other times experience a sense of anxiety and vagueness about who we are, how we represent ourselves and how we are perceived by others. At the same time, identities are subject to political struggles, such as when people argue about who is 'really' English or 'properly' an American, when politicians heatedly debate whether transgender people should be permitted to play sports in the gender with which they identify or when cultural mechanisms underrepresent those racially coded as 'other' on national television programmes. Much of our everyday lives involves having to undertake activities that relate to a sense of self-identity, whether that is carrying a drivers' licence, showing a passport to cross a border, using a personal key card to access an apartment or office building, logging in to a computer's operating system or a workplace server, building and maintaining a social media presence, putting up a profile on LinkedIn or providing our credentials to prove we are who we say we are to do a spot of phone banking.

The 'practice' of identity in everyday life also intersects with every facet of belonging. We belong to families, and much of the time are identified by the names (including surnames) they have given us. Most (not all) 'belong' to a nation-state, and part of that involves identity papers, citizenship documents and various degrees of national pride and participation in national events as an aspect of identity. We belong to schools and some-times wear uniforms that identify that belonging at first sight. Or we belong to univer-sities and have various practices of identity, such as graduating with diplomas and degrees which include our name and the stamp, seal or imprimatur of the university that has re-coded our identity from someone without a degree to a bachelor, a master, a doctor or other standing. We belong to workplaces, and through that belonging, our identity is formed in such a way that we attend to work, whether in a workplace or through video-conferencing from home, where our very sense of self is entwined with the work culture for several hours a day—and very often spills over into our non-working lives as well. It is therefore surprising that we don't talk more about identity, selfhood and belonging since its practice runs across so much of our everyday waking lives.

At the same time, however, it is perhaps not so surprising that we don't like to draw too much attention to it, since when we do, it calls upon us to ask difficult questions about ourselves: who am I? Who are we? How do we fit in with others? Am I normal? Can I prove who I say I am today? Whenever we look too closely at how identities are formed, we risk the possibility of showing that what feels authentic and essential to

DOI: 10.4324/9781003296652-1

ourselves is not always quite that secure, and a very close examination shows to ourselves all the little slippages in identity that make the ways we identify seem less real and meaningful. Nevertheless, by gaining the intellectual and conceptual skills to unpack what identity means, how it intersects with contemporary culture, how it frames our practices of belonging and feeling 'normal' and how it is constructed in the communication forms and languages we use to describe selfhood and belonging, we are often more empowered to find more ethical ways to live, to be more inclusive, to embrace diversity, to reduce fears of those who are different and to be less anxious about who we are.

I have been researching and writing about identity for around 15 years, particularly in relation to minorities, migrants and diverse genders and sexualities, and have often been focused on the role played by a range of everyday cultural practices in constructing how we think about and form our sense of selfhood, whether those everyday practices are watching television, engaging with physical space, desiring in particular ways, using social media, being a fan of a book series or conceptualising our belonging through concepts of population and community. Across this time, I've learned three main things about identity:

- There is no 'true' approach or theory that gives us the big picture of identity; no 'god principle' that reveals how identity, subjectivity and selfhood works; and no single philosophy that tells us a truth about identity. Rather, there are many different ways in which to think about identity, and most of those approaches or theories have something valuable to consider. It doesn't matter that there is no singular, all-encompassing theory—we benefit by coming at the big questions of identity from multiple angles.
- Identities change—they are a process and always in flux. Because that can be destabilising of our sense of self, our relationships and our forms of belonging, we tend to use practices of narrative and storytelling to 'play down' those changes and the kinds of inconsistencies in self-identity those changes reveal—often because that is easier than embracing the fluidity and change of performing identities over time. We re-read our own memories to make sense of the past, present and future *as if* it is always authentic, linear, innate and unchanging. And we use the many communication tools available to us to produce those stories, including particularly the tools of digital communication which have often proven to be well adapted to that form of identity storytelling.
- Identity is at the very core of how we live a liveable life and how we treat each other ethically and without violence. The extent to which we perceive ourselves as interdependent with others or in adversity with others can drive the kind of life we live and the ways of treating each other ethically. Digital communication has not always fostered a sense of identities as interdependent but, sometimes, has been misused to encourage aggressive difference and hostility. Wider cultural practices of reifying individuality and freedom feed into this and sometimes facilitate ways of being in the world that are unethical, that sustain inequalities and that leave some lives as less liveable than others.

With these three points in mind, it makes sense to have a greater understanding of the relationship between digital communication and identity, allowing us to navigate the contemporary social world and the future developments in media and communication; to be more informed about ourselves and our own identities and therefore potentially better citizens; and to help us keep in mind just how important ethical belonging is to living a liveable life.

1.1.1 Identity and digital cultures

There is no denying that in the 2020s, we live in a media-saturated world. The media and communication tools we engage with—films, television, social media, zoom, news, books, algorithmically generated feeds, artificial intelligence home devices—play a more-and-more central role in how we 'do' identity and how we think about selfhood. Media and communication are not of course the only influence on identity or, to use a more theoretical term, 'constitutive force' which means the social processes that give us the language, frameworks and examples by which to make sense of identity. Education, family upbringing, religion, informational guidance and the less obvious forms of language in how our bodies work and what they do also play important roles in constituting our identities. *However*, once we pay attention to the saturation of contemporary culture with screen-based devices and computer-generated communication, we can see that media, communication and digital engagement are increasingly at the centre of the knowledge we use to construct our identities and give meaning to selfhood.

There are three key facts about the centrality of media and digital communication in how they constitute our identities and sense of selves:

1. Media and digital technologies are at the very centre of almost all of our everyday communication now, whether that's being with a family watching television together, getting news updates on a feed on a mobile device, using study platforms via a browser or communicating about ourselves through video and images on TikTok or Instagram;
2. There is a lot of information at our fingertips (e.g., Wikipedia, broadcast news, social media feeds), and the ways in which much of what crosses our screens is in feeds generated by algorithms rather than our own choices. However, we are not *passive* consumers of information. Rather, much of our media engagement means encountering and making use of stories. Films, television series and social media pages are common forms of storytelling. Even a Wikipedia page tells a story about a topic, and news is constructed very much through narrative storytelling—this happened, then this happened, then this caused this to happen and so on. Stories align with identity because we perceive ourselves in our own story, and we often take on-board the practices of storytelling we have learned elsewhere to make sense of and describe who we are. We are active users of communication to tell our own stories in ways which shape how our identities are represented.
3. Media storytelling provides us with the tools, knowledges, frameworks and discourses (ways of speaking), to understand various categories, codes and demarcations of identity, including particularly around race, ethnicity, gender, sexuality, physical and mental ability. It is central to the production of stereotypes which tend to reduce a complex person to just one facet of identity or belonging. And it conditions the way we talk about inclusivity and diversity. And it provides opportunities for different kinds or storytelling that may give us new perspectives on selfhood and how to live.

To understand contemporary identity fully, then, we need to be able to make sense of the media and communication forms that play such a significant role in constituting identity. And if we truly want to appreciate how the relationship between media, communication and identity works, then we need to stay up-to-date with the fast-changing forms and practices of digital communication in our everyday lives. This includes approaching it as the setting in which our relationships and communication play out and making sense of the substantial shifts over the past few generations whereby digital communication, online interactivity, debates about privacy, the use of algorithms, the norms of digital engagement, the practices of online gaming, the reliance on artificial decision-making tools and the increasing disinformation online all play a very central part in how we identify, how we talk about identities and how our personal identities are articulated under the gaze of one another.

Sometimes, this means recognising the collapse of any idea that the 'Internet' is separate from embodied life or 'real' life (no communication happens without involving bodies in some way); paying close attention to new advances in digital communication that condition and adjust the way we enact our identities in front of others (such as the massive increase in the use of video-conferencing since the COVID-19 pandemic began); and making sense of the role of algorithms in conditioning the kinds of discourses, languages and concepts we encounter online (and *what* we encounter and do not encounter) that give meaning to our sense of selfhood. Given the increasing ubiquity of digital technologies for communication, there has been some impact on the ways in which we 'do' identity and the ways in which identities are made intelligible to us. However, that is not to say that digital communication technologies and online worlds have wholly changed the methods by which identity is enacted in everyday ways. Rather, what it means is that there is a clear, if very complex, articulation between the different forms and ways of communicating about ourselves and explaining our 'selves' to others, such as between spoken communication and creating TikTok content.

1.1.2 About this book

This book provides an accessible explanation about the role digital communication plays in constituting our identities, in shaping our debates about identity and belonging and how new digital practices sometimes play a role in upsetting or undoing identity norms. Each chapter explores different aspects of digital communication, from social networking to authenticity to deepfake videos to artificial decision-making practices, helping to keep us up-to-date with some of the remarkable advances in digital communication in everyday settings and what those advances mean for how we perform and think about identity. This book is written for students, for fellow scholars, media and communication professionals, health practitioners, community advocates and interested members of the community so that we can all share in the necessary work of navigating the intersection between complex theories of identity and selfhood and the exciting and sometimes anxiety-provoking advances in digital media and communication.

This book is therefore written for several different groups of readers to make sure we are all 'on the same page' about some of the debates and theories of the relationship between identity and digital communication. In that context, it should be read for five things:

- The need for everyone to have some reliable knowledge of the range of ways we theorise, discuss and know about identity and belonging and the role played by our participation in digital cultures;
- The role of digital media in advancing storytelling, particularly how we tell stories about ourselves and each other, about our communities and society, and how storytelling becomes more complex and convoluted in online settings;

- For media practitioners, gaining a sense of the importance of the professional work we do when we communicate and produce digital content and the impact that may have on the practices of belonging and the well-being of target audiences and those we seek to engage online;
- For health, mental health and well-being practitioners, to help guide the necessary work of understanding how clients and colleagues' identities and practices of belonging are formed and played out in the context of digital media and how complexities in communication sometimes create anxieties for how we are represented and engage with each other;
- And for those studying the world, whether as sociologists, humanities scholars, cultural studies researchers, literature specialists, applied scientists or people who are keen to participate independently in the study of meaning, having access to a clear and concise primer about identity and digital culture relevant to the 2020s.

This book begins by presenting theories of identity and adapting those for the era of digital communication. It is argued that identity is not only expressed through social relationships but increasingly through the conditioning of those relationships by social network platforms. It accounts for the role of the body as the 'fleshy connector' between systems, platforms and selves, particularly in the representation of the body visually online and the interface of the body and the digital through activities like gaming, online sexual expression, video-conferencing and selfies. The advent of the deepfake adds further dimensions to the question of identity online: The deepfake is software which relies on machine learning to produce very convincing fake videos of people, whether inserting an actor into a scene in which she never acted, making a politician appear to give a speech that was never given or an everyday person appear in pornographic content. Understanding what the future of computer-generated imagery and video means for the representation of the self (and for identity fraud) cannot be dismissed if we are to really make sense of the online self into the 2020s.

While the Internet was hailed as the setting *par excellence* of globalisation, recent regulation, online practices and digital cultures have worked to re-nationalise digital culture, creating an added layer of the global self as also articulated once again as a national citizen or subject. While the hopes of early adopters of online communication were that it would bring about interpersonal cooperation, collective intelligence and peaceful communication, the ongoing presence of cyberbullying and the recent increase in incivility online (from hate speech to pile-ons to exclusionary trolling) force us to ask what happens to identity when some users are actively and violently excluded from online participation and what this might mean for the future of public figures, identities and influencers who rely on digital communication to engage with the world. The further development of algorithms in conditioning the content, materials, images and ideas we encounter online has an effect on how we make sense of identity, selfhood and relationships, both making available some ways of engaging and consuming and making other practices and knowledges unavailable. At the same time, artificial decision-making and support or assistive digital applications open questions around agency, self-agency and the capability to navigate the complex world of relationships and sociality. Finally, this book addresses the persistent re-assertion of demands for authenticity over digital fakery—using the recent example of TikTok in which authentic identities are represented through creative uploads of dagginess, everydayness and the mundane alongside the high-end creative arts.

Overall, this book seeks to present an introduction, a starting point, for navigating the complexities of digital communication and identity from different angles, aiming to demonstrate that while identity and digital cultures are complex settings of *both* creative social engagement and sometimes painful or violent demands for conformity to norms or exclusion, there is no turning back from the infusion of digital culture in our lives. Any belief that identity operates today as it did in the pre-digital era is rooted only in a nostalgia that ignores our everyday communicative and social lives as we live them increasingly through or alongside the digital.

To start ourselves off, the next three sections provide some background on the different ways in which we can talk about, theorise and recognise identities and how those theories of identity change in relation to the developments in digital communication—from the early Internet 'cyber' identities approaches to the everydayness of Web 2.0 and social media. This chapter ends with a brief summary and chapter-by-chapter breakdown of the rest of this book.

1.2 Making sense of identity

At its most simple, identity usually refers to the set of traits, beliefs, appearances, experiences, memories, attitudes and behaviour that characterise a person—what makes a person seem to themselves unique and individual but also related to other people in our everyday belonging and social participation. Identity is inseparable from a concept of *cultural identity*, which is how a person perceives themselves (or is perceived by others) in relation to a range of categories and demarcations, such as ethnicity, gender, sexuality, class affiliations, social generation groups, shared histories and so on. And these all involve practices of *identification* to varying degrees, meaning there is always a process of communication, reading, interpreting and engaging that operates across different settings, not always consciously. I often like to refer to these as "coordinates" of identity (Cover 2016), meaning that the full range of demarcations, categories, experiences, beliefs and traits are ways in which we are multiply *oriented,* and that therefore identity is practised as a process of trying to shore up that complexity and articulate ourselves as coherent and intelligible.

At the same time, identity is always *relational*. This means that the processes of identification and articulation occur in relation to others through acknowledgements of similarity and difference (including politically problematic practised of 'us' versus 'them'). Relationality means our identities are formed in contexts that are not entirely in our control but are set by others. No person is fully formed individually, and no person lives in this world without a social relationship with others at some part of our lives. We engage with others sometimes by subjection to them (hence the related term: *subjectivity*) and sometimes in ways that are unconscious to ourselves (occurring in the *psyche*). At other times, we deliberately seek to transgress the boundaries those categories set for us, attempting to be something even more unique than we already are, even if that risks being perceived as marginalised or becoming socially excluded.

Finally, it should be noted that identity is always a *process*. How we navigate those complex coordinates is part of the process, and we often use practices of *storytelling* and *narrative* to make ourselves appear—whether to ourselves or others—as coherent and unified human beings. Stories are an important part of doing identity, because they are a mechanism to fend off criticisms of incoherence. For example, if I were an ardent vegetarian (and this were a major part of my *identity*, my self-conscious *subjectivity* and how I *represent* myself), I would appear to be an incoherent subject if I was suddenly eating a steak at a dinner. Under the surveillance or 'gaze' of others, I would be forced to explain or 'confess' *what am I*. And to respond to that surveillance and the social requirement for a confession, I will need to tell a story or provide a narrative that connects one with the other. I might explain that I was never quite that ardent a vegetarian and sometimes ate meat. Or I might tell the story of how I was a vegetarian for some time but recently was told by a medical practitioner that I have insufficient iron in my diet. Or I might explain how I only eat meat on special occasions or in restaurants. Those answers might be enough to restore my coherence and identity as a unified subject, although there may be further questions. Conversation is the setting through which we traditionally undertake that storytelling that connects the past, present and future of selfhood, although of course much of that storytelling now happens in digital settings, such as a Twitter feed or conversational responses to an Instagram post.

If we are going to explore identity, subjectivity and the setting of digital communication, the starting point is knowing a little about the range of theories and philosophies of identity so that we have, available to us, a few 'lenses' by which to assess the relationship between identity and digital culture. This section provides an overview of some of the most significant theories of identity to emerge in the late twentieth century, and to be refined in the twenty-first century is the critical account of subjectivity. The most important thing to acknowledge here is that there is no one, singular or 'true' theory of identity. Rather, different scholarship from different historical periods have discussed identity in a range of ways. Although that may seem to *undo* identity despite how very real and important it feels to ourselves, knowing about the theories available is valuable because it provides us with a 'toolkit' to do some useful investigation, analysis and assessment of how the practice of identity changes in relation to digital technologies and communication forms. Here, I discuss the philosophic notion of identity discussed by Descartes; liberal-humanist ideas of the unitary self (which is still the dominant approach to talking about identity today); Marxist approaches that argue identities are the product of 'relations of production' (the economic, ownership and labour structures in a society) and other economic factors; psychoanalytic theories that see identities as emerging from the psyche and the unconscious, postmodernism and consumerist approaches to identity; and finally poststructuralist theories that argue identities are not 'real' things we possess but are necessary fictions conditioned by language.

1.2.1 The origins of an idea of identity

Modern identity emerged as a concept in Western Europe during the fifteenth and sixteenth centuries, culminating in what we refer to as the 'humanist' idea of the subject as a free and autonomous individual in the eighteenth-century era of Enlightenment. This is the most common idea about identity outside scholarship, art and philosophy and the one that is most familiar to us in everyday speech. Humanist notions of subjectivity provide the conceptualisation of *self-identity* and *subjectivity* with certainty, truth and presence. Central to this conceptualisation and our everyday and 'common-sense' approach to identity and selfhood is René Descartes' (1596–1650) fifteenth-century notion of *cogito ergo sum* (Latin for "I think, therefore I am"), which operates as a first principle for the idea of an 'I' as a conscious and reasoning individual in which thought or 'mind' is given preference over corporeality and bodily sensations (Descartes 1968).

This notion of the autonomous, coherent, unified self was extended and solidified by numerous writers and thinkers over several centuries. These include the European liberal tradition that is found in the work of John Locke (1632–1704). Locke posited the idea of the human being as a liberal and free individual with some early concepts of rights. Jean-Jacques Rousseau (1712–1778) argued that the human subject was a self-same and knowing individual grounded in nature, while the philosopher Immanuel Kant (1724–1804) equated identity and consciousness. While each of these three trends emerged in slightly different times, they are part of what we sometimes refer to as an Enlightenment era approach to identity. The Age of Enlightenment is broadly considered the period starting around 1750, although it has its roots in the fifteenth and sixteenth centuries. The Enlightenment was an intellectual movement that had an impact on politics, governance, philosophy, science, literature, reading and many aspects of everyday life. It included concepts about knowledge and how we know the world and ourselves, putting forward the idea that 'reason' was the primary way of knowing things and arguing for systematic, scientific and evidence-based approaches to determine meaning, which includes using the evidence available to the senses.

These ideas seem, of course, very familiar to us today, because contemporary society and its key institutions (universities, government, the courts and the judiciary, education, the idea that the 'nation-state' is a good way to organise the world and so on) are built on Enlightenment notions of reason and rationality. And these govern how—in our everyday, shared and pedestrian sense—we perceive our identities. That is, from an Enlightenment perspective, we *can* know ourselves, we can determine aspects about ourselves by measurement and reflection and we can determine through reason that we are unique individuals with rights, responsibilities and desires. Society, then, is represented as that which is comprised of individuals, and the individual remains the core foundation on which that society is perceived to be built.

As valuable as such an approach to identity may be, Enlightenment thinking is also recognised as being very problematic. The primacy of the individual in much Enlightenment use today is sometimes seen as a framework that ignores inequalities or places responsibility for disenfranchisement on individuals themselves. Enlightenment thinking did not always appreciate the idea that human beings are rational and reasonable creatures to all persons, often excluding non-Europeans and women from being seen as rational. Late nineteenth-century and twentieth-century philosophies therefore actively critiqued such Enlightenment thinking, particularly focusing on questions over socioeconomic inequalities; gender; the place of the psyche and the unconscious; and—later—the role of institutions, language and culture in setting norms that sustain those inequalities. These critiques, then, led to alternative ways of approaching identity and subjectivity.

1.2.2 Marxist accounts of identity

Although the notion of the unitary, autonomous, coherent and essentialist subject remains the most common and ordinary understanding of identity in our everyday lives, theories and philosophies emerging throughout the twentieth century put this notion of identity in question and rejected the idea of human subjectivity as self-contained, unified beings who could know and understand their own conditions of identity. One of the most significant in the nineteenth and twentieth centuries was Marxist theory, and this was a very influential theory on social and media/communication scholarship in the second half of the twentieth century until about the 1980s.

Marxist theory refused to recognise the subject as a 'conscious' and self-knowing individual subject with agency over its own identity. Rather, Marxism attributed to it a 'false consciousness.' What that meant was that a dominant ideology about how society is structured obscured the *reality* of the conditions of class, particularly among the working classes (Curran et al. 1982). Classical Marxism worked within an 'economic determinist' perspective—that is, the economic structure (or 'base') of society conditioned the cultural practices across that society (or 'superstructure'). Here, individuals in *capitalist* societies are infused with false consciousness that allows the ruling class (those who own the 'means of production,' i.e., the profit-making companies, businesses, factories, etc.) to exploit the working classes (which is everyone else who is not an owner of the means of production) without us rising up in revolution.

From this perspective, the self-knowing, free subject of liberalism was considered part of that false consciousness. Rather than having a self-identity as an individual with rationally knowable desires, Marxist theory understands that people in fact are *not* able to access or truly know themselves or their conditions because without becoming conscious of the economic structure of society (through Marxism) a person cannot recognise how they are shaped by economic factors rather than having agency over themselves. From a Marxist perspective, the only way of overcoming this is to gain a class consciousness and thereby recognise that one's identity is built not on individuality as a worker but on a shared history of oppression and exploitation as a class.

Marxist approaches to identity are, of course, far more complex than can be described in a few paragraphs, as there are many different approaches and facets within Marxism. To give just one example, the structuralist-Marxist critique of identity and subjectivity undertaken by Louis Althusser (1971) questioned the economic determinist element while leaving some aspects of classical Marxist theory intact. While he argued that liberal idea of a universal individual subject was mythical, he showed that it was not merely a false consciousness determined by capitalist *economies*, but the core institutions of society (what he called "Ideological State Apparatuses") that 'interpellated' subject into incorrectly perceiving themselves as self-knowing (subject in the individual identity sense) and simultaneously *subjecting them to* social institutions (in the sense of political subjection). He compared ideology to the analogy of a policeman who 'hails' a person with "Hey, you there!" whereby hailed persons 'turn around' and in the act of turning becomes a subject because they recognise themselves as the *subject of* the hail. In being subject to ideology, self-identity is produced, inculcating in us values, preferences, attitudes, desires and ways of being.

1.2.3 Psychoanalysis and the unconscious

In Sigmund Freud's psychoanalytic critique of the late nineteenth and early twentieth centuries, we saw a wholly different approach to identity and subjectivity emerge. Psychoanalysis was popular among theorists and scholars through much of the twentieth century and provided the study of media and communication with a number of new ways in which to understand what motivates aspects of communication and spectatorship, the production of art and the value of more avant-garde texts to helping us see how the psyche is expressed.

Freud's conceptualisation of 'the unconscious' is key to a view that differed from liberal-humanist and classical Marxist approaches. For Freud (1984), the unconscious is the processes of the human mind that include memories, desires, motivations, repressions and other aspects of selfhood that we are unable to know ourselves because the unconscious is not accessible to our conscious, knowing mind. Importantly, a Freudian perspective sees the unconscious as the setting where thoughts to which we are adverse and cannot bear to know about (such as traumatic events) are processed, alongside our instincts and drives. What the 'discovery' of the unconscious did for identity, however, suggests that not only are we never self-knowing and fully self-aware subjects (as in the liberal tradition) or subject to false consciousness (as in the Marxist tradition). Rather, our identities are fragmented into the conscious self and the unconscious self. This did not mean that the unconscious identity was fully inaccessible or unknowable to a person, however. For Freudian psychoanalysis, the unconscious reveals itself in dreams, slips of the tongue, jokes and unintentional behaviours—but it takes a trained psychoanalyst to determine their meaning for us if we wanted to more fully know ourselves or explain the anxieties and neuroses that are caused by what happens in the unconscious.

Later theorists of psychoanalysis took Freud's ideas on the role of the unconscious in identity formation and selfhood further. Among them was Jacques Lacan (1977) who extended Freud's theory by drawing on structuralist semiotics, arguing for a greater role of unconscious *desire* in forming the subject. For Lacan, there cannot be a subject without a concept of desire. From a Lacanian perspective, then, we are understood to enter into language (or 'the Symbolic') as we grow up, which further separates identity from the unconscious self that then becomes *other* to us, resulting in a subject that is always described as 'split.' For Lacan, desire occurs in the psyche as a desire for the pre-oedipal stage of connection to our mothers, a state he referred to as *jouissance* (similar to bliss). Because we cannot desire or envisage that return due to prohibition on incest (the Oedipal Complex), the subject is driven—always unsuccessfully—to seek fulfilment by shifting our desires onto what he referred to as the *objet petit a,* or the 'little o' other—that is, some other object of desire whether a sexual object, a personal goal, private wealth, acclaim or something else. Because these desires are only ever false replacements for the desire for *jouissance,* they can never be satisfied, so we go on positioning our identities through an ongoing process of desiring again and again (Grosz 1990, pp. 32–33). In that sense, the subject is split, fragmented and all the actions of the subject are always about the attempt and failure to fulfil desire.

1.2.4 Constructionist and postmodern approaches

From the 1960s and 1970s, the Enlightenment humanist notion of subjective identity was put further in question by theories of social, cultural and discursive constructionism in which the subject is not born or the result of nature but produced within the environment, language and sociality. Both building upon and rejecting the dominant psychoanalytic critique of identity, this anti-subjective structuralist and post-structuralist criticism has become the prevailing approach in critical and cultural theories of identity, although it has by no means resulted in a wholesale rejection of the Enlightenment figure of the subject in contemporary public understandings of identity.

When postmodernism emerged in the 1960s and 1970s as an artistic, philosophic and intellectual backlash to early twentieth-century modernism in art and expression, it provided new ideas about the unknowability of the very concept of identity itself. In that sense, it differed from Marxist and Psychoanalytic thinking which still saw a 'real self' somewhere, whether that was obscured by ideology creating 'false consciousness' (leaving a real that can only be accessed through class consciousness) or hidden in the psyche that can only be revealed by the work of psychoanalysis. Rather, in most postmodern and poststructuralist accounts, there is no real, only a range of meanings about identity and range of ways of perceiving it. Postmodern accounts are very useful, because they disavow the *assumptions* that led to a belief in the liberal subject as self-same, knowable, unitary and coherent and instead open the field for coming at the idea of identity from more complex angles that critique basic assumptions. That is, they argue that there needs to be more interrogation of the underlying assumptions that lead us to perceive identity and subjectivity as real.

Arguably, we live today in a postmodern culture. While I usually suggest that this is a culture marked by many of its antecedents from Enlightenment, such as our main institutions, it is also the case that it is postmodern in the sense that there is an increasingly general feeling that rational ideas such as truth, evidence and meaning are more elusive than Enlightenment thinking would argue. There are many ways in which postmodernism is discussed, and it is not by any means a unitary theory or set of theories. Some of the discussions around hyperreality that we will deal with in Chapter 4 (where we explore deepfakes) draw on postmodern theories of the philosopher Jean Baudrillard, which share certain aspects of what I describe here but also differ in meaningful ways. A critic of contemporary postmodern culture is Fredric Jameson who provides a very good account as to how identity is made to seem fluid, unknowable or possibly never real to begin with in postmodernism. Jameson argued that in a postmodern culture setting, not only is the individual liberal subject of rights, authenticity and unity consider a thing of the past, but that in many respects, it is often considered to have "*never* really existed in the first place; there have never been autonomous subjects of that type" (Jameson 1985, p. 115). For Jameson, the autonomous subject has been a "cultural mystification which sought to persuade people that they 'had' individual subjectivity and possessed this unique personal identity" (p. 115).

Not all people who work from a postmodern or poststructuralist perspective believe that there is no such thing as identity or selfhood. Rather, many prefer to suggest that while identity stability remains meaningful and important (particularly for self-care, resilience, ethical relations and good social participation), the concepts put forward by liberalism, Marxism and psychoanalysis should not be treated as 'monolithic.' That means that they do not provide a *complete* picture to which we should adhere but are simply frameworks that tell a particular story about identity. This is useful, because it implies that the search for other stories or ways of knowing identity is an ongoing one. In some ways, this not only expands the possibilities of theorising but also frees us up personally from assuming that our identities are understood, thereby allowing us instead to take a critical perspective on who we are and how we belong, which may in the long run open up more ethical ways of being selves and of including those who are otherwise marginalised from being seen as fully human.

1.2.5 Foucault, institutions and disciplinary norms

Significant among constructionist approaches to identity has been the work of Michel Foucault who argued that identity is better understood not as a 'thing' but as an 'effect' of power, disciplinarity and biopolitics, which include processes and techniques of surveillance and normalisation. Foucault's historical, philosophic and theoretical work is among the most influential on the fields of media, communication and cultural studies, primarily because it provided new ways of making sense of the role of institutions (particularly those that play a disciplinary role and produce norms by which we are encouraged to measure ourselves), discourses (ways and limits of speaking about a topic), knowledge (including how it shifts over different historical periods), power (which is always seen not in terms of the domination by governments or rulers but as a positive force that produces various outcomes and ways of being) and biopolitics (an extension of discipline into the space of governance and regulation of whole populations).

Through these important concepts, Foucault furthered the postmodern and structuralist theories of identity, demonstrating that identity or selfhood is a *form* that is constituted in and by discourse (Deleuze 1988). For Foucault, the subject is inculcated by and through the deployment of power-relations, 'normalised' into identity categories through regimentary, disciplinary and biopolitical processes and institutions. The humanist or liberal identity as self-existent, coherent and consciously active is thus rejected by Foucault as an historical creation of institutions. He suggested, instead, understanding the self as produced by the active disciplining of bodies made 'docile,' by which he means generally conforming to sets of pre-given norms (Foucault 1977). That is, how we present ourselves in terms of gender, ethnicity, adulthood and other facets of identity are normalised by the processes of belonging through which we have been disciplined in such a way that we surveil and police our own behaviour in order to conform. That does not mean there is no one who fails to conform or who presents themselves in alternative ways—only that they do not necessarily get to enjoy social and institutional belonging to the same extent.

There are three further modes of identity construction we can discern from Foucault's work. The first is institutionally managed dividing practices, such as the isolation of the so-called mad (historically) in asylums which extends today to other dividing practices in institutions, for example, grading systems in universities, class streaming in schools, religious and political frameworks that mean cisgender people have potentially more liveable lives than transgender people and so on. Secondly is the Foucauldian concept of "scientific classification" arising from modes of inquiry given the discursive status of science. In the context of digital media environments, we might similarly refer to this as profile categorisation or 'naming'; a discursive practice whereby the recognition of identities plays a role in the constitution of the subject *as* subject. Finally, there is 'subjectification,' the processes of self-formation in which we conform to wider social expectations beyond the institutions of family, religion, education and health. This is where wider governance and administration come—governments and powerful corporations often rely on statistical data or, today, 'big data' as part of what Foucault referred to as a biopolitical technology of power. Biopolitics does not look to individual identity but to the wider continuation of (usually national) populations. Using a range of techniques from statistical measurement to health promotion to immigration controls, it governs populations not by calling upon people to conform with narrow norms but with wider normative curves of distribution. Biopolitics, as a form of power emerged historically a little later than institutional 'discipline' in the second half of the eighteenth century—it was part of the further development of governance for larger states. It is a form of power that produces identities by calling upon people to plot the extent of the normativity against those distributional curves (Foucault 2007). The extent to which one manages health, for example, in terms of health norms is part of it—producing certain ways of being or types of identity such as pre-diabetic, diabetic, the autism spectrum and so on. While these are useful categories for managing health, the practices of this power produce identities around those categories.

1.2.6 Judith Butler and performativity

The last theory of identity to discuss here is that of performativity. North American feminist philosopher, Judith Butler, has provided a very nuanced, poststructuralist account
of identity, subjectivity and selfhood that is perhaps the most significant and useful for
understanding the relationship between cultural practices (such as digital media use) and
identity today. Building on the work of Foucault (although also drawing on work by
Althusser and Lacan), Butler argues like other poststructuralist that there is no underlying 'real' identity that we can ever capture and understand. Rather, our identities are
constituted by repetitive 'performances' that are aligned with pre-given norms in such
a way as to lend the retrospective *illusion* that there is an inner identity core or essence
from which our identities emerge (Butler 1990). Identity is a normative ideal described in
language and called upon by our contemporary culture, rather than a descriptive feature
of experience. It is therefore to be understood not as a thing or property but an *effect* of
regimentary discursive practices.

The subject, then, is constituted by the very 'expressions' (ways of speaking, ways of
comporting the body, social engagement, attitudes, etc.) that have traditionally been
considered the subject's *actions*. As Butler notes, performativity is not a singular, deliberate
and self-conscious act but a reiterative practice that *cites the norms* in language and culture—
both of which always pre-exist us and in that sense are the source of identities. We perform
identities in ways which stabilise over time through the repetition of behaviours, ways of
being and actions so that we appear to ourselves and others to be consistent. However, for
Butler, because true repetition is always awkward (or, in some poststructuralist perspectives,
considered philosophically impossible), we remain forever at risk of being shown up as
inconsistent. In this powerful theorisation of identity as performative, we are socially compelled to perform in consistent, coherent, intelligible and recognisable ways under the gaze
of others, because a failure to do so upsets our capacity for belonging and social participation (Butler 1993). One important note here is that Butler has taken great pains to point
out that while she understands all identity to be performative, she does not intend that to
mean theatrical—performances of selfhood are not conscious, deliberate acts but occur in
non-voluntary ways to shore up our subjectivity and selfhood (Butler 1993).

One of the things Butler was trying to argue against in her theory of identity
performativity is the fruitlessness of what are sometimes called the essentialist/construc-
tionist debates. *Essentialism* (the belief that there is an inner set of characteristics that make
us who we are—an inner essence) has often been pitted against *constructionist* approaches
(that our identities are produced by society, sometimes exhaustively so). Butler points out
the ways in which *both* sides have often missed the point (1993, p. 8). While the essentialist
position, for Butler, is rooted in those early humanist and liberal traditions of identity,
constructionism also gets it wrong by suggesting that identities are universally and wholly
created by language. She argues that this position understands culture as exhaustively constituting identity, ultimately creating and determining our identities by naming us. Her
answer to these two positions is to dislodge both the fixity and foundationalism of essentialist views and the determinism of the constructionist position in favour of *performativity*
as establishing the subject as an *effect* of our participation in language and culture and,
more specifically, viewing the subject as a *process* that stabilises to produce the effect of
fixity over time.

Although Butler's theories are complex and difficult at first, they provide a very useful
framework for thinking about identity and digital communication. This is because rather

than assuming that our identities are formed as an effect of what we see, hear and read on our screens, performativity is an excellent reminder that our online engagement is an active performance—we upload, create content, comment, curate a social media profile and so on, and these are not necessarily all that different from the kinds of performances we do in bodily settings, such as practices of gendered ways of walking and talking or perform sexual identities through desiring or choosing certain foods as a vegetarian. I discuss Butler's work in more detail in Chapters 2 and 3 where we have an opportunity to work through in more detail how the performativity of identities occurs in a range of digital interactive settings. By looking back on Butler from a digital perspective, we can see further nuance and new perspectives to her theory.

1.2.7 Using theories of identity

As can be seen from the above, there is a trajectory from early theories that relied on the idea that identity, subjectivity or the self had an inner essence, was knowable to oneself, and was recognised as unitary, singular and individualist, through theories that outlined how fragmented identity really is, to constructionist approaches that placed identity as something unreal or unknowable to performative theories that explored why the unitary subject feels natural or normal but never quite is. The question, then, is what can we do with these theories?

By undoing essentialist approaches, theorists are not necessarily suggesting we should proceed *as if* there is no real identity or that it is meaningless. Rather, as many feminist and poststructuralist theorists have argued, we do not wish to dismantle identity altogether but to question the 'logic' that saw it as having a *knowable foundation*—primarily because failing to question that logic leads to substantial constraints on what identities might do or how we might do identity differently, more ethically or in ways that are more inclusive. As gender theorist Eve Kosofsky Sedgwick (1990) noted in discussing sexual identity, we ought to question the "natural, self-evidence" of identities based on differences (such as LGBTQ+ versus straight), but disavowing these identities meaningfulness would come at a large cost, because they have been important to people in their everyday lives and, for LGBTQ+ people, as a powerful way of gathering identities to fight for rights (p. 84). Likewise, Judith Butler argued that "there remains a political imperative to use these necessary errors or category mistakes" (Butler 1991, p. 16), acknowledging that while the logic that makes the dominant liberal-humanist sense of identity seem 'real' is always from the beginning flawed, we do need to persist with the idea of identities. Nevertheless, as I often argue, we are always better off by using critique not just in our study but in our own lives, because it opens opportunities to see ourselves as more than we currently do and perhaps may lead to more ethical ways to interact with one another.

The fact that there is a range of theories does not mean, then, that we must pick one and stick with it in attempting to analyse how digital communication has an impact on identity. Rather, what it means is that we can draw on the broad range of what has been discussed above—among other approaches—to build the right 'tool' for the task of analysing digital media. If we look at the range of theories as a sort of toolkit, we are able to draw on Marxist theory, for example, to describe the ways in which—say—digital workers such as moderators are produced as identities in the context of the relations of production between the employees of a major corporate and global digital platform and those who own it. At the same time, however, we might use aspects of Foucault's theories of identity to understand how exchanges that occur on a platform like Twitter have a disciplinary effect that calls upon people to adopt and align themselves with political poles or groups. We will work through some of the ways in which these theories can be used in the following chapters in this book.

1.3 Early Internet and the idea of identity online

In this section, I would like to spend some time considering the context of digital communication as an evolving factor in contemporary society so that we are better positioned to later map the relationship between identity and digital cultures. As with all studies of an artefact in history, it is important to begin in its early years so that we can understand how the practices that are familiar to us today came about.

Although the Internet has a long history of development across the second half of the twentieth century, it was in the early 1990s alongside the uptake of personal computing that what we understand as the Internet started to emerge. While the experience of digital communication in 1995 was very different from how we use online settings a quarter of a century later, many of the early practices have framed the concepts available to us to think about the relationship between communication technologies and identity. It is therefore important to have a brief overview of those early Internet experiences because many of the ideas that we need to critique are 'hold overs' from those early years, calling upon us to see what we might need to update or think about differently to understand our contemporary experiences.

The early years of the Internet were a period of slow communication speeds. For most people, connection was through telephone copper wire lines which involved deliberately dialling in during times one wished to be online and logging off when one was not—that is, our present experience of continued connectivity and 'always online' mode was unthinkable then. The slow speeds meant and therefore involved activities that centred on text, still image, decreased capacity for immediacy and access predominantly through non-mobile desktop computers, a number of approaches to online identity worked to produce a notion of cyberculture that was deemed separate from the 'real' of the 'real world.' This gave users the impression that there were different 'modes' of identity: a real, embodied and corporeal social experience that we had when we were doing something offline and, separately, a new, playful identity we experienced when doing something online such as using a text-based chat system such as Internet Relay Chat (IRC) and talking with other people in other parts of the world.

Important here is to emphasise just how different that experience was for those who predate the Internet. To be able to talk in real-time text rather than the phone with people we did not know and would never meet in 'real life' was a phenomenal shift in communication possibilities, and one that many users threw themselves into to explore this very new and exciting way of being in the world. Indeed, it is difficult today to imagine just how exciting sending an email across the world that was received in a few seconds might actually be when it is so mundane today. This development was about as significant as the uptake of the telephone in the early twentieth century whereby people overcame the limitations of distance and the previous social world in which communicating with someone in a different country meant sending a written letter or message taking days or weeks to arrive. What that did for identity was changed our sense of place and how it related to belonging and therefore identity—or, at least, this was the case for those who could afford to place a long-distance phone call. The early Internet resulted in a similar shift, primarily by making it relatively cheap to communicate in real time or send a written message—as long as one could afford the computer from which to send it.

The resulting shift in being able to participate anonymously in online chat opened some interesting ways of thinking about identity—particularly ideas about disembodiment, becoming 'mind' only and very utopian ideas about identity fluidity. Some of this drew on the cyberpunk fiction of the 1970s and 1980s, such as William Gibson's *Neuromancer* (1984), to *read* early Internet digital culture as a setting in which the identity constraints of the body were seemingly overcome by the capacity to experience identity otherwise through textual play, pretense, the affordances of anonymity, the formation of new ways of doing belonging and community, the idea of a 'virtual' life and the hope that this would overcome the identity inequalities linked to gender, sexuality, race, ethnicity and disability. Early approaches were therefore quite optimistic and tended sometimes to be highly utopian that playful fluidity in the realm of cyberculture would change how we relate to one another globally and reduce adversities across axes of identity, particularly in relation to gender, sexuality and race.

The example of early Internet 'cyber' thinking related to text-based communication in chatrooms, in combination with other speculative thinking, helped to produce the idea that digital communication could be thought of as an instance of identity fluidity. Theorist Mark Poster (2006), for example, suggested an approach to the anonymous speech afforded to Internet users producing possibilities for selfhood without limits, gender, religion, ethnic or national restrictions, opening wholly new ways of doing and being the self. Likewise, Mark Dery (1992) saw the potential of early Web 1.0 engagement for the subversion of identity and the rise of oppositional, resistant and revolutionary ways of practising identity. Discussing similar concepts and analysing online practices, early cyber theorist Sherry Turkle (1999) made a more nuanced argument by suggesting that new possibilities for online identity that emerge from this kind of thinking may be useful in contesting the older theories of identity as fixed, embodied and categorical, even though such approaches remained meaningful for most people in their everyday lived experience.

The early Internet did indeed open many opportunities to come at identity theories from different angles. The Web 1.0 text-based chatrooms offered technological opportunities that allowed postmodern understandings of identity as multiple, fluid, decentred and disembodied to be *explored* by facilitating experiential understandings of the illusion of a unitary self (Turkle 1997). In the often anonymous environments of text-based, virtual–reality multiuser domains (MUDs and MOOs), one could invest in and construct oneself in a simulated environment understood to be free of embodied territorial constraints. In effect, one could challenge the idea of unitary identity through the wilful experimentation with identity categories. Turkle (1999) introduced the well-known example of a user known as Case: a male industrial designer who maintains a 'Jimmy Stewart versus Katharine Hepburn dichotomy' of online personae to exemplify a notion of identity as distributed and heterogeneous, facilitated by text-based online forums. For Case, presenting himself as a feminine 'Katharine Hepburn ideal' online allowed an externalisation of an aspect of himself that he would be unable to fully explore in 'real-life' masculine embodiment.

From today's perspective, examples of identity play such as that of Case is not only already outdated but arguably on the creepy side, given our changing relationship with online anonymity, concerns about user safety and the increasing emphasis of the visual over the written textual as the form in which we use digital media. At the same time, we have also moved away from the real/virtual distinction that marked this possibility of identity play, resulting primarily from the technological shifts that allow pervasive, mobile and always-connected Internet use in contrast to the 1990s practice of dialling in and leaving later. That is, the dualism of the real versus virtual is far more complicated and perhaps even completely collapsed in the Web 2.0 era that followed from about 2005 onwards. Although celebrated as examples of identity fluidity, these early Internet online performances were much less a new way of doing identity, and much more a mechanism to engage in theatrical play with concepts of identity rather than to offer new ways of being for the self.

Two areas, however, where early cyberculture did indeed have an impact on identity involved new access to information in ways that did were unthinkable before the 1990s. In pre-digital cultures, consulting texts meant taking a book off a shelf or physically visiting a library, and knowing what was happening in the world meant reading a news-paper or tuning in to radio or television news—all of which were moderated by media gatekeepers. The increased capacity to access alternative forms of information was a sub-stantial change that opened new opportunities for aspects of identity. For example, even in the early 1990s, LGBTQ+ peoples and communities continued to be relatively invisible on film and television screens (Cover 2000), but early Internet websites made available the information that helped many younger people who would otherwise have felt excluded or isolated to have a sense that there was a wider community, resources for self-esteem and opportunities to chat with others. There is no doubt that early Internet culture's capacity to provide this kind of information resulted in identities of pride and played a very sub-stantial role in creating a widespread culture of tolerance, acceptance and social belonging over the following two decades (Cover 2016).

At the same time, the early Internet allowed new kinds of 'virtual' communities to form across newsgroups, forums, websites, chat programmes and email. Although these were often represented in idealistic ways as a future world of harmonious, online settings for belonging and engagement (Rheingold 1993), they had an important impact on the relationship between belonging and identity. Prior to this, communities of people who had genuine contact with each other were limited by geographic bounds, such as a village or town. Or they were experienced without face-to-face engagement as forms of sym-bolic belonging, such as among a community of migrants living across the United States (Cohen 1985). Or they were bound by the regular consumption of daily newspapers (Anderson 1983) and gained a sense of belonging and affiliation by that shared practice, such as among a national community. The early Internet, however, allowed the formation of alternative communities by bringing together people from dispersed locations who did not have the necessary resources to gain a symbolic sense of belonging, such as through print news and broadcast media.

One famous example that emerged through the affordances of the early Internet is the formation of the 'furries' community. Furries are a subculture within science fiction and fantasy fandom, and practices involve dressing as non-human anime characters. While this is often theatrics and not necessarily about a bodily dysmorphia (Dobre 2012), the identification as a Furry—that is, as a person whose sense of selfhood is defined by the engagement in such play—is deeply felt, an attachment that is subjective and meaningful. Such play, of course, may involve more serious identification with animals themselves as some choose to live lives in an everyday sense through the theatrics of being a wolf or a cat (Dobre 2012). The Furry community and the construction of identity did not simply emerge by itself. Nor was it about pre-existing furries suddenly finding they had an opportunity to talk to each other through digital means and thereby, as individuals, coming together as a community. Rather, the community itself came about, developed and gained a shared sense of identity because the affordances of digital media allowed the gathering online of very dispersed voices of those who were otherwise disenfranchised from identity norms and forming the name, language and shared symbolic belonging that stabilised as an identity.

The early Internet was therefore a setting that had an impact on identity and belonging but in complex ways. On the one hand, the idea of identity fluidity enabled by online chat and playing with identity representation in chatrooms was a bit of a non–starter: it did not revolutionise how we think about or do identity today, even though it opened a new opportunity among some early theorists to think about how new communication tools might enable alternative ways to approach identity. On the other hand, the vast access to information, representations that were otherwise unavailable in more traditional media forms, and the emergence of new communities by bringing disaffected and disenfranchised people together to communicate and gain a shared sense of identity was a vast and substantial shift in identity practices.

1.4 The changing digital world

While the concepts of real/virtual and community connectivities that emerged in the early Internet remain part of how our contemporary global culture continues to think about many aspects of digital communication, it is important to consider some of the subsequent changes and developments in digital culture in the era beyond the early Internet. The starting point here is to recognise that while our current digital culture is built upon the foundations of the early Internet, very little about it, how it is used, the practices of engagement, the make-up of users or the ways we conceive it are the same. Much of what follows in the remainder of this book relates to the era from 2005 and onwards and into the 2020s, and it is important to keep in mind that digital culture continues to change over that period and will continue to do so in the next decade. It is therefore sensible to give a brief summary of the key developments since 2005 and what they began to mean for how we approach concepts of identity.

1.4.1 Web 2.0

From the mid–2000s, the world began to see the real development of what came to be called Web 2.0, whereby digital communication was much less about email and text-based chat and less dominated by those with the skill to develop websites and early blogs. Rather, it was marked by a substantial development in facilitating *user-generated content*. That is, the early Internet (now referred to as Web 1.0) involved a lot of real-time engagement, but much of the work involved in developing websites had remained limited to a relatively small number of users. Web 2.0 facilitated a revolutionary change by providing the tools and capabilities for vast numbers of users to generate and share their own content, and collaborate with others, across a range of platforms. Common among these in the mid-2000s were social media (LiveJournal, MySpace, Facebook), wikis (especially Wikipedia but also fandom-oriented wiki platforms that allowed vast numbers of users to contribute material) and video-sharing platforms (particularly YouTube, which started life as a platform to share user-generated content such as vlogs). There were also a number of blogging sites. Key here is that platforms provided the framework and tools for the curation of users' content, encouraging a substantial increase in sharing.

Behind the scenes, significant changes in communication technology facilitated the advent of Web 2.0. The introduction of broadband connectivity allowed an always-on approach and overcame the previous difficulties of dial-up connectivity which prevented multiple users in a single household wishing to communicate online simultaneously. Computer processing power increased substantially such that they could process image and video downloads more quickly. Browsers became more stable and enabled faster upload and processing of content. Thus, while it built on the assumptions and practices of the early Internet as a space for sharing, communication and user-generated material, technological advances provided a major boost that enabled very large numbers of everyday people to start spending more time online and facilitating the curation of material that reflected one's identity without the need for website management and HTML skills.

Social media was obviously one of the most significant affordances made available to everyday users, and it is perhaps this most of all that has had an impact on how we practice online identity. Where the early cyberculture theorists imagined a future of unbridled expansion of identity categories and identity fluidity, the success of social networking platforms like Facebook suggests, instead, that identity is articulated online in ways that are constrained by the curation limits of the sites. At the same time, the image-based sharing that marks so much of Facebook activity is one through which our identities are not so much played with (by text-based pretense and theatrics) but are articulated in meaningful ways through sharing the stories and narratives of our lives (Walther et al. 2011, p. 26). This is not to say that everyone using social media does so in the same way, and that there is no identity fraud or identity privacy. Rather, it is to suggest that we utilise platforms to present ourselves in intelligible, coherent ways and in ways that link our 'off-line' time with the 'online' representation.

1.4.2 *Collapsing the real/virtual divide*

Despite the shift from Web 1.0 text-based personal hyperlinked webpages towards Web 2.0 social networking—characterised by participation, audio–video sharing, interactive remixing and up-front non-anonymous engagement—older theories of online identity presenting the notion of the digital self as theatrical and, sometimes, fraudulent have continued to frame much public discourse on subjectivity in online contexts. This is particularly the case in the occasional representation and re-circulation of a so-called real versus digital distinction.

Much of the way digital communication is discussed in everyday contexts, some journalism and some scholarship is framed by those early Internet and cyberculture notions of a 'real' versus 'virtual' distinction. This is often presented *as if* everyday people's sense of identity is split between what they do online and how they perceive themselves as a subject in non-digital spaces and settings. It is part of what Kristian Møller and Brady Robards (2019) have described as the continuing propensity to look at digital communication through concepts of spaces—in this case, as spaces that are seen to varying degrees of separation from radically different to overlapping. Following this point, I argue that the continued perception of a more extreme difference is problematic for making sense of identity for a few reasons:

- A real/virtual dichotomy is built on the idea of early Internet access and having to make a conscious decision to 'go online' (such as dialling in through a modem; going physically to a desktop computer, etc.), which always implies an instance of leaving, departing or dialling out from so-called cyberspace.
- It also relies on cyberculture metaphors of an online identity comprised only of one's 'mind' *as* if the 'body' is somehow irrelevant (despite the typing, seeing and hearing the body performs when engaging with digital media). The metaphor extended to the idea that one was somehow disembodied when 'jacked in' to the Internet and then returns to the body or what, in Cyberpunk writing, is sometimes called 'the meat' when one jacks out again. As discussed in Chapter 3, the body is *never not* part of the picture of digital communication.
- As a dichotomy, framing an idea of 'real' (or embodied) communication versus or 'virtual' (digital) communication leads to a framing of the former as beneficial and healthy, while the latter is depicted as risky, dangerous and unhealthy. The reductionist depiction of digital settings as unhealthy includes the inaccurate perception that it has properties which are inherently addictive (Cover 2007), or that it drives moral panics which substantially over-state the risks of, say, echo chambers and filter bubbles to the quality of public communication (Bruns 2019).

This is not to suggest that the so-called space of the real and space of the digital are completely collapsed into each other. Rather, there is substantial evidence that everyday people do indeed perceive a distinction in the quality, form and type of engagement they experience, the sorts of friends they have 'in real life' versus those who are labelled friends 'online' and the kinds of information that people are willing to share in one setting but not the other (Third et al. 2020). Certainly, the practice of 'disconnecting' either temporarily or permanently has become more marked as people do in fact find that there are unhealthy aspects about overexposure to certain toxic online environments or that spending too much time scrolling through TikTok content detracts from the time available for healthy exercise. While this draws on a real/digital distinction that I've described as artificial and constraining, the old distinction forms part of how, as a culture, we *think about* digital communication; the distinction is thus often used by many of us as a way to frame our lived experience as we navigate the many identity facets of communication, privacy, well-being and time. In other words, the distinction is artificial but is sometimes meaningful.

What is significant, however, in arguing that such a distinction is no longer as defined as it was in the days of the early Internet is that we are now in an era in which machines themselves remain connected to the network, in which very large numbers of households (obviously not all) have access to wireless connectivity, multiple computers and mobile devices, meaning it is possible for each person to engage without waiting a turn, as was once the case (Green 2008). It means we are physically surrounded by devices that are connected from fridges to mobiles to networked speakers to virtual assistants such as Google Home and Alexa. Even when we refuse to have these in our own home, we are often surrounded by similar networked and tracking devices in shops, workplaces, schools and the homes of our friends and family. In that respect, if we are to consider our identities as aspects of selfhood that are articulated by physically being in places and communicating ourselves in those spaces (Woodward 2002, p. vii), we need to acknowledge that it is no longer easy to find ourselves in spaces in which the digital network is fully absent.

Perhaps more importantly, we have to acknowledge the fact that connection is not just about the *technical* aspect of machines connected or people using them but is also a *conceptual* factor in which it is increasingly impossible for other forms of communication to happen without reference to the digital. For example, contemporary journalism often draws on Twitter not only to promote stories but as a source for news; watching a television show on a digital network often provides links to further information about the show online, and many of our everyday activities require us to utilise digital networks, whether that is banking or using check-in applications on mobile phones to demonstrate COVID-19 vaccination to enter physical spaces. TikTok is referenced in contemporary films and books. Again, the discourses by which we make sense of identity are no longer ways of speaking that exclude networked and digital settings—our lives are infused by digital communication even if we refuse to have a social media account.

1.5 Angles of identity

The following chapters each take a different angle on the relationship between digital communication and identity. This chapter has introduced some of the key concepts for beginning to think about identity in the context of digital cultures. It has discussed why digital communication and its related cultural practices are central to identity formation and belonging today and presented a summary of key theories of identity, subjectivity and selfhood. It has covered some of how identity has been framed in early (Web 1.0) Internet settings in terms of fluidity and a perceived separation of the 'real' (embodied) and the 'virtual' (online; mind) and how that changed during the later phases (Web 2.0) in which digital communication became more ubiquitous and permanently connected in our everyday lives. It has discussed some of the implications of critiquing identity as an approach to understanding the significance of digital culture as a core aspect of communication, society and self and has argued that any theory of identity today needs to take into account the increasing pervasiveness of image and text, fast-changing developments in digital media, changes in the speed and reach of communication and the role of digital creativity in governing our emerging frameworks for making sense of identity, subjectivity and selfhood.

The second chapter explores concepts of online interactivity. Interactivity is a concept that differentiates digital media from other, more traditional forms such as print, film, radio, newspapers and television. This is primarily because digital settings are built around enabling interaction through *user-generated content* (posts, uploads), the *manipulation* of existing texts (editing, re-utilising, photoshopping, remixing) and *collaboration* with others (social media comments, friending, tagging, reading news feeds, group zoom chats, etc.). Drawing on Judith Butler's important contribution to the theory of identity performativity, the chapter works through the ways in which identity can be said to be 'performed' by users in Web 2.0 online settings as a process of engagement. Significant is that while social media and other aspects of digital engagement permit us to articulate our identities online in ways that are different from but not wholly separate from how we articulate and represent ourselves in face-to-face, bodily settings, social media also provides the tools for others to critique, police, surveil and sometimes 'upset' identities as well. In some senses, then, social media has become the setting not just for identity performance but for identity anxiety as well.

Chapter 3 explores the role of the body. While early Internet 'textual' practices were often perceived as being disembodied experiences, the body has always been a core part of identity in the context of communication, since it is always a part of the 'doing' of identity. Bodies have been strongly represented in online communication since the early years of this century, particularly in image and video, and they are a core part of how we play online games, engage with virtual–reality devices and utilise the affordances of mobile devices to remain connected. In the Web 3.0 era of networked devices and appliances, it is our bodies that interact with digital culture. This chapter does four things: (i) introduces readers to a range of theories that help us define the body in digital, technological and communicative frameworks; (ii) discusses the digital visual representation of bodies of difference in the context of identity signifiers of gender, race, (dis)ability and the ways in which stereotypes both persist and are disavowed online; (iii) addresses some of the ways in which the embodied practices of online gaming demonstrate how the body is active rather than passive and sedentary; and (iv) provides an account of the relationship between identity, health, well-being and fitness as it plays out through the widespread use of digitally connected body-tracking and fitness devices and the digital cultural framing of the body as a project of betterment.

Chapter 4 begins our discussion of some of the implications of digital communication and identity. This chapter explores one of the more exciting and creative (or alarming and dangerous) forms of digital production to emerge in the past few years—the 'deepfake' video. The deepfake is a technologically enhanced false video and audio content that draws on both real and existing images but reconfigures and re-juxtaposes them to produce 'fake' video and audio material that appears to be credible. Discussing some of the contemporary issues around the digital distribution of disinformation, misinformation and fake news, this chapter explores how deliberate deepfake videos affect how we perceive the authenticity of identity and create new opportunities for identity fraud. Deepfakes are discussed here not exclusively as a surreptitious practice but as something which sits at the intersection between the digital practices of interactivity and co-creativity, on the one hand, and the contemporary framework of postmodern hyperreality, on the other hand. The deepfake belongs to and extends the boundaries of 'fake news,' posing a greater threat to the quality and control of evidence, information and communicative norms, and thereby to the reliability of the normative discourses through which identities are made intelligible, coherent and recognisable. Its implications for how we 'do' identity are only beginning to emerge, and it may well be a new departure for digital communication.

Chapter 5 presents an overview of how local, national and global 'spaces' intersect with identity and digital networks. In the era of the early Internet—and perhaps still often today—we thought about digital communication as being part of a wider move towards 'globalisation' and the 'global village.' The capacity to communicate easily across national borders in Web 1.0, the under-regulated global platforms of Web 2.0 and the vast access digital media has given to real-time image and video from across the planet has often made the experience seem synonymous with globalisation. However, new moves to regulate the platforms (to combat disinformation and trolling in particular) and other digital corporations (to prevent tax avoidance among some of the highest profit-generation companies in the world) is part of a process in which the nation-state comes back into framing communication and media. That is, while digital, networked media and the Internet have been understood across the past quarter century as symptoms of the process of globalisation because they changed our relationship with the 'space' and 'time' of communication, they are increasingly seen as objects to be curtailed by national regulatory frameworks, national interests and local needs—particularly to curtail cybersecurity threats, stem the power of major platforms and sometimes manage flows of information and content. How we position ourselves in identity terms as global users and national citizens is, therefore, increasingly in flux. By identifying some of the push-and-pull factors between the global and national, introducing theories of globalisation and revisiting older theories of the nationalistic framework of communication, Chapter 5 points to the multiplicity of discourses and practices through which identity as national and global citizens is conceived and performed.

Chapter 6 takes us into the contemporary problems of online hostility and hate speech and what the toxicity of many online settings means for how we practise and perform identity. The experience of hostility, hate speech and adversarial behaviour in everyday online spaces has increased substantially in recent years, with known health and mental health outcomes for users. This chapter discusses some of the ways in which new forms of digital hostility, beyond the more familiar cyberbullying, represent a new departure for digital communication due to the 'massified' form of contemporary hostility experienced in the Internet 'pile on' and in the persistence of trolling. Exploring how digital hostility is a problem of culture rather than one of technology, this chapter explores the impact of the online pile-on as a key example of how hostility has taken advantage of the affordances of networked engagement in ways which identify victims as unliveable and ungrievable selves.

From an everyday, liberal-humanist perspective, we usually think of identity and selfhood through concepts of agency, choice, freedom and free expression. From a post-structuralist perspective, a concept of agency is sometimes regarded with suspicion—for example, when an idea of endless consumer choice is recognised as a cover for the curtailment of other kinds of agency, including actions that permit the expression of subjectivity at the margins of social normativity. In relation to digital culture, however, we have seen an increasing movement concerned about how to uphold freedoms, choice and agency in light of the use of algorithms (especially for search engines and managing content feeds), artificial decision-making applications (that provide particular outcomes for us without showing the full range of choices that may otherwise have been available) and targeted content (particularly news and other essential information). The rise of algorithmic culture is often discussed publicly as bringing about a curtailment of agency. In extreme cases, it is claimed that the only realistic choice a user can make is to remove themselves from digital settings. This chapter analyses the popular 2020 Netflix documentary *The Social Dilemma*, which used an alarmist discourse of techno-pessimism to suggest that human agency was being taken by social platform algorithms in ways which fostered both passive consumerism and violent extremism. Interrogating the underlying discourse of the suspicion of digital media as anti-agency, the chapter introduces readers to key concepts in machine learning and artificial decision-making and locates emerging public anxieties in the longer history of technology and anti-digital nostalgia.

Chapter 8 considers how claims about identity authenticity re-emerged in surprising ways in discourses about video-sharing platform TikTok. Despite the advances in hyperreal, computer-generated imagery such as filtering on Instagram images, and machine-learning applications such as deepfake videos, identity authenticity—being true to oneself, performing in everyday, grounded ways—clearly has some continuing public appeal. Investigating some of these arguments, this chapter suggests that we may be confusing authenticity and amateur or non-professional content in contrast with the increasing professionalisation and filtering found on other, older platforms. Rather, what is at play on TikTok, I argue, is an 'aesthetic of authenticity,' a set of tastes and values and an appeal to 'realism' over 'glossy' where the tone and form of videos is deliberately playful, silly and unpolished rather than curated. This chapter also discusses some of the ways in which influencers and celebrity culture both infiltrate and emerge upon TikTok to compete with the authenticity aesthetic and what it means when unethical virtue signalling presents itself as the false 'proof' of an authentic identity.

A final, short chapter explores some of the future directions for identity in the context of digital communication. It revisits theories of identity and corporeality, issues of authenticity and agency, cultures of relationality and exclusion and examines a few examples of digital technology developments that are publicly thought to impinge upon or open new opportunities for performing identities in new ways.

Key points

- Identity is one of the most complex concepts in contemporary society, and crosses personal, community, social and cultural frameworks—all of which include communication practices.
- There are many different approaches to identity (or 'theories'), and none of them are necessarily more correct than others. However, in a complex digital world, some are more *useful* than others to help us understand the relationship between digital cultures and who we are, how we are represented and how we practise belonging online.
- The early (Web 1.0) Internet was often discussed as a setting for identity play, representing it as a 'virtual' space separate from our 'real' lives. Some of these ideas have passed down into how we continue to discuss digital communication, although we have to be careful not to be held back by older ideas that are not reflected in our everyday experiences of the digital.

References

Althusser, L., 1971. *Lenin and Philosophy and Other Essays,* trans. B. Brewster. London: NLB.

Anderson, B., 1983. *Imagined Communities: Reflections on the Origins and Spread of Nationalism.* London:Verso.

Bruns, A., 2019. *Are Filter Bubbles Real?* London: Polity.

Butler, J., 1990. *Gender Trouble: Feminism and the Subversion of Identity.* London: Routledge.

Butler, J., 1991. Imitation and Gender Insubordination. *In:* D. Fuss, ed. *Inside/Out: Lesbian Theories, Gay Theories.* London: Routledge, 13–31.

Butler, J., 1993. *Bodies That Matter: On The Discursive Limits of 'Sex.'* London: Routledge.

Cohen, A.P., 1985. *The Symbolic Construction of Community.* London: Ellis Horwood & Tavistock Publications.

Cover, R., 2000. First contact: queer theory, sexual identity, and 'mainstream' film. *International Journal of Gender and Sexuality*, 5 (1), 71–89.

Cover, R., 2007. Gaming addiction: the role of narrative and play in the production of the addiction myth. *Game Studies: International Journal of Computer Game Research,* 6 (1). Available from: http://gamestudies.org/0601/articles/cover [Accessed 2 February 2022].

Cover, R., 2016. *Digital Identities: Creating and Communicating the Online Self.* London: Elsevier.

Curran, J., Gurevitch, M. and Woollacott, J., 1982. The study of the media: theoretical approaches. *In:* M. Gurevitch, T. Bennett, J. Curran and J. Woollacott, eds. *Culture, Society and the Media* . London: Methuen, 11–29.

Deleuze, G., 1988. *Foucault*, trans. S. Hand. Minneapolis: University of Minnesota Press.

Dery, M., 1992. Cyberculture. *South Atlantic Quarterly*, 91 (3), 501–523.

Descartes, R., 1968. *Discourse on Method and the Meditation*, trans. F.E. Sutcliffe. Harmondsworth: Penguin.

Dobre, C., 2012. *Furries: Enacting Animal Anthropomorphism*. Plymouth: University of Plymouth Press.

Freud, S., 1984. The unconscious. *Penguin Freud Library*, vol. 11. London: Penguin, 159–222.

Foucault, M., 1977. *Discipline and Punish: The Birth of the Prison*, trans. A. Sheridan. London: Penguin.

Foucault, M., 2007. *Security, Territory, Population: Lectures at the Collège de France, 1977–78*, ed. M. Senellart, trans. G. Burchell. Hampshire: Palgrave Macmillan.

Gibson, W., 1984. *Neuromancer*. New York: Ace Books.

Green, L., 2008. Is it meaningless to talk about 'the Internet'? *Australian Journal of Communication*, 35 (3), 1–14.

Grosz, E., 1990. *Jacques Lacan: A Feminist Introduction*. Sydney: Allen & Unwin.

Jameson, F., 1985. Postmodernism and consumer society. *In:* H. Foster, ed. *Postmodern Culture*. London: Pluto Press, 111–125.

Lacan, J., 1977. *The Four Fundamental Concepts of Psycho-analysis*, trans. A. Sheridan. Harmondsworth: Penguin.

Møller, K. and Robards, B., 2019. Walking through, going along and scrolling back: ephemeral mobilities in digital ethnography. *Nordicom Review*, 40 (1), 95–109.

Poster, M., 2006. *Information Please*. Durham, NC: Duke University Press.

Rheingold, H., 1993. *The Virtual Community: Homesteading on the Electronic Frontier*. Reading, MA: Addison-Wesley.

Sedgwick, E.K., 1990. *Epistemology of the Closet*. London: Penguin.

Third, A., Collin, P., Walsh, L. and Black, R., 2020. *Young People in Digital Society: Control Shift*. London: Palgrave Macmillan.

Turkle, S., 1997. Multiple subjectivity and virtual community at the end of the Freudian century. *Sociological Inquiry*, 67 (1), 72–84.

Turkle, S., 1999. Cyberspace and identity. *Contemporary Sociology*, 28 (6), 643–648.

Walther, J.B., Carr, C.T., Choi, S.S.W., DeAndrea, D.C., Kim, J., Tong, S.T. and Van Der Heide, B., 2011. Interaction of interpersonal, peer, and media influence sources online: a research agenda for technology convergence. *In:* Z. Papacharissi, ed. *A Networked Self: Identity, Community, and Culture on Social Network Sites*. London: Routledge, 17–38.

Woodward, K., 2002. *Understanding Identity*. London: Arnold.

2 Interactivities

Performativity, social media and online participation

2.1 Introduction

If we understand the history of pre-digital-mediated communication to be one marked by the 'control' of the text (the printer, the filmmaker, the television producer), then it is easy to suggest that the language, stories, norms and ways of perceiving our identities have overwhelmingly been put in the hands of everyday people in a digital era. What marks out the digital Web 2.0 era, then, is our capacity to publish our own storytelling and to interact with other people's texts by making changes, re-utilises, photoshopping, video edits, remixes and other forms of interaction and engagement. In that context, digital communication has meant entering an era of interactivity, and this means changes to ways in which our everyday identities are thought, articulated and performed.

In Chapter 1, I described some of the ways we can theorise identity and subjectivity and argued that Judith Butler's theory of performativity is the most sophisticated and useful for making sense of the relationship between digital communication and identity. At the time Butler first introduced the theory of identity performativity in her book *Gender Trouble* (1990) to discuss how gender identity comes to be formed by citing norms given in language and repeating them to stabilise an identity, she described a cultural environment in which we encounter, access, read and interpret language and knowledge through institutions, texts and disciplinary practices (Cover 2004). Over 40 years later, the setting where we access texts, knowledge and information has changed, because we now interact with it, adapt it, share it and engage with it much more on *our own terms* than we did at the time Butler introduced her version of performativity. Once we understand ourselves to be in the realm of digital interactivity, those texts are no longer quite so fixed in the 'published' or 'broadcast' sense but available to a very different kind of engagement. This shifts the relationship between identity and media very substantially.

Using Judith Butler's approach to identity performativity approach here, this chapter has three main areas of focus:

- How interactivity has changed the practice of reading and engaging with media and thereby has shifted how media is implicated in identity formation;
- The role of social media as a setting for the performance of identity in which we curate our stories of selfhood as an *act* of performativity not much different from how we do so in other contexts such as dress, speech, consumption choices, employment and so on;
- How social media is also a site in which we are subject to surveillance and critique by others which risks undoing all the work of performing a coherent and intelligible self or at the very least makes the 'work' of doing identity more labour-intensive.

DOI: 10.4324/9781003296652-2

To understand digital identities today, we need to be attention to how much has changed historically since the introduction of digital interactivity; how much our identities are shaped by our encounter with language, discourse, norms and knowledge; and how we continue to respond to the cultural demand to be coherent, intelligible subjects through performing identity in online settings.

2.2 Participatory digital creativity

In this section, we work through some of the ways in which digital interactivity (loosely: the capacity for users to generate, share and manipulate content) radically shifted how we engage with the kinds of knowledge frameworks we depend upon to produce and perform coherent and intelligible identities. The entire foundation of the digital media era is, in fact, one framed by an expectation that users will engage with *existing* texts through a range of editing techniques to produce new meanings, intertexts, artefacts and ways of seeing. For example, major contributor to the development of the World Wide Web platform, Tim Berners-Lee (1999), imagined a future in which texts were edited, changed and further developed freely by other users. As he reflected in a 1999 speech:

> I wanted the Web to be what I call an interactive space where everybody can edit. And I started saying "interactive," and then I read in the media that the Web was great because it was "interactive," meaning you could click. This was not what I meant by interactivity, so I started calling it "intercreativity" ... A few fundamental rules make this possible. As you can read, so you should be able (given the authority) to write. If you can see pictures on your screen, why can't you take pictures and very easily and intuitively put them up there?

The web was to be, for all users, a read–*write* medium in which manipulation of existing texts, images, footage and words was part of the co-creative potential that underscored the development of tools and protocols (Lessig 2008, pp. 58–59). While the Web 2.0 era of social media and platform-based curation of content has adapted how users (or machines) interact with texts, including particularly the use of platforms which provide the framework for the curation of user-generated content, the capacity of interactivity remains a central feature of digital culture. In identity terms, that means it is both the form through which we express ourselves online, while simultaneously giving us additional capabilities to adapt the very texts we read that provide us with cultural codes, norms and frameworks of identity itself.

2.2.1 What is interactivity?

We often use the term interactivity to describe the face-to-face conversational way in which people engage with each other, and that metaphor of interactivity began to apply to the early Internet because digital engagement was marked by the shift from engaging with earlier, traditional media that did not have a mechanism to allow us to change or utilise the text in different ways (e.g., radio, film, books). The term was a buzzword in the early to mid-2000s (Cover 2006), often presented as a 'selling point' in the marketing of home computers, technologies and digital commodities. Put in very simple terms, the notion of interactivity describes some of the ways in which digital communication and networking re-figured practices of authorship, co-creativity or co-participation in the production of texts, remixes and mash-ups, thereby producing new texts and new ideas and the changing nature, role and function of audiences.

The interactivity of digital communication has resulted in several tensions in what had previously stabilised as the author–text–audience relationship, primarily by blurring the line between author and audience, eroding older technological, policy and conventional models that provided a 'control' over the text such as the printed page, the broadcast television episode and the film—all of which could be said to prevent the text from being *easily* changed, adapted, re-sequenced or redistributed. Many authors, media producers, content-creators, government officials, experts, medical and psychological practitioners and teachers continue to operate in the dominant paradigm of intellectual property that is deemed to be the way in which texts—including popular culture and those texts that serve either deliberately or unwittingly as resources for identity formation—are controlled, stabilised and made permanent and fixed. Such practices are seen to disavow engagement by not inviting participants to contribute, change, alter, rearrange, remix or otherwise interactively co-create. An era of interactivity, then, is not merely a throwing over of the old ways of controlling a text. Rather, we might describe it as a deep-seated human desire to *participate* in storytelling and distribution or sharing that occurs within a kind of *push-and-pull struggle* between those who wish to control a text and keep it fixed and those who wish to manipulate, change or redistribute it (Cover 2006).

The idea of digital interactivity as occurring within a struggle is important to the study of identity, because the texts that we use to make sense of what identity is are subject to that struggle in ways which only occurred marginally through alternative arts practices in the past. This, then, is a sociocultural push-and-pull relationship in which interactivity opposes itself to the political and social protection of the text that is enacted through all of legal (copyright), social (respect for authors) and technology (digital control) protections.

Audiences continue to fight back with new disregard for copyright regimes (for example, peer-to-peer distribution and torrenting of texts; digital downloads of films, etc.), with new frameworks of understanding authorship (for example, through the concept of the 'prosumer' or, increasingly, through a breaking down of the professional and the amateur in terms of contributions to the public sphere) and technological innovations (such as new hacks that release technological limitations of texts thereby opening them up to manipulation or redistribution not by the 'author' but by everyday users). In making sense of interactivity, then, it is important to look not only at how this contestation emerged, but how the development of interactive technologies can be seen as a new field of engagement in a much older struggle around the concepts of author, text and audience, as we do in Section 2.2.4.

2.2.2 Participatory digital creativity

Another way of describing interactivity is as *participatory culture*. Theorist Terry Flew explained the shift from Web 1.0 to Web 2.0 as one characterised by a

> move from personal websites to blogs and blog site aggregation, from publishing to participation, from web content as the outcome of large up-front investment to an ongoing and interactive process, and from content management systems to links based on tagging.

(Flew 2008, p. 19)

That is, in a Web 1.0 environment, most everyday users tended to *retrieve* information, with only a few who were building websites and generating their own texts. In the Web 2.0 environment that emerged from 2005 onwards, platform architecture was more frequently being built around the idea of users as *participants*. Think of Facebook or Instagram, which has no real purpose for most people if they are not generating content for distribution and engaging with other people's content through commentary and sharing.

Participation, then, occurs due to some changes in the 'affordances' of digital communication. This includes primarily the shift in the level of skills needed to participate in media creativity: digital skills in development, content-creation, film production and writing are no longer the province of professionally trained media practitioners. Rather, they became increasingly available to vast numbers capable of producing and editing their own short films for YouTube, sharing their own music online without the need for a record company and so on. Computer-related activities shift from being understood as the domain of the 'nerdy hobbyist' to an everyday pursuit that allows a continued uptake of digital skills and content-creation activities and, indeed, a broad desire to engage in such settings and interactions. YouTube's primary affordance is its useability (Burgess and Green 2009, p. 64), and this is a powerful shift in how we are able to think about the relationship between the self as a spectator engaged in a media world, and the self as a creator of media content that can be made available to potentially very huge crowds. Who we are as digital selves is something which needs to be thought through the frameworks, nuances and complexities of interactivity as a theory of digital relationality, as a popular taste for engagement, as a marketing term and as an element in the larger history of human communication.

2.2.3 Discerning interactivity and participation by type

Although interactivity has been difficult to define due to its widespread 'buzz-word' use in the early 2000s, there have been some good attempts to define its different forms and types, and these are useful to know if we want to understand its role in identity practices. It is useful to think of it not as something wholly determined by digital technologies, platforms, programming and authorial 'permission' to alter or redistribute a text but as emerging from a culture in which people have always expressed a deep-seated desire to participate in the stories that give us meaning. That means, in this case, to participate in the *textuality* of a text, its *narrative*, the course or temporality of its *narrative flow*, its *structure* and its *situatedness*. That is, interactivity always implies some level of engagement with the text in the act of reading or usage that self-consciously shapes the text or the experience of its reception. Digital media environments promote convenient and comfortable ways of altering a text: to co-participate, re-sequence or interactively transform a printed book would require *literally* cutting and pasting pages, whereas the opportunity to cut-and-paste in order to re-sequence or substantially transform a digital text has become not only easier but a matter of normal engagement with texts.

Defining interactivity is therefore broad and sometimes vague. Spiro Kiousis (2002) argues, however, that there should be no alarm expressed at the difficulty of coming up with a clear definition of interactivity: "as long as we all accept that the term implies some degree of receiver feedback and is usually linked to new technologies, why should there be a problem?" (p. 357). In the widest of definitions, receiver feedback might constitute the changing of television channels or the use of a pause button on a DVD player or selecting a song on an iPod—the exercising of user choice is not, however, necessarily interactive. Other writers have presented more precise understandings of interactivity. Lelia Green (2002), for example, suggests that interactivity implies the capacity of a communication medium to be altered by or have its products altered by the actions of a user or audience, as well as suggesting a technology which requires input from a user to work effectively (p. xx). This definition would cover such products or texts as electronic games, but the extent to which this form of interactivity depends on the technology is more complex—the key question here is one of diverse useability in which different levels of user interest and effort intersect to create a sense of the extent to which a text, medium or channel is interactive. While the latter is not often a built-in feature of a film, and while the *technology* does not specifically direct this sort of choice, it does involve receiver feedback and considerable engagement with a digitally manipulable text.

Sally McMillan provided a very useful, although early, typology of interactive forms. Drawing on the work of Bordewijk and van Kaam (1986), she outlines the concept of interactivity into four different (sometimes intersecting) types:

1. *Allocution*, in which interactive engagement is minimal and is set within the context of a single, central broadcaster and multiple receivers on the periphery. This would ordinarily include most mass media forms such as television, as well as real-time events like the lecture or the play (McMillan 2002, p. 273).

2. *Consultation*, which occurs in the use of a database or static website, where a user actively searches for pre-provided information (p. 273). We might say undertaking a Google search or consulting a page on Wikipedia is an ordinary form of consultative interactivity. Interactive feedback is therefore relatively minimal, even though behind the scenes most engines record the *fact* that a search has been undertaken or a page has been consulted and generate new information about the person who consulted it (often to provide recommendations or advertising in the future). This form of interactivity therefore does not alter the content, the narrative or of the information requested.

3. *Registration* is a form McMillan described as responding to inputs from users because it records those inputs and thereby causes a change to occur in a text (p. 273). We could, perhaps, see the example of a Wikipedia page being *edited* by an everyday user as a good example of registration—it records the typed inputs and changes the page. Similarly, *writing a comment* on someone's Facebook page can be seen as a form of registrational interactivity, because the platform takes the input, registers it and it is published as part of the post. Or we might consider our Instagram feed whereby *uploading an image* has changed the page of our images by adding to it. Or a digital game, in which interaction with the text by *game device inputs* that are registered by the application and change what is happening in the game is another good example.

4. Finally, McMillan identified the most interactive form of interactivity, being what she labelled as *conversational*. Conversational interactivity occurs when individuals interact directly with each other, mimicking aspects of face-to-face (F2F) contact through digital platforms and sites (p. 273). Again, to use an example from Facebook, while commenting on someone's post might be understood as registrational, if you and I engage in a non-real-time conversation by continuing to post, this setting has shifted from being a registrational interactivity to a conversational one. This last one is an important point, because it demonstrates how difficult it is to decide on what form of interactivity a digital user is involved in and implies there may be intent.

McMillan's definitions tend to focus on the affordances of different aspects of digital formations and the kinds of interactivity they facilitate, suggesting to some extent that it is determined by technology. Others, however, have suggested that interactivity is located more in the process of use than in the affordances of a technology or medium. For example, Rafaeli and Sudweeks (1997) argued that:

> interactivity is not a characteristic of the medium. It is a process-related construct about communication. It is the extent to which messages in a sequence relate to each other, and especially the extent to which later messages recount the relatedness of earlier messages.

What they have done by focusing on process is ensure the *user*—and their decisions about what they do—is a key part of the picture of interactivity.

Likewise, Denis McQuail (1997) reinstates the question of the audience member, user or receiver as human subject in a communication process:

> this would seem to run counter to the general trend of media history, restoring a human scale and individuality to mediated social communication, restoring the balance of power of the receiver at the periphery as against the dominant centralized sender. But it also increases the individuation of use and fragmentation of the mass audience. It is also still unclear how far the audience wants to be interactive.
>
> (p. 10)

This leads back to the idea I suggested earlier: that there is a deep-seated desire among audiences or users to engage with texts in interactive ways. In that sense, we might say that the authorial control over the creation of traditional *recorded*, *broadcast* and *published* content has always been a sort of constraint on that desire, and that digital interactivity is a cultural response or workaround that enables participation in storytelling and sharing as we desire it. In that sense, interactivity is not something given to us by a technology but the result of a grassroots resistance to textual control.

2.2.4 Interactivity and the author–text–audience relationship: synergy and struggle

For Mark Dery, who wrote the important work 'Culture Jamming' (1993), the kind of resistance that early digital interactivity took was in the form of media hacking, informational warfare, terror-art and the guerrilla tactics of work which sought to point out the Derry controlled foundations of media texts. This conception of an emerging, diametric war between media creators/industries and audience participation was therefore part of the early era of the Internet, although, of course, most media industries have seen the benefit of 'capturing' the potential of interactivity rather than alienating their audiences.

Considering the form of registrational or participatory interactivity, it is useful to think of this in terms of the longer history of audiences and authorship—none of which should ever be seen as natural but constructed cultural relationships. It is useful to start with the idea of the author. The very concept of the author as the central 'authority' of a work is, as historian Michel Foucault (1977a) pointed out, one which emerged at a particular moment in history as a result of a range of cultural factors and change. Foucault re-theorised the concept of the author not just as the creator of a text but as the cultural figure which helped 'organise' how a text was read, controlled, distributed, copyrighted and so on—that is, we read Shakespeare in a way different from how we read your comment on a TikTok video.

Questions over, for example, intellectual property illustrate the two poles of authorship in which, on the one hand, a work can be disputed as having needed the protections that accord its 'ownership' to an author and, on the other hand, as defending a set of rights asserted by an author not to have that work *altered* or *distributed* outside of their control. Such rights are a major aspect of the hangover from Enlightenment culture, publishing and mass media forms of the past. Foucault (1977a) demonstrated how the author is not only historical, but that the idea of an author is one which is threatened at various times and in various forms:

> The 'author-function' is tied to the legal and institutional systems that circumscribe, determine, and articulate the realm of discourses; it does not operate in a uniform manner in all discourses, at all times, and in any given culture; it is not defined by the spontaneous attribution of a text to its creator, but through a series of precise and complex procedures; it does not refer, purely and simply, to an actual individual insofar as it simultaneously gives rise to a variety of egos and to a series of subjective positions that individuals of any class may come to occupy.
>
> (pp. 130–131)

This suggests, therefore, that the emergence of digital interactivity that encourages participatory manipulation of a text is part of a cultural *pleasure* of engagement with the text. It puts into question the functionality of authorship and, perhaps, makes the idea of an author less secure. As he noted: "We can easily imagine a culture where discourses would circulate without any need for an author. Discourses, whatever their status, form, or value, and regardless of our manner of handling them, would unfold in a pervasive anonymity" (Foucault 1977a, p. 138). Am I the author of my Instagram page? Or have you contributed to that authorship by using the interactive tools to make comments, likes and so on? Which part is the text, and if we divide it up, which part is my text and which is yours?

Textuality itself, then, becomes something that is put into question in a digital interactive culture. The idea of the text persists, of course, but no longer as a unified, coherent and fixed whole. For example, I might finish a short film and upload it to YouTube, but with no guarantee that it hasn't been downloaded, remixed, had an alternative voice put to it, had scenes deleted and so on. While I might resent what is done to my film because I perceive myself as its author and try to claim a right of authorship, those who manipulated it are simply participating in the culture of interactivity and using my film to tell a different story (even if it looks bad or discredits me).

That's the story of authorship in a digital communication setting, but what about the *audience*? How does the concept of an audience change in a culture of interactivity? Once interactivity is deemed to make available forms of textual creation, participation or co-creativity with authors, the ability to alter, transform or redistribute a text is, on the one hand, the *empowerment* of audience (McMillan 2002, pp. 279, 285) and, on the other hand, the dissolution of the traditional concept of audiencehood (Brooker and Jermyn 2003; Webster 1998). Definitions of audience are, of course, diverse and contested, but by necessity have been subject to various forms of categorisation, particularly where such categorisations occur in ways which give the power of the audience to interpret, act, transform or redistribute in other ways.

In her canonical work *Desperately Seeking the Audience* (1991), Ien Ang, for example, categorises the audience across two paradigms as, on the one hand, a *public* and, on the other hand, a *market*. Ang's distinction is also of significance in demonstrating the gap between the audience desire for participation and the authorial desire for textual control (p. 29). However, Ang's dualist system is open to a reinterpretation in terms of the rise of interactive engagement: for Ang, the audience-as-public paradigm locates the audience in a transmission model of communication, viewing the audience as that which requests and, under paternalistic systems, requires information and meaning. This view of the audience is of a mass group of 'receivers' within a system of more-or-less ordered transference of meaning (p. 29). The desire for narrative interactivity under such a view would be seen to be a disruption of this order of transference and would dissolve the centrist model on which transmissional systems are based. The audience-as-market notion, however, gives the question of transfers of meaning—or, indeed, material from which to make meaning in an 'active audience' conception—only a secondary level of importance, after the primary business of providing goods and services to potential customers, aroused in order to maintain their interest (Ang 1991, p. 29).

However, Ang's pre-digital dualist system is open to reinterpretation in terms of the rise of various forms of interactive engagement: for Ang, the audience-as-public paradigm locates the audience in a *transmission* model of communication, viewing the audience as that which requests and, under paternalistic systems, requires information and meaning. This view of the audience is of a mass group of 'receivers' within a system of more-or-less ordered transference of meaning (p. 29). The desire for interactive engagement and participation under such a view would be seen to be a disruption of this order of transference and would dissolve the centrist model on which transmissional systems are often thought about. We might view the interactive audience—where such interactivity involves participation in the transformation or co-creation of the text—as a new category to describe both an ancient form and its re-emergence alongside digital media technologies.

In his book *Communication as Culture* (1988), media theorist James Carey identified two views of communication practices that include the figure of the audience in two different ways—the *transmission* view and the *ritual* view. The transmission view is the standard, pedestrian account of communication as it occurs in most simplistic communication models of sender-message-receiver. It is, for Carey, defined by key terms such as "imparting," "sending," "transmitting" and "giving information to others." Texts in the pre-digital framework are transmitted or distributed *across space* to audiences, whether that's a book sent to a bookshop or a television series broadcast through terrestrial aerials (p. 14). He described the ritual view, on the other hand, as communication acts that were about "sharing," "association," "fellowship," "possession of a common faith" among audiences. Here it was much less about the content of the text that mattered, and much more important to consider the ritualistic engagement or viewing or reading practices of an audience that gave us a sense of commonality and community as readers or audiences.

We might argue, however, that seeing the audience as interactive in a digital era constitutes a *third position* (Cover 2016). It is this third position or view that works to blur the distinction between author, text and audience by suggesting that such a distinction was always from the beginning a constructed one that attempted to 'shore up' the idea of the author as the *authority* over the text and position the audience as secondary in the process of creativity. The interactive position is one which is located in the push-and-pull struggle between author-industry and audience-user over the right and ability to access and utilise the text in ways that meet the audience members' desires to participate.

Certainly, audience members and those who would ordinarily be defined by media industries as content-receivers or content-users are aware of the push-and-pull relationship between authorial/narrative control and audience interactivity. This was the case even in the early days of the Internet before social media. Edward Downes and Sally McMillan (2000) interviewed a number of users on the impacts of computer-mediated interactive communication, finding responses categorisable across the three areas of the revolutionary potential of interactivity, the general consequences to media consumption and an uncertainty over the future of media use. What is interesting about the interview extracts used by the authors is the location of questions of interactivity within the language of threat (to authorial control), empowerment (of audiences or users) and opposition to media industries (as controllers). As one respondent put it, interactivity "threatens whole industries, threatens whole professions" (p. 164). Another found that the ability to access and utilise knowledge was in general empowering and located this empowerment in controller/user and corporate/media citizen dyads: "Because I have a voice now. I think the threat is to existing institutions and the old ways of doing things" (p. 164). Although it appears their respondents valued the concept of a *threat* to authorship diversely, others seemed to speak more in terms of wresting control from the author (p. 170) and in creating a territory or space as a sense of 'place' within new computer-mediated environments (p. 166).

This notion of online environments as having separate kinds of spaces in which authorship is done differently is, perhaps, a moot point today in a digital network in which such diversity of material is available. One of the key questions, then, becomes not a matter of whether traditional institutional controls, content-creators, news-producers (etc.) can or will exist alongside the entry of newer start-ups and individuals writing, but the extent to which a democratically feasible mix of alternatives is available and how they will be accessed in a search engine regime that can seemingly give preference to larger corporate distribution networks. This is highly significant for how we practice identity, given that an interactive environment that preferences the potential of interactivity can make available new, democratically creative and potentially radical formations of identity that are right now unknowable but may have value either to individuals or socially beyond that.

2.2.5 *Push-and-pull: audience interactivity in history*

Another way in which we can understand interactivity as a struggle between the concept of the author and the concept of the audience or user is across the wider history of mediated communication. This is to make an argument that a deep-seated desire to participate in storytelling and meaning-making, and a struggle to control the text's distribution, has been part of the very long duration of media. In some ways, therefore, we might argue that if identity is always performative in the sense that it involves citing and repeating the categories and knowledge frameworks of identity given in discourse itself, then one aspect of how identity is done has always depended on the kinds of controls, battles, dominances and alternatives over the communication of texts that convey and mediate that discourse. Here, I would like to briefly trace some aspects of this push-and-pull juxtaposition between authorial control and interactive dissent across a longer period with some brief examples drawing on the evolution of media forms from theatre as a real-time event through recorded analogue media forms such as cinema and television—all of which are different from but underpin and lead to the development of contemporary digital cultures and practices, including digital gaming and social media.

The practice of the theatre as a media and communication form is a good example. Our usual experience of the theatrical text is one based in cultural practices of audience limitation: any attempt by the audience to interfere or involve oneself in the storytelling, to disrupt, change, shout out or otherwise participate (unless invited) is to cross a line. That is, the penetration of the sacred space of the stage would be considered abject behaviour, disrupting both the social and the ritualistic processes of language and the coherence and intelligibility of the actors (communicators) versus audience (recipients) as a cultural form (Kristeva 1982). Such a breach is to *upset* the integrity of the theatrical work as a text. Of course, doing so risks not only keeping our seat in the theatre but being perceived by others as having lost our right to social belonging.

The very architectural aesthetics of the standard, contemporary Victorian model of the theatre that remains normal today—with its neat line between the audience and the stage—can however be contrasted with the much earlier model of the Greek amphitheatre. The amphitheatre with its circularity fosters a kind of interactive engagement with the text/play and across the audience who are better positioned to see each other. The Victorian model of the theatre, however, is familiar and enduring, and it became the spatial setting for the cinema and reinforced that dividing line, because the screen itself (and the fact the film was already finished before it was screened) halts any possibility of interaction and destabilisation of the text as a finished text. Television, building on the form of radio broadcast, likewise presents its dividing line—like cinema in a public setting, the private viewing of a television screen provides no opportunity to interact creatively with the text.

This is not, of course, to suggest that the impersonality of the film screen, the television screen, the one-way television broadcast and other media forms that did not afford interactivity and personal engagement with the story are necessarily inferior. Indeed, Raymond Williams pointed out that it is common to contrast, say, television viewing with in-person conversation and to see the latter as the superior form, but what such anti-television arguments did was ignore the fact that television (or film) did not *replace* conversation but added a media choice that was made available in contemporary culture (Williams 1997). In the same way, cinema did not replace theatre but added a media form to the range available. Arguably, then, the rise of digital interactive models of engagement with texts and meaning has not replaced the traditional non-interactive forms of media either but helped fulfil a cultural desire for participation by adding to the available media forms.

Nevertheless, it remains that traditional media forms are marked by a radical separation by space or time between the author and the audience that prevented interactivity: the television live broadcast from somewhere other than where we are viewing, the book that was written 20 years ago that we are now reading (Meadows 1994, p. 133). However, various developments across history did allow users and audiences greater control and interactivity in what I have been describing as the push-and-pull struggle between authorial control and audience desires for manipulation. For example, in the case of television, the advent of the video recorder not only released the text from the broadcast imperatives of time (Cubitt 1991, p. 42) but allowed a user to control various aspects of viewing a television programme—to watch at various speeds, to forward through segments of little interest, to rewatch the entire text a second or third time and, for the more advance, to utilise two video recorders to reorder sequences, delete sections or otherwise 'interfere' with the text (Penley 1997, p. 114; Jenkins 2003), thereby allowing an early form of narrative interactivity which provided an outlet for creative desires to participate in and expand existing texts. Indeed, the very substantial uptake of video recorders in households during the 1980s and 1990s is one, among many, strong indicators of a broad public desire to 'take control' of texts in ways that television itself did not make available.

Bearing this in mind, it can be suggested that one way in which we can view the historical development of various media technologies is from a perspective which understands their emergence as driven by a cultural demand for the *democratisation* of control over the text. This is a demand to participate in creativity *alongside* recognised authors, creators, broadcasters and so on and to achieve gratification through interactive participation. In this sense, digital interactivity is not to be understood as an invention that suddenly enabled people to engage with texts and with one another, but the *fruition* of a long-standing, deeply seated and highly meaningful desire for participation. In this sense, digital technologies afforded the restoration to audiences of their capacity to participate, share control and engage in storytelling practices of their own.

2.2.6 Identity and interactivity

In the context of the forms of co-creative interactivity, I have been describing here as something which is a key element of the contemporary Web 2.0 digital culture, we might ask what the experience *does* for thinking about identity. In this section, I would like to return to some of the approaches to identity opened up by Michel Foucault and Judith Butler as poststructuralist critiques of older, liberal-humanist understandings of identity, subjectivity and selfhood. This will allow us to turn away from the idea that we come to digital media with agency, fully intact identities and a sense of authenticity before we participate. Instead, it opens the chance to ask how interactive and participatory media cultures *shape* us in our acts of participation. That is, where we may have utilised traditional media as texts which provided the norms, categories and intelligibilities so we could perform a coherent and recognisable identity, we now participate in and adapt texts so that we are now also their co-creators and adapters—substantially changing the framework that governed the role of media texts in guiding identity.

Butler (1990, 1993) argued that identity is always performed through *citing* categories, signs and norms that circulate in culture and always precede us. Contemporary culture and the holdovers of Enlightenment demands for identity coherence encourage us to 'take on' certain norms of identity—such as gender, ethnicity, sexuality, class affiliations, 'human' and so on. We do this in order to fulfil the cultural demand of being a coherent and recognisable subject, which allows us to belong and to participate in society as a full subject (Butler 1993, pp. 225–226). This does not mean that we do not vary those categories in ways which are diverse, nor does it mean that there are no political arguments about the legitimacy of some categories of identity or that some are not marginalised socially. Rather, it means that identities are always *relational*: they are performed, practised and made sense of in the context of pre-existing languages, discourses and texts that are social to begin with and that we encounter in many different ways.

In the second half of the twentieth century, we might say that much of that encounter occurred in television, print, radio, popular song and film—we encountered narratives that told stories about how 'we' should look, feel, behave, react and otherwise 'be' our identities. Once we acknowledge that we are now living in a digitally saturated world, we have to consider how digital practices such as interactivity dominate that 'encounter' with pre-existing discourses and, therefore, what interacting with those texts we encounter might do for that process of 'citation.' In other words, the way in which we encounter the languages, discourses and texts that convey categories of identity and make them sensible is *conditioned* by digital practices which, today, involves participation in the making and remaking of those texts.

In a traditional framework, for example, a subject might encounter the discourses, categories, norms and codes of behaviour that make a *national* identity meaningful—perhaps across the media matrix that includes news services, national television series and soap operas, a national war hero film, some books read at school, public articulations of 'national pride' and so on. For some people, this might mean citing the behavioural norms that are conveyed in those texts in order to better perform that national identity. Those norms might include attitudes of national pride, nationalism and patriotism; or bodily norms related to choice of dress, a particular accent; or taste-based norms such as choices of further films and television to watch, books to read, attendance at ceremonies on national days, the acquisition of ornaments and objects that convey help demonstrate our national feeling (Noble 2002). Or it might include performing attitudes that refuse to see the difficulty of experience among migrants, a revulsion towards citizens from foreign origins or intense affiliation with a political party. Most of these will 'feel' like decisions made with agency, but from a performativity theory perspective, the norms of that national identity have come from discourse and may include paradigms that were mediated across a range of communication forms. Obviously, this does not mean that many of us do not resist even having a national identity, and that there isn't variation and diversity. Rather, what it means is that national identity is performed through acts that broadly *align* with the knowledge frameworks we have encountered. So *how* those knowledges are made available is important. It also means that once we recognise the dominance of a digital interactive culture in which people participate in a great outpouring of communication, creativity and textual manipulation (Andrejevic 2011), the fixity and coherence of those texts that communicate the norms of a national identity are now much more in play. They are also becoming more complex and contested.

For example, a subject might encounter digital video that meaningfully conveys norms about national identity but subject that text to video manipulation and remixing. There has been a substantial proliferation of remixed (audiovisual) texts such as fan music videos, slash video, mash-ups and digital stories utilising and combining both existing and new visual and audio material on sites such as YouTube, opening important new ways of thinking of media engagement as predicated on interactive and co-creative formations. Remixed texts can be understood as a new and transformative form of user engagement with media that, despite industry copyright concerns, do not compete with existing texts but make use of them as 'found material' in order to produce an ostensibly intertextual experience (Lessig 2008, pp. 11–12). For Lawrence Lessig (2008), remix is a form of creativity that puts in question the separation between reader and writer and, instead, emphasises the participatory form in which read–write creativity (or co-creativity) becomes the normative standard of high-level engagement with extant texts through both selection and arrangement (p. 56). Remix culture, Lessig suggests, makes use of digital technologies that have been developed for other purposes and practices and delivers forms of collage, complexity and co-creativity directed towards a broader audience.

A user might, say, take a number of scenes from that video, re-sequence them into a new order, juxtaposed and aligned and place them against a three-minute audio track of Madonna singing "Justify my Love." In the act of remixing them and hearing them 'speak' back against Madonna's unrelated lyrics, new meanings emerge. This is not simply the *productive activation* of meaning in the act of reading and interpreting a text, but the *active production* of new textualities that come to have meanings for identity, creating new, unexpected and unanticipated categories, significations and attributes for a set of identities in which the reader recognises something different about the norms of national identity. In other words, rather than simply 'citing' the norms as they are given in the text and the wider cultural discourse, a subject now has the capacity to co-create those texts and give them new, perhaps unintended meanings. This does not mean such an act fully undoes the norms of nationalism (in fact, it might exacerbate them), but that our *relationship* with texts has substantially changed in an interactive era.

Butler theorised that identity is not only constituted in the citation and performance of pre-given cultural norms of identity, but that in the encounter with new, alternative and different discourses a subject may be reconstituted as something other, making a shift in identity not only possible but a normal part of the *process* of stabilising identity over time (Butler 1991). In this context those new discourses are not only texts one stumbles upon that might change an outlook and be incorporated into identity—such as the encounter with anti-nationalistic texts that disrupt the significance of national identity to a subject. Rather, the subject is potentially participating in the creation of alternative texts by remixing, changing and co-creating, allowing wholly new configurations of identity possibilities available for citation. In other words, the possibilities of doing identity differently are substantially increased not merely by the proliferation of discourses made available online but by the very practices of interactivity that actively encourage co-creativity in storytelling, which includes the national stories that make a national identity intelligible and meaningful.

2.3 Identity performativity and social media profiles

Social media platforms are, of course, one of the main settings in which we simultaneously conduct online interactivity and perform our identities. While uses of platforms are very diverse, much of the time we do what we might call 'identity work' in these spaces—maintaining profiles, telling stories from our everyday life, indicating our attitudes and preferences towards politics or popular culture, connecting with other people, uploading selfies and other images and so on. All of these are part of the practice of performing an identity, and it is in the act of engaging with social media we not only reveal who we are to a wider social group but effectively produce our identities.

Some scholarship on social media has tended to think about platforms merely as a medium through which we communicate our lives or identities *as if* our identities are already fixed and our communications are directed from a pre-existing self (e.g., Donath and boyd 2004; Liu 2008; Livingstone and Brake 2010). This is what we call an *a priori* identity approach, whereby the identity is always seen to precede the act of communicating about it. In contrast, if we use a poststructuralist approach, we can see that the act of communicating is just another way of performing the self and in ways both (a) directed by how the platform sets norms and limits on how we curate our profiles and self-stories and (b) opened up by our interaction with other knowledges through commentary, likes, sharing and adaptation. All performance of identity is relational in that it requires the citation of discursive categories of identity, is performed for recognisability and operates within constructed 'truth regimes,' and these are also conditioned by the additional *surveillance* from others enabled by the social media settings whenever we post, engage or perform. In this section, we work through some of the ways in which Judith Butler's theory of performativity is both useful for understanding social media and requires some further adaptation in light of interactivity.

2.3.1 Social media and the performativity of identity

Much of the early literature on social networks is grounded in an idea that there is a conscious, wilful *use* of an online platform like Facebook, Twitter or Instagram—that we make decisions about what we post and then return to our 'real life.' This position continues that early cyberculture approach that maintains the 'real life' versus 'virtual self' dichotomy and, effectively, the reification of a 'real' identity out of which the 'virtual self' could be voluntarily created. However, several more effective and theoretically grounded approaches to understanding the relationship between social networking and identity build on the work of Erving Goffman (1959). Goffman's analysis of identity performance offers a convenient framework for the analysis of identity expression only. Social networks, situated in the broader cultural practices of individualism, self-narration and interconnectivity, offer many parallels to Goffman's work. Goffman points to the self-conscious presentation of selfhood in different contexts as well as the symptomatic elements of performance—that is, what people 'give' and what they 'give off.' An individual, for Goffman, performs identity through both of the forms of intentional and unintentional expression. In the context of social networking and other online forms of relationality, Goffman's approach to the performative expression of selfhood points to the ways in which the online acts of typing, updating, uploading photos and videos and other activities serve as both intentional and unintentional forms of expression to varying degrees depending on intent and context.

Beyond the anthropological work of Goffman and its reliance on ideas of a front-end and back-end performance of selfhood, the poststructuralist and feminist approaches since the 1990s have contributed to a broader understanding of identity as contingent, multiple and fluid, constituted in historical, cultural and narrativised structures and frameworks. This approach was critical of Goffman's perception of a front-end (public) and back-end (private) identity split and instead argued that not only is identity more complex but that the idea there is a private self which directs and produces the public identity is mythical. Indeed, the very distinction between private and public is more complex, has many grey areas, changes and is not something which is clearly agreed among all of us. That is, poststructuralist theory was critical of the Enlightenment framework which had long perceived identity to be innate and fixed with an inner essence, and by which we direct our public and social representations as if the public identity practices are consciously shaped.

Butler's work on performativity was particularly useful in helping us make sense of how such behaviour, communication, articulation and activity was not just a 'front end' of our real selves but actively constitutes identity—that is, what we do in the face of others is not merely a representation that may be more-or-less the same as our core selves but actually forms that core self through repetitive practices aligned with norms, categories and signs of identity. Although Butler's work is complex and wide-ranging, there are four nodes of her approach to identity performativity which are significant for studying online, interactive behaviours and experiences on social media. These can be summarised as follows:

1. Building on the work of earlier theorists such as Nietzsche, Foucault and Lacan, Butler argued that there is no knowable core essence or inner self from which behaviours and actions, whether online or offline, emerge. Rather, there are only sets of performances that retroactively produce an illusion of an inner identity core.

There is no doer behind the deed, no actor behind the acts. The sense we have of an inner identity self is only ever an *effect* of those performances (Butler 1993, p. 12). *In that sense, what we write, post, upload on social media or how we otherwise engage with social media are performances of the self not merely expressions.*

2. Our identities are performed 'in accord' with discursively given norms, categories, stereotypes, labels and expressions. These norms are given to us in culture, and while we vary them substantially we culturally compelled to perform our identities within normative limits. *In the context of social networking, such norms occur under the surveillance of those in our networks and through practices of platform curation that help direct the 'norms' of posting, liking and so on.*

3. Identities are constituted in discourse but can be reconstituted or reconfigured differently in the encounter with different, new, alternative discursive arrangements (Butler 1991, p. 18). *In a social media context, these can be understood to include alternative discourses that were not previously available to us, for example, encountering alternative ways of perceiving gender norms among those in our networks.*

4. The process of performing identity within regimentary norms occurs within a narrative of coherence *over time*, motivated by a cultural demand or imperative that we are coherent, intelligible and recognisable to others in order to allow social participation and belonging (Butler 1997, p. 27). *Although there is substantial diversity in any social media space, it is one among many institutional and social practices that call upon us to perform identities in coherent, intelligible and recognised ways in order to participate. Incoherent or unintelligible selfhood risks always losing members of our network, being questioned or criticised by others or losing the rights to post.*

In other words, a Butlerian perspective argues that our identities are produced through the citation of culturally given identity norms in a reiterative process and played out across all our actions, speech and behaviours in ways which give a sense that there is an individual, inner self. In this theoretical framework, then, it would be a mistake to think of social networking participation and engagement as being in any way different from other aspects of performance, whether that is—to use gender identity as an example— norms of comportment, dress, voice, desire and so on. In social media settings, that might be the kinds of images we post, the attitudes we take and express, the choices around liking or ignoring the posts of others—all of which are part of the wider performance of identity that helps shore up our gender in accord with certain norms, including norms of diversity.

When we bear in mind that contemporary culture *compels* coherent, rational, recognisable identity performances in order to belong in some way (Woodward 2002, p. 89), social media platforms are therefore available to be understood as one tool or mechanism for attempting to be *effective* in articulating that coherent and intelligible identity. As the *work* of self-coherence becomes ever-more difficult in the face of an increasingly complex world, the time we spend in curating our profiles and posts may best be understood as a response to that demand for coherence. Coherence is, of course, never fully possible because identity is always a *process* rather than a completed artefact of selfhood—from Butler's perspective, we are driven to perform in coherent ways but will always fall slightly short, hence the need to continue the performance through repetition over time.

We can therefore argue that participation in social media can be said to be the tools *par excellence* by which to perform as a coherent subject. As Helen Kennedy (2006) has pointed out about online settings generally, they are a media form which is never entirely finished, just as identity performance is a continuous process—both are constantly "under construction" (p. 869). A user posting on Instagram as an aspect of performing identity in a never-ending process towards coherence and intelligibility is, effectively, doing what we do when we have a conversation, perhaps in a café, with a friend and speak of ourselves, desires, experiences, recent actions and tastes. Within a disciplinary society of surveillance (Foucault 1977b), we police each other's identities for coherence, often in line with stereotypes and easily recognisable 'norms' and narratives: one subject's taste for classical music but punk outfits demands an explanation for consistency, intelligibility and uniformity in order to belong and maintain participation in the social. Within cultural frameworks that posit the stereotype that, for example, gay men are particular about interior décor (an old but persistent stereotype), one's gay identity but images of a messy and unkempt household are seen as non-complementary or 'failure.' The fail to conform to that knowledge stereotype demands explanation. Similarly, two conflicting political views must be smoothed over as in conversational language: "But you said earlier…" demanding the *work* of bringing the performance, articulations, expressions back into coherence and stabilising once again the project of identity.

On social networking sites, the tools for producing and articulating oneself in coherence and unified intelligibility are effectively *supplied* in the profile management interface, providing a discursive framework used to give performative acts of identity consistency and coherence. For Sonia Livingstone (2008), whether those choices are limited or expansive, such choices are always acts of biographisation of the self, in which users "select a more or less complex represent of themselves" (p. 403). The profile basics can be said to include gender, birth date, gender of sexual/romantic interest, relationship status (and who), a biographical statement, political views, religious views, a short written biography, a profile photograph or image, a favourite quotation, education and work, likes and interests. Notably, sites such as Facebook have responded to the increasingly popular idea of microcategorisations of identity by expanding the possibilities for how one represents oneself. For example, while early Facebook profile management tools required people to select the profile gender from a list of two (male or female), it was later expanded to include a wider range and eventually to permit custom terms that align with the widening range of gender identity labels (Cover 2019).

What is significant here is not merely that social media profile management interfaces typically call upon us to *announce* our genders and other demarcations of identity, but that the *act* of making a selection is itself a performance of identity, no different from other kinds of bodily, corporeal performances in other aspects of our lives. This does not mean that we do not mis-choose (by mistake) or play (for the purposes of humour, disruption or resistance). What it does mean, however, are the following:

1. the first of the four key aspects of Butler's performativity theory is enacted online by the act of articulating and stabilising our identities by making a selection—it may feel like a deliberate act that merely represents ourselves, but it is one among the many identity performance acts we undertake every day that retroactively stabilises our identity *as if* it is something that emerges from within our very core. In Butler's (1990) terms, like discourse, these are "constitutive categories that seek to keep gender in its place by posturing as the foundational illusions of identity" (pp. 33–34).

2. the second aspect of Butler's theory is also at play—that we cite from the available languages, categories, norms, signifiers and codes of behaviour that always *precede* our identities and come before us. Here, we choose from the available categories

provided by a social media platform, aligning with the ways in which we have already been positioned to articulate our gendered identities in other aspects of our lives. As platforms increasingly tend not to direct to a list of available choices (such as male/ female) but to be open to letting us articulate those identities on our own (Cover 2019), we respond with what aligns with our curated profile, with our coherent performativity of selfhood.

3. Noting the important point that the encounter with alternative or previously unavailable discourses has the potential to reconstitute or shift a stabilised identity, the encounter with any kind of drop-down list of alternative identity labels or what we see on other people's profiles has the potential to reconstitution how a user recognises themselves, potentially prompting a change in gender identity or, indeed, a refusal of gender labels altogether.

4. Finally, the fact that one is called upon to state identity terms such as gender is a call to abide by the cultural demands for coherence and intelligibility. This is not simply a demand to select a gender identity (indeed, it is increasingly optional on platforms worried about the demands this places on people). Rather, it is a demand to align our performances, selections, articulations and statements with recognisable norms in a coherent way. For example, if I choose or state the perceived 'wrong' gender category, what will my friends or family on Facebook say when they stand in for wider society and demand an explanation (demand that coherence)?

What is important about the profile pages of Facebook is that the information, often provided as an initiation into social networking (boyd 2008, p. 128) and subsequently updated as the 'narrative' of our performed identities might change, shift or stabilise over time, responds to the cultural demand for coherence and provides the tools for smoothing over the inconsistencies into an intelligible, recognisable presentation of selfhood. This is not the site of the Web 1.0 chat-room identity experimentation (Turkle 1995) I described in Chapter 1. In the era before social networking platforms, there was substantially greater opportunity for play, theatrics, pretence, trying things out or tricking other people. Rather, in the face of the surveillance by the network of known users on a platform, we are routinely encouraged to produce ourselves with greater attention—and all the extra labour that entails—to the demands for coherence and intelligibility, for normative identities that operate in ways which are recognisable to others.

2.3.2 *Interacting across the social network*

Section 2.3.1 discussed profile management tools on social media. This, however, leaves out the wider aspect of contemporary digital communication that was approached earlier in this chapter—interactivity. While interactivity has been discussed in terms of engagement with the texts that precede us and give our identities meaning, it is useful to now think about how *interactivity with others* is part of the identity process online.

Although not wholly disconnected from profile management, the act of friending and relating to others through social networking on Facebook is a separate set of performances of identity expression. This second 'field' of online performance focuses on the social or relational, producing conformity through interactive identification with others: friends, acquaintances, strangers, persons known only online, co-workers, employees, students and teachers, parents and family—all typically presented under the problematically simple label of 'friends.' Online relationality is developed through:

1. the creation and maintenance of friends lists through reciprocal adding and accepting of friends (Lewis and West 2009, p. 1210); and
2. engaging with those friends to varying degrees through interactive communication such as updating, commenting, responding and tagging (Green 2008, p. 7).

Just like profile management, both of these are performative acts of identification that occur in relation to others and in terms of belonging. They are specific activities which produce, constitute and stabilise our identities. Who we are friends with, how we describe them, who we choose not to add or accept as online friends, who are stated as family and other aspects of articulating kinship and peer networks are substantial aspects in the performance of identity (Lewis and West 2009, p. 1210).

Within this theoretical approach, it can be argued that the act of coherent and intelligible identity performances are not only to maintain norms for social participation but are done in the context of those in our circle of friends who—often unwittingly but within disciplinary society—surveil. Those who will engage with the narrative of my performance, those who will look for coherence and those who will recognise my self as a subject do so on behalf of power formations of normalisation. This is something that occurs within a construction not just of identity norms, categories and names as given discursively but within a matrix of *identification* and *belonging*.

In some older work on how users present themselves through social networking on the now more-or-less defunct early platform LiveJournal, Hodkinson (2007) argued that social media friending is always an individualised set of choices as to how one interacts and customises the self within shifting personal priorities rather than fixed and ongoing group structures (p. 646). Building on some of Donath and boyd's work (2004), Liu similar points out that a user's friends and network connections on other social media are an expression of identity and "the public display of friend connections constitutes a social milieu that contextualises one's identity" (2008, p. 254). They are, for Liu, "willful acts of context creation" (p. 254) that aim to produce group identifications through solidarity between a user's tastes and a social group's taste norm (pp. 261–262). This perspective is notable for the way in which it places identity within the context of surveillance through spectatorship and interaction with others within a social network. Liu sees this as a self-conscious act by which performers are reflectively aware of the impressions fostered within the network of friends. However, the relationality of social networking can be understood as a non-ostensible activity taken up unwittingly by users as part of the "biographical 'narratives' that will explain themselves to themselves, and hence sustain a coherent and consistent identity" (Buckingham 2008, p. 9).

In line with Butler's more nuanced approach to identity performativity, we might argue that the performances of identity which may appear to be wilful and reflexive are acts which constitute the *narrative* of selfhood, retroactively establishing the subject who speaks—or in this case, 'speaks that identity' through interactions with friends and acts of friending. The performative interaction and relationality with others online comes in the two forms of: (1) friending and friend list maintenance and (2) synchronous and asynchronous communication between those 'friends,' both of which I will outline below.

Friending: To understand the identity implications of the act of friending, we need to keep in mind how the performance of identity operates in the context of online social networks: that is, by asking what acts of friending might do to constitute our identities. In the first few years of Web 2.0 social networking, there was interest among scholars in how online friends are categorised variously by users relying on platform mechanisms that allowed certain information to remain private from certain groups (Diaz 2008); others explored how friendship online was being understood as a weak form of relationality as opposed to social contact in a fully embodied, offline sense (Baym et al. 2007; Ellison et al. 2007; Tong et al. 2008); and still others suggested that social networking sites' singular conceptual category of friend (regardless of various privacy distinctions on Facebook) is a flattening out of the complex relationships and multiple categories of friendship, kinship and acquaintanceship experienced in offline spaces (Lewis and West 2009).

We can advance these important points by noting that the act of friending—of adding a friend, whether that be an acquaintance, a stranger, an old friend or some other category of relationship—is an act of identity performance in and of itself. But that act is channelled through a concept of *identification*. This means acknowledging and thereby producing and stabilising some relationship and some sense of like (whether that be liking in the sense of fondness or being akin to an other, noting that Facebook frequently uses the signifier *like* as a means of response to friends' comments and the terminology for joining a group fan page). Choosing to add a friend may, of course, feel like a voluntary act of seeking information or gaining access to another's profile. However, in Butler's performativity framework, it is what that act 'says' about a user that retrospectively makes it a factor of identity performance—remembering that all performances of selfhood are non-voluntary and non-conscious acts.

In the case of most social media networking and friending practices, one thus forms an identification with an other through the performative act of adding a friend or liking a group, and this responds to the very grey set of distinctions between identifying with an *other* in relation: possessing an other as a friend on a list and possessing a particular 'friend count' (Tong et al. 2008). Given that friending on Facebook, as on several other social networking platforms, is also an action which allows access to one's profile of 'managed' self-information, prior postings, photographs and other artefacts (Tufekci 2008), the act is a sort of double-performative—it is an identification that is simultaneously an articulation of the history of identifications given through that profile, a simultaneous act of relationality and of speaking the self. None of this is to suggest that there is some flattening out of all persons on a friendship list, as if a group has come together through sameness. Rather, identifications can be constituted in difference and distinction (Butler 1995). For a singular user, what can occur is a set of identifications that are marked by varying gradations and fragmentations of identification, of sameness and difference, of closeness and distance and of other categorisations which may not be stated obviously through Facebook's friends lists. The act of adding—and, by corollary, the decision *not to add*—friends is therefore an act of performance that constitutes the self through a complex array of claims to relationality and sociality.

Networked communication: As for the second form of performativity through friendship and relationality, identifications are *stabilised* through commentary, updates, discussions and communication with those in our network. The performativity of relationships and belonging in social networking is, in other words, not limited to (a) owning a list of friends and/or (b) being on another's list of friends but on maintaining flows of communication through the multifarious vectors of friendship and relationality on social networking sites. These are, of course, not the only ways in which we perform our identities relationally: most users utilise a multiplicity of communication platforms both offline and online, through synchronous and asynchronous means and across more than one platform. Communication and comments are not always necessarily simply updates on one's actual status, thoughts and feelings; responses to others' comments; and other engagement with networked friends. Rather, they operate within various sets of connotations and significations that may be recognised by others—common experiences, shared amusements, in-jokes among a close inner circle (Lewis and West 2009, p. 1222) or "seemingly random statements that only their recipients could truly appreciate" (Walker et al. 2009, p. 686). What this means, then, is how we perform our identities is recognised in different ways by others, and the intelligibility of the self may be more *easily* recognised by some in our network as opposed to others.

For example, a user makes a status update that is able to be seen by all or some on a friends list who have access to that profile's wall and appear in their feeds. One friend can begin a commentary that surreptitiously questions how that update fits within the user's recognisable identity: "But you said last week that you preferred ..." demanding an explanation. The complexity occurs not because the borders of a community are being policed through surveillance and the imperative to confess for normalisation, coherence and recognition but because the original status update is open to a multiplicity of "activated meanings" within a complex set of discursive reading formations (Bennett 1983, p. 218). For different friends, this will depend not on *where* they are located within a network morphology but on *how* they are located in relation to that user. Friends lists are neither a flattened group of individuals but identify with users variously, through multiple typologies: family/friend/acquaintance, extent of experience with the user, shared identity experiences, production and maintenance of online and offline knowledge.

Of course, each user's set of friends and their individual and group practices for communicating and engaging with each other on a network of relationality will differ (perhaps rapidly) over time and will include how other meanings and identifications are produced in other ways across the network—such as how that user commented on a photograph on the friend's sister's partner's site. In other words, complexity is found in the variances in knowledge around a user and the considerable variety of networkers but is *managed* through the technological paradigm of a social networking site. Simultaneously complex and easy, belonging becomes not a thing but a momentary intersection between different dimensions of identification managed but always persistently in flux. Online relationality, identification, mutuality and performance, then, are constituted by a structural logic of "nodes and hubs" (Castells 2000, p. 443) whereby we relate in complex ways to others across a fluid network of relationships.

2.4 Complexifying identity on social media

In Section 2.3, we worked through the complex ways in which two aspects of social media settings play a role in the performance and stabilisation of identity, that is, both profile management and interactivity with others. What happens, however, when we begin to think about the two of these together? In the final section of this chapter, I discuss some of the ways in which these two facets of identity performance might be seen to make our identities even more complex, might be understood as creating greater risks that the façade of coherent and intelligible identity is seen through and might be approached as a factor that makes the labour (and the anxiety) of contemporary digital identities more strenuous and problematic.

While profile maintenance and online friendship or relational networking are, in a Butlerian perspective, both sets of performative acts that constitute identity, and both are very effective tools of identity performativity, there is a critical perspective that can be raised in relation to how these two aspects risk undoing or destabilising the identity narratives we so carefully curate in order to be coherent selves. That is, while they both provide useful and effective means by which to articulate self-identity in ways that aim to fulfil the cultural demand for intelligible selfhood, viewed together they open either the possibility of revealing the basic incoherence and multiplicity of identity or adding to the task of 'identity work.' It is important to remark here on some of the ways in which the use of digital communication generates *inconsistencies* in the performance of a coherent identity. This incompatibility of the two activities might be said to be one of those 'gaps' in citation, reiteration and repetition of which Butler (1990) has demonstrated "shows up" the persistent instability of coherent identity (p. 145). In fact, it may only be by taking the risk of showing identity's incoherence that identification with others—the networking with, for and by friends in their various formations—can occur.

The profile, as I have been arguing, is the site of a reiterative performance or practice of identity that, carefully constructed, works as part of an overall narrative and a strategy towards the coherent performance of a unified identity/subjectivity, answering the Enlightenment imperatives for intelligibility and recognition in order to participate socially within a disciplinary society of norms. While social media platforms provide a convenient tool for the construction and clarification of selfhood online (and one that is capable of being utilised as an archive for offline performances for others and the self), they also present the greatest risk to narrative coherence through the possibility of a misalignment with the interactive engagement with the network (aside from the possibilities of misalignment across the multiple platforms people use every day). This might be said to occur in three ways:

1. Through the capacity of social media's commentary function whereby a 'friend' is effectively able to undertake surveillance on our posts and, in front of others, point to a breach in the coherence of our identities—for example, ask questions when a person's post indicates that they are of mixed-race identity rather than identifying by a singular race;
2. through the possibility of disruption by being able to point to the specific moments in the *record* of identity narrative represented by past posts and status updates. We may have changed, developed new facets of identity or been reconstituted in accord with some alternative practice of identity. For example, a cisgender male who, over time, has begun to identify as non-binary but has done nothing with the past narrative or story that prior posts tell about us;
3. by the fact that the narrative of the self is not entirely 'managed' by the user (in the way, perhaps a diary maintained over time has been), meaning their performance of coherent selfhood is regularly added to by the comments, cross-posts, taggings and so on *about* that person, some of which may be unwanted and may complexify the identity we perform and practise in a social media setting.

I would like to give more detail on each of these three instances of identity 'disruption' in more detail below.

2.4.1 Commentaries

The fact is that participants in the culture of social networking are in a position to surveil each other's profiles and posts (to varying degrees, of course, as privacy settings become more sophisticated). This creates the possibility for undoing our carefully curated identity coherence. From a poststructuralist perspective, that is not always a negative thing, since genuine coherence and intelligibility is always mythical, and there is significant empowerment in facing the fact we may be more complex than can be captured in our identity storytelling. However, for some people, such destabilisation of identity can be damaging and problematic, particularly if they do not have the resources for identity resilience.

The fact that the conversational policing of identity occurs through social media commentary (perhaps on an image posted) presents what in pre-digital times may have been a spoken request with a more sustained cultural perception of authority that comes with written/produced text (Foucault 1977a, p. 128; Biriotti and Miller 1993, pp. 2–6, 12). At the same time, however, it should be remembered that this is not a one-sided form of conversing whereby an author-user is interrogated by a reader giving feedback. Rather, it always goes both ways: the request for a clarification in a comment or a caption made by another user on the platform is also *their* act of subject performance, an articulation constitutive of the self within the nodes-and-hubs arrangement of the network morphology of online identification. It may be, therefore, a performance that reveals a racist aspect of their identity (although it is more likely simply to be interest or lack of understanding). The multiple directions of the flow of such performative commentary and conversation is an interactivity which, for Mark Andrejevic (2002), has an element of the confessional culture that stems from a contemporary desire for subjection to "a discursive regime of self-disclosure" (p. 234).

In the approach to culture taken by Michel Foucault (1977b), we are understood to live in a society that surveillances us in order to produce the normative self through discipline. Foucault used the metaphor of the institution of the prison and its panopticon—the tower used by guards that allow them to watch every prisoner, but in which the prisoner can never be sure they are being watched. Foucault's argument was that the idea that we *might* be being watched helped shore up an identity in which we are compelled to conform to a set of recognised norms, and that this framework infused contemporary society to produce docile subjects. Put this now into the context of social media, and it is no longer that we might be being surveiled by those who will ask us to confess the 'truth' of our identities but in the *certainty* of that surveillance within the network flows of relationality. Friends are no longer thus those who *might* surveil and normalise; rather, their relative placement as nodes and hubs in an interactive flow of question-and-answer constitutes their performativity as Facebook friends within a framework of regularisation and normalisation. In that sense, social media is the disciplinary regime of surveillance and confession *par excellence*. But due to the multiplicity of flows that contrasts with the centralisation of the panopticon metaphor, we do not see its effect as surveillance from the tower; rather we normalise ourselves across the multiple and conflicting spaces and aspects of online engagement. The user and their narrative of recognisable identity risks being forcibly fragmented or, at the very least, require even greater 'identity work' to perform, retain and stabilise coherence and intelligibility under this super-surveillance culture.

2.4.2 Disrupting the past: the archive

Confession in the face of the other is, as Sally Munt (2002) has pointed out, a technique of the self which renders the subject "visible and plausible to itself, and to others" through a reiteration which gains the force of a plot and involves a persistent and retrospective reordering (p. 19). But what happens to that retrospective remembering and reconfiguring when the momentary articulations of an identity performance and the many conversations and regimentary instances of surveillance and confession are laid out across a social networking profile as a written history of the self over time? What Brett St Louis (2009), following Stuart Hall, has referred to as narratives which account "for peoples' arrival at the present through a past that is imaginatively reconstructed and dramatized" (p. 565) and Buckingham (2008) points to as part of the "project of self-hood" in which biographical narratives articulated over time are both useful in pointing to the ways in which the narrative of performative selfhood that is developed by the user through profile management is put asunder by the friendship wall discussions, additions, commentary and tagging that act as an *archive*.

That is, the memorialisation of the past is not as easily re-figured, reordered and re-remembered when an order, a history and a set of collective memories are laid out as an archive. Just like an autobiography, a reflective construction of a user's online profile involves storytelling as a memorialisation of a past which retrospectively narrates and justifies the *current* moment of identity coherence in order to lend the illusion of an ongoing fixity of selfhood across time (Mendelson and Papacharissi 2011). In a lurker-ish mode, for example, we might scroll back through a new friend's profile—or, more creepily, a stranger's—in order to get a sense of who they are, reading their past posts to reveal aspects of their identity to us. The identity archive of the past is precisely that which opens up the possibility of incoherence by having documented the past identity configurations at various moments. This profile may have been revised a dozen times, but when read *as* a profile, there is no necessary reason to tease out its constructedness. But reading the *posts*, all the commentary, their other friends' views and contributions, who is a member of their friends list and so on, there is an *alternative* story of their identity that has emerged from their relational engagement with others. That is, I can see an archived record of momentary fragments of a fragmentary self that has not been shaped into performance masquerading as a representation of intelligible selfhood. My friend's intelligibility and coherence as an identity may, therefore, be at risk if the *profile* and the *posts* give conflicting stories.

What is important to note, however, is that online commentary can be, to use Vikki Bell's (1999) phrase, "the constitutive moments and modes of identity" (p. 7), but that for performativity to 'work,' those constitutive moments must be smoothed over, disavowed, forgotten or re-memorialised into something else, something otherwise. And it is precisely this that the documentary record of these moments does not allow, instead making visible the fact that any subject may have had a multitude of those moments and the corresponding shifts in identityhood. In that way, the labour of performing identity in digital settings is vastly increased and made more problematic.

2.4.3 *Tagging*

Finally, there is the disruptive role of tagging by other people. Tagging of images and other artefacts, adding hashtags on Twitter posts, shares and re-shared and other activities that create even greater complexity than I have described in the two areas above. Tagging has sometimes been a slightly controversial element of social media, given that it allows a user to link the name of another user to a photograph of which the tagged person may not have been aware existed or authorised its distribution among others. Tagging is very much the epitome of an interactive, relational culture of social networking (Munster

2008; Walther et al. 2008). They create identificatory links by making associations between the user and other people, as well as activities and behaviours—some of which may be in conflict with how one perceives oneself.

For example, let's say that a major part of my identity is disavowing elitist and conspicuous consumption, and that is how I recognise myself as a subject. But what about that occasion, long forgotten, in which I went for a champagne breakfast on a yacht, dressed up for it, ate smoked salmon and mixed with over-dressed, image-conscious people. When one of the party posts that old image and tags me in it, I am confronted by a representation of the self that is—effectively—a performative act; it constitutes who I am under the surveillance of others. It may call upon me to confess to myself an added complexity that is in conflict with how I perceive my identity. Or I might simply accept the tag, allow it to appear on people's feeds identifying me in way that may make me appear less coherent among others. We therefore have much less control over how we are represented and therefore performing our identity in a culture in which there are so many images and in which others can share those images with a very wide circle of others.

This, of course, is part of the increasing capacity of digital environments to organise data and online artefacts in ways which are more easily accessible through classifying, filtering and tagging, even though it replicates older conceptual issues around the relationship between image and word (Prada 2009). An image of a user may be captioned, but for anyone searching for those images, without digital tagging they would be difficult to find, similar to, for example, a handwritten caption in an analogue, physical album in Grandmother's attic. This element of rationality has raised a number of concerns and panics around privacy and control of information over the past couple of years in the popular press.

Significant here is that rather than thinking of social networking as singular activities, the ways in which social networking sites have developed through the growth of applications, user-uptake and favoured user activities has provided us with a multiplicity of activities and communicative forms which are not always mutually compatible with the process of performing a coherent self. This theoretical account is one among several ways in which we can approach social networking and identity; additional empirical work will reveal other understandings of this significant tool of everyday identity.

2.5 Conclusion

Using Judith Butler's theories of identity performativity is only one of the available ways to assess and understand how digital interactivity and social media engagement are sites of both identity performance and play, on the one hand, and increased risk of identity incoherence and unintelligibility, on the other hand. It is, nevertheless, one of the most powerful accounts of the complexity and out-of-our-control nature of identity and selfhood, and that makes it significantly useful for making sense of our digital lives in identity terms. Despite the framework I have presented here which describes some of the risks of identity incoherence and destabilisation through our use of social media, it is important to recognise that—on the whole—most people are not necessarily going to be reflective on the extent to which identity incoherences or 'slippages' matter, and that is absolutely fine. We also play with our identity in sometimes self-conscious ways, and people are generally very resilient in shoring up identity.

Key points

- Interactivity with texts and with other people is a major shift between traditional (print, broadcast) media and today's digital world.
- Interactivity comes to fruition in the post-2005 digital era of Web 2.0 social networking and platform-enabled curation.
- When using Judith Butler's theories of identity performativity, we need to update the idea that we 'cite' the categories, norms and signifiers of identity from static texts to recognise that interactivity means we now participate in the co-creation of those texts.
- Social media enables us to perform coherent identities. However, when we bring together the incompatibility of (a) what we put up on profiles and posts and (b) what others post about us or how they interact with our posts, we are potentially 'shown up' as incoherent or more complex than we necessarily wish to represent our identities.

References

Andrejevic, M., 2002. The work of being watched: interactive media and the exploitation of self-disclosure. *Critical Studies in Media Communication*, 19 (2), 230–248.

Andrejevic, M., 2011. Social network exploitation. *In:* Z. Papacharissi, ed. *A Networked Self: Identity, Community, and Culture on Social Network Sites*. London: Routledge, 82–101.

Ang, I., 1991. *Desperately Seeking the Audience*. London: Routledge.

Baym, N.K., Zhang, Y.B., Kunkel, A., Ledbetter, A. and Lin, M., 2007. Relational quality and media use in interpersonal relationships. *New Media & Society*, 9 (5), 735–752.

Bell, V., 1999. Performativity and belonging. *Theory, Culture & Society*, 16 (2), 1–10.

Bennett, T., 1983. Texts, readers, reading formations. *Literature and History*, 9 (2), 214–227.

Berners-Lee, T. 1999. Keynote talk to the *LCS 35th Anniversary Celebrations*, Cambridge MA, 14 April. Available from: www.w3.org/1999/04/13-tbl.html

Biriotti, M. and Miller, N., 1993. *What Is an Author?* Manchester: Manchester University Press.

Bordewijk, J.L. and van Kaam, B., 1986. Towards a new classification of tele-information services. *InterMedia*, 14 (1), 16–21.

boyd, d., 2008. Why youth (heart) social network sites: the role of networked publics in teenage social life. *In:* D. Buckingham, ed. *Youth, Identity, and Digital Media*. Cambridge, MA: MIT Press, 119–142.

Brooker, W. and Jermyn, D., 2003. Conclusion: overflow and audience. *In:* W. Brooker and D. Jermyn, eds. *The Audience Studies Reader*. London: Routledge, 332–335.

Buckingham, D., 2008. Introducing identity. *In:* D. Buckingham, ed. *Youth, Identity, and Digital Media*. Cambridge, MA: MIT Press, 1–24.

Burgess, J. and Green, J., 2009. *YouTube: Online Video and Participatory Culture*. Cambridge: Polity.

Butler, J., 1990. *Gender Trouble: Feminism and the Subversion of Identity*. London: Routledge.

Butler, J., 1991. Imitation and gender insubordination. *In:* D. Fuss, ed. *Inside/Out: Lesbian Theories, Gay Theories*. London: Routledge, 13–31.

Butler, J., 1993. *Bodies That Matter: On The Discursive Limits of 'Sex.'* London: Routledge.

Butler, J., 1995. Collected and fractured: response to *Identities. In:* K.A. Appiah and H.L. Gates Jr., eds. *Identities*. Chicago: University of Chicago Press, 439–447.

Butler, J., 1997. *The Psychic Life of Power: Theories in Subjection*. Stanford, CA: Stanford University Press.

Carey, J., 1988. *Communication as Culture: Essays on Media and Society*. London: Routledge.

Castells, M., 2000. *The Rise of the Network Society*, 2nd edition. Oxford: Blackwell.

Cover, R., 2004. Bodies, movements and desires: lesbian/gay subjectivity and the stereotype. *Continuum: Journal of Media & Cultural Studies*, 18 (1), 81–98.

Cover, R., 2006. Audience inter/active: interactive media, narrative control & reconceiving audience history. *New Media & Society*, 8 (1), 213–232.

Cover, R., 2016. *Digital Identities: Creating and Communicating the Online Self*. London: Elsevier.

Cover, R., 2019. *Emergent Identities: New Sexualities, Gender and Relationships in a Digital Era*. London: Routledge.

Cubitt, S., 1991. *Timeshift: On Video Culture*. London: Routledge.

Dery, M., 1993. Culture jamming: hacking, slashing and sniping in the empire of signs. *Open Magazine*. Revised edition. Available from: http://markdery.com/?page_id=154 [Accessed 19 June 2012].

Diaz, J., 2008. Facebook's squirmy chapter: site's evolution blurs line between boss and employee. *The Boston Globe*, 16 April. Available from: www.boston.com/bostonworks/news/articles/ [Accessed 28 November 2008].

Donath, J. and boyd, d., 2004. Public displays of connection. *BT Technology Journal*, 22 (4), 71–82.

Downes, E.J. and McMillan, S.J., 2000. Defining interactivity: a qualitative identification of key dimensions. *New Media & Society*, 2 (2), 157–179.

Ellison, N.B., Steinfeld, C. and Lampe, C., 2007. The benefits of Facebook 'friends': social capital and college students' use of online social network sites. *Journal of Computer-Mediated Communication*, 12 (4), 1143–1168.

Flew, T., 2008. *New Media: An Introduction*, 3rd ed. Melbourne: Oxford University Press.

Foucault, M., 1977a. *Language, Counter-Memory, Practice: Selected Essays and Interviews*, ed. D.F. Bouchard, trans. S. Simon. Ithaca, NY: Cornell University Press.

Foucault, M., 1977b. *Discipline and Punish: The Birth of the Prison*, trans. A. Sheridan. London: Penguin.

Goffman, E., 1959. *The Presentation of Self in Everyday Life*. Garden City, NY: Doubleday.

Green, L., 2002. *Communication, Technology and Society*. St. Leonards, NSW: Allen & Unwin.

Green, L., 2008. Is it meaningless to talk about 'the internet'? *Australian Journal of Communication*, 35 (3), 1–14.

Hodkinson, P., 2007. Interactive online journals and individualization. *New Media & Society*, 9 (4), 625–650.

Jenkins, H., 2003. *Interactive Audiences? The 'Collective Intelligence' of Media Fans*. Available from: http://web.mit.edu/21fms/www/faculty/henry3/collective%20intelligence.html [Accessed 12 June 2012].

Kennedy, H., 2006. Beyond anonymity, or future directions for Internet identity research. *New Media & Society*, 8 (6), 859–876.

Kiousis, S., 2002. Interactivity: a concept explication. *New Media & Society*, 4 (3), 355–383.

Kristeva, J., 1982. *Powers of Horror: An Essay on Abjection*, trans. L.S. Roudiez. New York: Columbia University Press.

Lessig, L., 2008. *Remix: Making Art and Commerce Thrive in the Hybrid Economy*. London: Bloomsbury Academic.

Lewis, J. and West, A., 2009. 'Friending': London-based undergraduates' experience of Facebook. *New Media & Society*, 11 (7), 1209–1229.

Liu, H., 2008. Social network profiles as taste performances. *Journal of Computer-Mediated Communication*, 13 (1), 252–275.

Livingstone, S., 2008. Taking risk opportunities in youthful content creation: teenagers' use of social networking sites for intimacy, privacy and self-expression. *New Media & Society*, 10 (3), 393–411.

Livingstone, S. and Brake, D.R., 2010. On the rapid rise of social networking sites: new findings and policy implications. *Children & Society*, 24 (1), 75–83.

McMillan, S., 2002. A four-part model of cyber-interactivity: some cyber-places are more interactive than others. *New Media & Society*, 4 (2), 271–291.

McQuail, D., 1997. *Audience Analysis*. Thousand Oaks, CA: Sage.

Meadows, M., 1994. At the cultural frontier. *In:* J. Schultz, ed. *Not Just Another Business: Journalists, Citizens and the Media*. Leichhardt, NSW: Pluto Press, 131–147.

Mendelson, A.L. and Papacharissi, Z., 2011. Look at us: collective narcissism in college student Facebook photo galleries.' *In:* Z. Papacharissi, ed. *A Networked Self: Identity, Community, and Culture on Social Network Sites.* London: Routledge, 251–273.

Munster, A., 2008. Welcome to Google Earth. *In:* A. Kroker and M. Kroker, eds. *Critical Digital Studies: A Reader.* Toronto: University of Toronto Press, 397–416.

Munt, S., 2002. Framing intelligibility, identity, and selfhood: a reconsideration of spatio-temporal models. *Reconstruction, 2* (3). Available from: www.reconstruction.ws/023/munt.htm [Accessed 29 December 2002].

Noble, G., 2002. Comfortable and relaxed: furnishing the home and nation. *Continuum: Journal of Media & Cultural Studies,* 16 (1), 53–66.

Penley, C., 1997. *Nasa/Trek: Popular Science and Sex in America.* London: Verso.

Prada, J.M., 2009. 'Web 2.0' as a new context for artistic practices. *Fibreculture,* 14 (2009). Available from: http://journal.fibreculture.org/issue14/index.html [Accessed 4 January 2010].

Rafaeli, S. and Sudweeks, F., 1997. Networked interactivity. *Journal of Computer Mediated Communication, 2* (4). Available from: www.ascusc.org/jcmc/vol2/issue4/rafaeli.sudweeks.html [Accessed 19 June 2009].

St Louis, B., 2009. On the necessity and the 'impossibility' of identities. *Cultural Studies,* 23 (4), 559–582.

Tong, S., Van Der Heide, B., Langwell, L. and Walther, J.B., 2008. Too much of a good thing? The relationship between number of friends and interpersonal impressions on Facebook. *Journal of Computer-Mediated Communication,* 13 (3), 531–549.

Tufekci, Z., 2008. Can you see me now? Audience and disclosure regulation in online social network sites. *Bulletin of Science, Technology & Society,* 28 (1), 20–36.

Turkle, S., 1995. *Life on the Screen: Identity in the Age of the Internet.* New York: Simon & Schuster.

Walker, K., Krehbiel, M. and Knoyer, L., 2009. Hey you! Just stopping by to say hi!: communicating with friends and family on MySpace. *Marriage & Family Review,* 45 (6-8), 677–696.

Walther, J.B., Van Der Heide, B., Kim, S., Westerman and, D. and Tong, S., 2008. The role of friends' appearance and behavior on evaluations of individuals on Facebook: are we known by the company we keep? *Human Communication Research,* 34 (1), 28–49.

Webster, J.G., 1998. The audience. *Journal of Broadcasting & Electronic Media,* 42 (2), 190–207.

Williams, R., 1997. Mass and masses. *In:* T. O'Sullivan and Y. Jewkes, eds. *The Media Studies Reader.* London: Arnold, 18–27.

Woodward, K., 2002. *Understanding Identity.* London: Arnold.

3   Bodies

Digital corporeality and identity

3.1 Introduction

Unlike the 1990s early cyberculture, we no longer think about digital communication as being radically separated from our everyday lives and our everyday bodies. Some aspects of cyberculture drew on fictional accounts to describe the Internet as a kind of separate 'space' in which we interact at the level of the 'mind' but leave behind our 'body' which was sometimes described in a derogatory way as 'the meat.' This is a mythical approach to the body, communication and interaction that is familiar to viewers of *The Matrix* film series (1999, 2003 and 2021), although the concept of this separation of mind and body had a much older history in science fiction and fantasy, including in a 1976 episode of British series *Doctor Who*, in which the Doctor is plugged in to a computer (interestingly also called 'the Matrix') interacting with others in this computer-driven mental space while his body remains inert and seemingly unaware of his surroundings. The idea that this is what 'being online' meant is, of course, ridiculous.

The concept of a separation between bodies and mind is, indeed, even older and predates contemporary science fiction. Writing in the first half of the seventeenth century, the philosopher René Descartes (1968) articulated an idea that has become a staple throughout the ensuing centuries on how to perceive our identities in the context of our corporeality: that we are comprised of the body as a material and unthinking substance and of a mind that is thinking and conscious of itself. This has come to be known as the principle of mind/body dualism. While separate substances of human identity and selfhood, Descartes articulated them as joined—not just as like a pilot (mind) manoeuvring a ship (body) but as a unit functioning together. This enduring philosophy has governed much of how we perceive ourselves, although in science fiction and early approaches to digital communication and 'virtual reality' (VR), we saw a more substantial break from Descartes with the perception that somehow the mind could operate without the body.

In this early framework of digital communication, then, whenever the user dialled up to the Internet, they were understood to be 'jacking in' in their mind into a collective intelligence of other users and experiences. The body, however, was perceived as redundant and unnecessary in the experience of VR (despite the obvious fact that it is seeing, hearing, typing, speaking, recording and the brain is doing the work of thinking). However, once we come into Web 2.0 and subsequent iterations of digital communication, the body is shown to be not only redundant or a separate substance from the mind but as equally represented in the experience of digital communication and identity. It is recognised as *active* and *present*, whether in the context of online gaming, communicating,

DOI: 10.4324/9781003296652-3

uploading selfies, conducting a video-conference, touching the wireless communication devices, typing or wearing digital tracking technologies. In that sense, there is no frame-work for thinking about the mind as if separate from the body in digital contexts of identity, nor is it helpful to assume that the body is always passive in a digital context in the 2020s when 'being online' no longer necessarily implies being sedentary at a desktop computer.

This chapter explores the role of the body, embodiment and corporeality as signifi-cant to the relationship between digital communication and self-identity. I am keen to break from the Web 1.0 cyberculture and mind/body dualist accounts that perceive the body as passive and inferior to the communicative work of 'mind,' and instead to keep us remembering that the body is always present in the act of communicating. Even more pertinently, perhaps, in the Web 2.0 and Web 3.0 era of the 'Internet of Things' in which we are surrounded by connected devices, wearable technologies, mobile connectivity and other digital tools and technologies, it is not a connection with mind, but a *surrounding* of the body with technologies that come ever closer to us personally and play a distinct and ongoing role in our embodied lives. I therefore want to begin with a few ways in which we can unpack the definitions of the body in Section 3.2. In Section 3.3, we explore how the body is very well represented on-screens as a key practice in digital communication of identities. Section 3.4 discusses some of the ways in which digital technologies and their 'closeness' to our bodies play a constitutive role in our identities. Contemporary approaches to the body as a 'project' are closely related with the development of digital communication tools used to track, enhance and improve the body in ways which are active and which inform our identities as embodied selves.

3.2 Defining the body

The mind/body dualism approach that has been so important in how we perceive identity began to be criticised among philosophy, social psychology and in the social sciences in the second half of the twentieth century. Part of this was a criticism of the way in which the body was perceived as the *inferior* party, while the mind was *superior*. Another angle was critical of the way in which the mind was associated with European civilisation, masculinity, high art and the pursuits of the upper-middle classes, while the body was more associated with other races and ethnicities, femininity, low-brow entertainment and the manual labour of the working classes. Critical engagement with the idea of the body to find better ways of understanding human identity—and what *counts* as fully human—meant critiquing the mind/body dualism and the perceptions of the body as a machine controlled by the mind of the human subject. A renewed interest in philosophies of the body in the 1990s has been referred to as the 'corporeal turn,' and this has informed much subsequent scholarship about identity, overturning some of the precepts of Western philosophy that were ascribed by Descartes (Grosz 1994, p. 5).

As a result of this 'corporeal turn,' the body started to be recognised not simply as a biological machine or a neutral, natural object separate from culture, language, social dis-course and the 'higher things' of civilisation. Rather, it was better understood as something complex, formed and perceived by the languages and practices available to us that help us make sense of the body, where it begins, where it ends, what it does, how it performs and how it remains central to identity practices. That is, there was more attention paid to how our philosophies, languages and ways of thinking produced a concept of corporeality that had tended to define bodies, present them as objects separate from each other and the environment.

The more common contemporary conception of the body as whole, unified, natural and fixed is, however, limited by being a *linear* conception. According to philosopher Alphonso Lingis (1994), we perceive our bodies as "constant" and "stable" (p. 155). If subjectivity is dependent on reiterative performativity, then a linear performance of the 'constant' and 'static' body is *constant* and disguises the fact of reiterative performance. In other words, it is not that reiterative performativity is a *series* of independent 'acts' as such, but that in the *perceived* linear and stable conception of the body, it is an ongoing reiteration in continuity and linear temporality. This is not to suggest that there is no possibility of undermining subjectivity. As we'll recall from the discussion of Judith Butler's (1990) theories of identity in the previous chapter, *repetition* of our identities is a necessary part of shoring up who we are, but such repetition is always at risk of failure. In pointing out the necessity of repetitive citation, Butler (1997) makes clear the ultimate impossibility of consolidation of the dissociated unity of the subject (p. 93). The linear constancy of the body as an unchanging object is just as mythical, an illusion that is itself dependent on repetitive performativity. Nevertheless, in its linear presentation in contemporary Western society, it certainly makes it more difficult to undermine the notion of fixed and essential bodily subjects.

One angle of theory that sought to restore the body to philosophical importance while critiquing some of our everyday assumptions about bodies was found in feminist psychoanalytic and poststructuralist theory. Elizabeth Grosz is a theorist who drew of feminist, psychoanalytic and cultural theories to reframe how we think about the material of bodies. For Grosz (1994), the body itself is not an innate and passive object acted upon or controlled by our minds but is itself constituted and produced within frameworks of social, cultural and psychic representation, discourse and language (pp. x–xi). Today, we can therefore say this includes social, cultural, psychological and communicative factors of how we use digital communication in ways which produce a corporeal normativity.

According to Grosz (1994), "bodies must take the social order as their productive nucleus. Part of their own 'nature' is an organic or ontological 'incompleteness' or lack of finality, an amenability to social completion, social ordering and organization" (p. xi). Grosz (1995) presents the body as a complex formulation of matter, psyche and the social:

> By 'body' I understand a concrete, material, animate organization of flesh, organs, nerves, and skeletal structure, which are given a unity, cohesiveness, and form through the psychical and social inscription of the body's surface. This body is, so to speak, organically, biologically 'incomplete'; it is indeterminate, amorphous, a series of uncoordinated potentialities that requires social triggering, ordering, and long-term 'administration.' The body becomes a human body, a body that coincides with the 'shape' and space of a psyche, a body that defines the limits of experience and subjectivity only through the intervention of the (m)other and, ultimately, the Other (the language- and rule-governed social order).
>
> (p. 104)

While this includes a perspective drawn from psychoanalytic theory by invoking the psychical *map of the body, we can infer from this that the body is 'materialised' (made 'matter' in a way that is thinkable) through that inscription. In other words, the body does not start off as whole, unified, separate, individual, natural and knowable, but in the act of forming identities, we form a*

sense of our own bodies, their bounds, how they work, what they might and might not do and how
they interact with one another. We rely on knowledge frameworks engaged in everyday communica-
tion for that sense to develop.

Butler presented a related but slightly different framework for understanding the production of the body in her book *Bodies That Matter* (1993). There, she pointed out that the
materiality of the body and the performativity of identity are linked, primarily through
the normative arrangements of "regulatory ideals." That is, rather than using the concept
of the psyche, she drew on philosopher and historian Michel Foucault's work to argue that
the body is the *product* of various cultural, social and historical knowledge frameworks that
actively discipline a body into shapes, forms and concepts that serve a wider set of social
or institutional goals. Since identities are performed not as a singular or voluntary act but
through the repetition of a citational practice, the body provides one of the sites of that
repetition. The repetition of our bodies as if they are constant and unchanging becomes
one of the myths that upholds a sense of linear identity (p. 2). In unpacking the idea of the
body as constant, Butler proposed a critique of the very idea of matter, which she argued
is not as a natural site or a surface, but "*a process of materialization that stabilizes over time to*
produce the effect of boundary, fixity, and surface we call matter" (p. 9, original emphasis).

For us, this leads to questions as to the rituals, normative practices and regulatory
norms through which particular *kinds* of bodies are materialised; which kinds of bodies
are excluded from the full definition of the human by virtue of those norms; and in
what ways the body is given intelligibility in the context of objects, tools, communicative forms and extensions through space and time. In this way, for Butler, the body is
something that is 'materialised,' but this is not to say that it is an unreal, imaginary thing
that comes into existence from language (p. 3). Rather, the idea of materialisation calls
on us to acknowledge that while there are such *things* as bodies, we only 'know' them
(including our own bodies) through the concepts and logics that make them knowable
and perceivable, and all of these come from language. In this philosophical perspective,
there is nothing that can be thought that is outside of language and culture and that
includes bodies.

To make sense of how language and culture acts upon us to produce the body, we need
to draw on Michel Foucault's thinking. From a Foucauldian perspective, the body is also
not thought of as an *a priori* given: real, material and self-contained. That is, a body is not
to be understood as 'real' and 'material' but as itself the product of cultural and historical
formations. Bodies come to be understood, then, as the site at which certain kinds of
disciplinary powers 'normalise' us (Foucault 2004, pp. 25–26). When the body comes to
be understood as able to be produced—and produced differentially—through discipline,
we can see the ways in which bodies are malleable and adaptable through technological
production (Miller 2011, p. 209).

In this way of thinking, then, technologies of communication, entertainment and digital
creativity everyday social participation (such as social networking, electronic banking or
using eBay, for example) can be understood as being developed and made available for
the instrumental production of bodies rather than merely being *tools* which help our
bodies do things (represent ourselves, go shopping, etc.). They effectively shape our bodies
according to particular sets of norms, ways of being and devotion to activities related
to labour and consumption. Disciplinary technologies here include surveillance (which
incorporates activities of self-surveillance, such as the filling out of forms and surveys
online or posting images of ourselves that others rate and comment on or using wearable
technologies that measure and shape our fitness and capability). This is not to suggest,

however, that all technologies are used in disciplinary endeavours; rather, technologies are sometimes taken up in ways which resist discipline and the disciplining of bodies. For example, technologies that enable obesity or failures of fitness and forms of digital communication that, on the one hand, produce certain efficiencies while, on the other hand, reduce the long-term efficiency by making the body less fit (such as overwhelming use of email in the workplace as distinct from walking up the corridor).

3.2.1 Digital identities without bodies? Never

In writing about concepts of cyberspace, Kath Woodward (2002) asks if identities continue to *need* bodies. This is recognisable as a pre-Web 2.0 era notion of identity and digital communication of the sort that reifies 'mind' over 'body' and assumes the latter is redundant. Woodward draws on utopian discourses that had emerged in accounts of online communication and, interestingly, cybersex, suggesting that digital communication had the potential to offer opportunities "to escape the body, especially the constraints of a body which is marked by race, age, gender and corporeal needs, such as eating and sleeping" (p. 113). Cybersex in its early accounts was often viewed as an element of activity in which unusual desires could be practised without the need to involve or risk the body itself (Green 2002, p. 182), although we might actually wonder if cybersex is truly disembodied or the pleasures of aural, visual, screen-based remote haptic stimulation and other aspects are not always from the beginning bodily experiences. Certainly, the body has to be present and part of the picture to experience pleasure from cybersex.

The notion of the body-less self that is aligned with an ideal of the 'projection' of the self *into* cyberspace here is problematic because it draws on an idea that the things happen without bodies. Woodward (2002) points out that subjects have always presented themselves without being physically presents by letters, telegraph and telephone, suggesting that these are not only disembodied but are the antecedents of contemporary digital communication (pp. 113–114). However, rather than imagining that the telegram, the letter or the phone call are disembodied forms of communication just because the people communicating are not face to face, it has to be remembered that a *body* wrote or typed that letter (and licked the stamp to mail it), that telegram was input and sent around the world by a series of bodies and that the voice coming down the phone lines was the voice enabled by a body with vocal cords. In the same way, the email is typed by a body, the game is played by a body and so on. As Woodward (2002) put it in dismissing her own arguments about the possibilities of disembodied virtual spaces: "Cyberspace may be disembodied but it is still 'real' bodies who press the keys and write the scripts" (p. 117).

Cyber-fictional accounts of subjectivity as post-corporeal proliferated in the 1990s and early 2000s and remain common ways of thinking about a future identity that leaves the body behind (which is impossible). Nevertheless, these accounts were philosophically useful, because they helped provide a way to critique how bodies are also central to various kinds of communication exclusions (for example, in racial and gender demarcations and subordinations). However, they were problematic in suggesting hope for a future in which the individual and universal limitations of the body might be escaped as the solution to racism, sexism and so on, primarily because such ideas were ultimately grounded in the notion of the superiority of the mind over the body, and moreover, such ideas are absurd in assuming it is actually possible to *have* an identity without a body.

Rather than the pretence of the body-less subject floating in the digital ether, or the idea of the subject who can express an identity online differently from that which is coded and constituted in representations of the body, or the very fanciful science fiction notion that we all are on the way to becoming semi-robotised creatures as cyborgian losing our own flesh, it remains that digital media and communication use in Web 2.0 and 3.0 frameworks is very much *about* the body. This includes, and is not limited to, representations of the self online as a visual presentation, the drawing-together of bodies and digital interactivities through new relationalities that focus on the body such as wearable technologies, citations of bodily practices and norms from online representation in the materialisation of the body.

While I am somewhat dismissive of the radical utopianism of early Internet and cybercultural notions of completely disembodied identities running around online without our bodies involved, they are ideas which contribute some useful thinking when we take it *beyond* the mind/body dualism. For example, theorist Donna Haraway's (1991) conceptualisation of the cyborg that melds human biological flesh with the technology of the machine provides a framework for thinking beyond a number of dichotomies that subordinate the body. By pointing to the collapse of the distinction between bodies and machines (or human beings and machines), Haraway opens the possibility of a new way of critiquing the mind/body dualism of Descartes. Her work helped draw attention to the fact that a mind/body dichotomy often aligned in our contemporary culture with other cultural reductionisms such as masculine/feminine, heterosexual/homosexual, Western/non-Western, Christian/Muslim—and many others—which suggest the former identity category is dominated by the mind, while the latter is base and focused on or emerges from an undisciplined body.

Approaches which recognise the centrality of the body to communication are therefore important, but we can also learn from the histories and representations of texts and practices that tried to think about our communication practices differently, including the cybercultural concepts of the disembodied self—as long as we place them in their philosophical and historical contexts and recognise that they may be less meaningful for contemporary approaches when they are adequately critiqued. What is at stake here is that once we start to think about bodies as being more complex, less-knowable and more central to digital communication, we can start to think about how they perform a core role in the production of identities in the context of digital media.

3.3 Representing bodies on the digital screen

As I have been arguing, a pivotal shift occurred in the mid-2000s was increasingly represented on digital screens. Prior to this, writers would often frame digital communication as a space that was absent of bodies and present identities as communicated primarily through the written word, claiming, for example, that: "any aspect of social role performance, presentation of self and physical appearance are within the written text" (Wiley 1999, pp. 134–135). Once broadband and mobile connectivity became more widespread, and with the development of new platforms that enabled significantly faster upload and download speeds, the improvements in computer processing power and the increased use of cloud storage, the underlying cultural interest in sharing *visual stories* of our lives came to fruition. Naturally, we still tell stories that express, construct and constitute our identities in written form, whether that be textual tweets, Twitter posts, commentary on a photo shared on Instagram, comments and tags on other people's posts, forum entries and answers on Reddit and Quora and—of course—old-school digital use such as email. Thus, while we have undergone an incredible shift towards the visual across a number of platforms, for example, using TikTok without visuality would make little sense, this does not necessarily mean we have eradicated the textual or that there is no 'play' around identity using the communication tools available to us. That is, there is plenty of identity fraud when we use platforms that do not require our image or physical presence or for which we substitute a photo that does not represent us or through which we construct a false identity to use as a sock-puppet and so on. What has shifted, however, is a set of cultural norms over representation: the fact identity fraud is not the construction of a supposedly separate online identity but very clearly the conscious and knowing production of a fraudulent one (and that this is recognised widely as inappropriate and unethical) is a significant change that comes from the visuality of identity in our contemporary forms of digital communication as they've developed over the past 15 years.

The body is represented in very substantial ways through digital communication, with visual images of our embodied selves online, the curatorial relationship subjects have with images of themselves on platforms such as Instagram, Facebook, TikTok and Twitter, as real-time audiovisual representations when attending a class by Zoom, as profile photographs that routinely accompany our work and education profiles on sites like LinkedIn and in a host of other online practices. In this context, I would like to make a few points about digital, interactive media as a site for the knowing, conscious and meaningful dissemination of images of the body and what these might mean for how we construct ideas of the body that are meaningful for identity.

3.3.1 Stereotypes: image, movement and categories of discrimination

An important aspect of the contemporary visuality of digital communication is that it exposes people to discrimination based often on the visuality of identity. We explore some aspects of this further in Chapter 6 where we investigate the relationship between identity, hostility and hate speech online. However, it is useful here to examine how *stereotypes* that promote discriminatory communication are at play in digital settings of visuality. Digital media is often thought about as a setting that promotes diversity, particularly in its capacity to provide images, conversations and stories from all over the world, exposing users to more diverse cultural, identity and narrative expressions. However, it is also a space in which discrimination based on visual stereotypes and the violences of sexism, racism, homophobia, transphobia and other practices that respond violently to the bodies and identities of others is at play in ways less seen in physical face-to-face encounters and in other forms of media that use traditional gatekeeping practices such as television and film.

Stereotypes are a key element of this concern because they bring together bodies, identities and communication. Stereotypes are a form of communication which links an identity-based image with a set of attributes, behaviours or beliefs, circulating throughout culture and fixing that view through constant repetition (Rosello 1998). It is never pleasant to give examples of stereotypes (because doing so puts them into further circulation, even when we're just trying to analyse or explain them), but we can give a relatively benign one here in the hope it doesn't accidentally create more stereotypical views: the stereotype of an accountant. I did a Google search for the word 'accountant' and hit the images tab. While we need to account for any cookies that might be at play, personalised search algorithms and other factors that might make my search appear different from the next person's, Google came back with a lot of images of white men, thin and short, wearing glasses, a bit nerdy in style, always at a desk, always with a computer screen, often a spreadsheet open on the screen, typically a pile of additional papers on the desk that look a bit messy, usually in a corporate-style office setting or background, mostly urban views outside the window or almost always with their fingers on a calculator.

If no one could see the search term, the stereotype is strong enough in contemporary culture that people would make a reasonable guess that these are images of accountants. What happens here is that a lot of information is communicated in a simple image, such that anyone who looked at that image would draw on the cultural knowledge of the stereotypical accountant to recognise that person as an accountant. That, in itself, is not problematic. Rather, what is a problem is that the repetition and circulation of these images—and the fact they come up in a search engine this way—presents a view that skews the reality of diversity among accountants: not all accountants are white men, not all wear glasses, not all work in corporate settings or with numbers on a spreadsheet. And it opens questions then about how someone who might wish to become an accountant would consciously or unconsciously react to the overwhelming visual information that might suggest they would not belong in the narrow group.

Stereotypes are typically centred on the image and representation of particular categorisations of body, and most of the more serious ones include racialised bodies, gendered bodies, the bodies of a minority sexual orientation or the bodies of persons with a disability. The image or idea of that particular body is 'fixed' to particular notions which, for example, might be to suggest that particular racialised groupings behave in particularly violent or ignorant ways or that women are unlikely to catch a ball or that all gay men are fit and toned or that persons with disabilities hold bitter, negative attitudes. There are many such examples that are not worth putting into further repetition. In all cases, stereotypes work to bind the visual image of a subject defined by a facet of identity by producing particular sets of borders that articulate some subjects as more patently that identity than others.

In a digital culture and information ecology where sound-bytes and opinion dominate and judge, and in which knowledge made available digitally in the forms of information, entertainment, gossip, user-generated commentary and interactive contributions in all sorts of forms from text to image to moving visuals is widespread, the stereotype has become an even more significant form of communication. This is in spite of the logic that might suggest stereotypes are less likely to circulate the more media we have. Rather, they become ubiquitous because they are used in stock image databases which are drawn upon by advertisers, marketers and website designers (for example, if I want to produce a brochure for an accounting firm I might just search a stock image database for 'accountant' and have results return similar to the ones above. Even if they are diverse, I may feel encouraged to choose the most stereotypical because that would be *efficient communication*).

Stereotypes are also very ubiquitous in fast-paced information ecologies because they communicate information—rightly or wrongly—in very simple, easily read 'bytes.' An online brochure that is trying to attract attention to accountants does not have the space, time or value in giving a paragraph description about diversity among the accounting profession. Rather, it relies on the *instantaneity* of recognition and that means relying on viewers' existing knowledge of a stereotype—thereby putting the same stereotype into further circulation and fixing it further. That is, by working with existing cultural knowledges and falsities that reduce an identity category to a particular set of attributes and behaviours, they circulate through images of bodies in which readers and users actively *recognise* that body as doing particular things or behaving in particular ways. In this sense, when the body of a lesbian is more easily recognisable through, say, a visual representation of butchness, the image is *read* through the stereotype in a way which provides a set of norms by which lesbians are called upon to judge themselves and the wider viewers' recognition of the stereotype as 'true' is potentially reinforced.

In other words, stereotypes are a necessary fact in a digital environment in which communication is, on the one hand, rich and diverse, but, on the other hand, effective communication relies on viewers making very quick interpretations of visual information, including the bodies represented on-screen. Not all users will have had access to alternative discourses informing the more critically minded and digitally literate that bodies, identities and people are actually remarkably diverse (Nakamura 2008, p. 30). This is not, of course, to suggest that any ignorance over stereotypes is the fault of the viewer. Rather, ignorance is a socially cultivated framework of viewership among the fast-paced media and information overload within that digital ecology. The circulation of stereotypes is, nevertheless, a matter of ethics, and there is something remarkably unethical about any deliberate circulation of some stereotypes, particularly in relation to gender, ethnicity, race, sexuality and bodily ability.

While we have been encouraged by early cyberculture perceptions to see the digital space as a disembodied one, it is important to think about what the contemporary emphasis on visuality does *for* our bodies, particularly when stereotypes circulate online. Stereotypes produce and fix a knowledge framework about bodies in relation to particular identities, and assign those bodies/identities with attributes. In that sense, they are implicated in what Butler (1993) has argued is the discursive and regimentary materialisation of the body discussed above. Alternatively, we might see them as doing what philosopher Alphonso Lingis (1994) understands as cultivating the body's "capacities, skills and inclinations" (p. 53). In other words, they circulate online in ways which tell us what bodies 'do.' By 'doing,' I mean the movements, spatial relations and gestures of the body and the expectations we have of our bodies. The very movements, comportment and adornment (clothing, jewellery, hair, etc.) of the rudimentary body constitute it as an explicit *type* of body, and stereotypes make those aspects of the body available to be recognised *as* a particular identity—often in relation to minority members of society. Through the cultural force of stereotyping, a dynamic is produced such that the image, identity and body formation will be compelled to move, dress and behave in specific, knowable and recognisable ways.

This relates to the element of 'knowledge' that accompanies, informs and is communicated by the stereotype, whereby it employs visuality and connotation to provide bodies and identities with attributes. For Lingis (1994):

> bodies are sensory-motor systems that generate the excess force which makes them able to move themselves, systems that move toward objectives they perceive, that thus code their own movements. Our bodies are also substances that can be moved and that can be coded. Subjected to regulated operations of force, our bodies become subjects of capacities, skills and inclinations.
>
> (p. 53)

Assigning identities to bodies through particular kinds of stereotypes is not just a painful experience for some who are demeaned by those stereotypes. Rather, they involve gratifications because they help determine particular kinds of norms which allow even minorities to 'fit in' with society's expectations about what particular identities and bodies can and should do and what they cannot or should not do—for example, that girls should not play rough sports (Young 1990, pp. 141–159). In other words, the link that a visual stereotype reinforces between a body and what that identity's body should do is a recirculation of a discourse that, for Foucault (1977), sanctions "an infinitesimal power over the body" by compelling specific "movements, gestures, attitudes and rapidity" (pp. 136–137).

In thinking about bodies and identities in the context of digital communication, then, it is important to take account of the way in which on-screen representation of bodies relies on stereotypes, circulating and reinforcing cultural knowledge that is always *reductive* of the genuine complexity of human lives and human corporeality. They circulate because they are useful for providing a packet of information very quickly and easily, but they are often unethical because they reduce not only our ability to recognise diversity among others but because they actively encourage us to conform to those stereotypes as well.

3.3.2 Gaming bodies, corporeal avatars and characters

Gaming is one area where we can think about the online representation of the body in another way—the production of the on-screen avatar. Digital games have become more and more sophisticated over the past decade, primarily as a result of improved processing power of our devices. This has meant our on-screen avatars have very often become better, more recognisable bodies and much less 'cartoonish' than they once were. However, they remain a very interesting area for thinking about the relationship between identities, bodies and digital media because they are implicated in all sorts of arrangements around how we choose avatars and on-screen representation and how our bodies interact with the game setting through devices. One aspect of that interaction is through a concept of *immersion*.

The idea of immersion has regularly been used in connection with digital gaming experiences in which it is often argued that the gamer's identity extends into and beyond the screen into the setting of the game. This is not quite the same as those early cyberspace theories of leaving the body behind—perhaps because a body that is gaming is perceived as more active and engaged than a body that is simply typing, scrolling or uploading (although they are, of course, all very active). Miroslaw Filiciak (2003) makes the following point in relation to gaming, bodies and identity:

> The process of secondary identification taking place in cinema theaters depends paradoxically on distance while in the case of games we encounter something more than just intimacy. Identification is replaced by introjection—the subject is projected inward into an 'other.' We do not need a complete imitation to confuse the 'other' with the 'self.' The subject (player) and the 'other' (the onscreen avatar) do not stand at the opposite sides of the mirror anymore—they become one. While using an electronic medium in which subject and object, and what is real and imagined, are not clearly separated, the player loses his identity, projecting himself inward becoming the 'other,' and identifies with the character in the game. During the game, the player's identity ends in disintegration, and the merger of user's and character's consciousness ensues.
>
> (p. 91)

This account of playing digital games helps us to think more about how a player's identity is not something that is fixed while we choose an alternative identity for the game. Rather, our identities are conditioned by the performances we make in playing a game such that there is a complex relationship between our bodies and the body images that represent us on-screen. We are immersed in the game, although, of course, our bodies are not. However, at the level of the psyche our actions using game controllers perform particular actions on-screen in ways that are not as easy to separate. This is not, of course, to suggest that playing a violent digital game changes our identities to make us more violent selves. Rather, it is that in the context of playing games we lose ourselves in those immersions for a while such that we do not necessarily maintain a sense of our embodied self in the same way as we might when doing something else. In other words, a relationship with our body that differs from other activities similar to using other tools such as driving a car, canoeing or playing the piano.

Attempts that frame gaming through the older mind/body dualism described above perceive the metaphor of immersion in a way that overly separates the two spaces, suggesting that two spaces are crossed, much like leaving the land to dive into the sea. Of course, within certain practices online, there are real, genuine separations between the corporeal real and the virtual activity, and we see that most commonly in the actions of subjects while playing digital games. While we would not necessarily want to argue that gamers leave behind a sense of the body and *only* embody a character or avatar on the 'other side of the' screen, intent is part of the practice of gaming. Filiciak (2003), for example, makes this point in underscoring how the mundane activities of everyday life are left behind in gaming in ways in which the on-screen body performs actions that would damage the body. As he argues:

> the effort put into the development of a game character do[es] not necessarily need to be the opposite of what happens to us in everyday life. Even worse, it often happens in games that we encounter things we would not want to do every day, and yet we do them .... In reality I wouldn't like to do such a monotonous thing as carrying crates. Within online games there are even more examples of repetitive and boring actions. While playing EverQuest, I spent long hours running around the forest and looking for some creature or artefact. It would be boring in a real life, but in the context of the game it was fun.
>
> (p. 99)

If we take this query to the extreme levels of games of a generation ago, we would note that the barrel-hopping undertaken in Donkey Kong (to be old-school about it) would be something we may be physically capable of doing in a real-world, corporeal existence, but something most of us would not seek or wish to do. In the same vein, we could consider how using our bodies to fight, harm or kill others in a first-person shooter is something we would *never* do in our corporeal existence as social subjects, but this activity forms a particular staple of gaming narratives and digital interactivity with other characters. The space of play on the so-called other side of the screen is, therefore, one in which a practice differs from the ethics that are involved in our embodied lives.

Performing identity online is, of course, one possible experience of digital communication as I have described over the past two chapters. This does not suggest, however, that in playing a game we are necessarily performing a disembodied identity—rather, we are playing with theatrics in conceptual spaces, much as a stage actor does not embody the identity of their character. As we know from Johan Huizinga (1949), who wrote one of the most important analyses of play, there is always a conscious boundary between the act of playing a game (whether playing Rugby, Monopoly or Grand Theft Auto) and a conscious knowledge of the distinction between play and non-play—no matter how immersed, invested or wrapped up in it we become. We protect our bodies in ways which we do not necessarily protect our avatars or on-screen characters when gaming because we *know* there is neither a collapse between bodies and gaming. In other words, they are intertwined in ways which affect, shape and constitute identity, but this is never to say that we *assume* the identity of a game character. This is also not to suggest that we do not form deep attachments to the interactive representations and avatars we engage with on-screen, and there is a bodily aspect to that. The body is active in playing a game, which, of course, includes the brain chemistry, the cognitive processing (Grodal 2003, p. 130), the adrenalin, the movement and the use of controllers—all of which are actively corporeal and experienced by ourselves as embodied identities.

I want to suggest here another way we can understand the body as active in gaming in ways which constitute identity. Sociologist and theorist Pierre Bourdieu (1990) argued that, in the context of social practices: "The body believes in what it plays at: it weeps if it mimes grief. What is 'learned by the body' is not something that one has, like knowledge that can be brandished, but something that one is" (p. 73). In this context, we might therefore suggest that by playing a game, the body comes to feel and experience aspects of what is insinuated for our characters on-screen through acts of imagination—in the same way, an actor experiences the joy or the pain of their on-stage character through the theatrics of performance. To underscore a point I often make: this is not to suggest that one comes *to be* their on-screen character or identify with their avatar and become, say, a violent subject. It is to suggest that there is an engagement with the character that is complex, nuanced and that this promotes a rethinking of identity rather than a subsumption of our identities by those on-screen representations. Gaming, in that sense, may not necessarily disrupt the identity of the subject, but it informs the performativity of that self by adding experiences and perceptions that are simultaneously felt as 'real' in a real bodily sense and as separated from the narrative, cultural and social space in which that body moves and, indeed, *must* move as part of biological and social existence.

This section has addressed two ways in which the body is implicated in our digital lives: through its representation on-screen and through the bodily engagement with on-screen gaming. Key here is moving away from the mind/body dualism as a way of understanding bodies in digital settings which are not quite as simple as seeing us in the older cybercultural concepts of performing in real (embodied) space and cyber (disembodied) spaces. Rather, it is to recognise that the body is key to identity. If our digital communication, interactivities and utilisation of communication are implicated in the constitution of our identities and the knowledges and practices that give us a sense of who we are, the labels of identity and the ways of describing ourselves to others, then it remains important not to fall into the trap of assuming that just because that communication occurs digitally the body is suddenly less important to how we perform our identities.

3.4 Body–technology relationalities

In this section, I would like to consider four ways in which the interfacing between the *body* as a core component of how we perform identities and the *technologies* of digital communication play additional roles in constituting identity and belonging: firstly, the digital technologies we encounter through touch; secondly, the digital practices that discipline our bodies and thereby condition our identities; thirdly, the ways in which digital technologies are used to emphasise contemporary practices of seeing the body as a 'project' of the self; and finally, to return to put these and the above arguments into the context of what I have elsewhere referred to as the 'seam' between digital communication and the body.

3.4.1 Touch-friendly and wearable technologies

Digital technologies are increasingly incorporated into our everyday lives in ways which bring them into close contact with our bodies. Earlier technologies tended to be more distanced from the body, whether the desktop computer of the late 1980s and early 1990s that was in the form of a box under the desk, attached by wires to its interface devices (keyboard, monitor and then the mouse). The proliferation of laptops and notebook computers from the late 1990s brought the device and the body into closer contact with much advertising showing the supposed benefits of using a computer perched on one's knees—not without some controversy about the effect a warm computer might have on a man's reproductive potential. The evolution of touchscreen technology brought the devices even closer to the body, such that what was visual is now also interacted with more directly, shifting digital technologies into something that is more closely embraced, caressed and touched—and *marked* by the body which leaves the residue of our corporeal existence on the screen as smudges, oils and marks.

These historical shifts indicate a process of increasing 'closeness' between our embodied selves and our digital communication devices. At the same time, the development of increased portability of digital tools is a significant historical advancement inseparable from corporeality: smartphones brought the tools of digital communication even closer to the body, to the point that they are a device we take about with us, that sits as close to the body as possible in pockets, and spend a lot of their time not only 'at hand' but also 'in hand,' whether we're using them or not. Increasing ubiquity of 4G and 5G mobile cell towers and the dominant use of Wi-Fi routers in the home mean our bodies are—very literally—surrounded by digital communication tools that are no longer located in a space for communication (a study, an office, a shared computer in a lounge room) but go where our bodies go.

The format of the smartphone adds to this close relationship, being one that is fingered regularly even when not involved in talking to others remotely. However, cultural changes bring it into such close proximity to the human body in regularity that it becomes part of the body. In the first episode of the third season of the HBO television series *Veep*, one of the Vice President's senior aides is distraught at the idea of having to relinquish her mobile phone into a storage bowl for a wedding ceremony. "I can still feel it, like a phantom limb," she points out. The phantom limb is figurative of the body as a psychic ideal, whereby the part that is missing is felt as if it is there, always startling when one discovers it is not (Grosz 1994, pp. 70–73). In the same way, the mobile phone's movement in relation to the body from being a device that is always 'at hand' to one that is always 'in hand' and which creates anxieties when it is not being held indicates the ways in which it is so closely associated with the body it becomes part of the psychic map of the body. Much as clothes can be understood as a technology that become part of the assemblage of bodies in space in which nakedness is the sensation of their absence and a matter for anxiety (Cover 2003), the absence of the phone from its position in hand, *with* the body, *against* the body is a sensation of nakedness, since it produces a sense of incompletion as a material body.

A broad range of gaming devices and technologies likewise put the body into close contact with digital technologies in ways which have an effect on how embodied subjectivity is produced and how the body is materialised and given a sense of unification through contact with objects of technology and communication. Hand-held games, for example, have been common entertainment pastimes since the Game-and-Watch phenomenon of the 1980s and the Nintendo Game Boy of the 1990s. Today, more recent versions include the playing of games on smartphones in ways which provide both entertainment and engagement with text, interactivity and play through digitality by placing the device as a whole directly in the hand in close, regular and ongoing contact and touch. In many cases, the 'fit' between bodies and digital technologies is a deliberate result of design decisions (Benford et al. 1997, p. 93), and the emergence of such devices should never been seen to be alien and exotic but purposefully built to work with the existing perception of the body's senses, most obviously the eyes and ears, and limbs, typically the arms but also sometimes the feet. For example, while the dance pad was a particular kind of game controller for specific sorts of games based around dance, they have also been trialled as devices for typing (Sydney Morning Herald 2006), although they have clearly not taken off as a device of ubiquity replacing the more recognisable keyboard that developed in response to norms of dexterity through the building of the typewriter. Again, however, a move towards the placing of the device or its connectivity alongside, on, against or held by the body indicates a pathway towards bringing the body and the digital device closer together.

This increasing closeness of bodies and digital technologies is not, however, a fully linear historical progress in which we come ever closer to incorporating the technologies alongside or upon our bodies. Google Glass represented an interesting example of a wearable technology that closely associates digital connectivity with corporeal everyday life, but in a way did not become as popular as imagined. First announced in 2012 as a development in-progress in the Google X Lab and reported as being capable of recording what is in front of our faces while displaying information to the user on the screen of the glasses, they were reported as being "Terminator-style," with reports often accompanied by images of Arnold Schwarzenegger in sunglasses (Olivarez-Giles 2012)—an image which serves as the contemporary depiction of the cyborg creature who, whether for uses of good or evil, merges flesh and technology for efficiency (Ruston 2012, p. 31). While Google Glass would not really have produced the human cyborg—the device was effectively a smartphone assemblage worn above the nose rather than *within* the body—the metaphor drew attention to how digital communication tools are perceived as refiguring bodies and identities, including the identity of being 'human.'

However, anxieties about the technology emerged very soon after the announcement, with considerable concerns over privacy and, particularly, worries about whether or not it would be clear if someone was surreptitiously recording in setting where it is normally considered culturally inappropriate (such as the locker-room at the gym, where it is typically obvious if a person is taking images on a smartphone but may be less so if a person wearing glasses is simply glancing around). At the same time, discussions around the ability of users to draw information quickly without participants in a face-to-face conversation knowing also indicated some apprehension about the ethics of wearing glasses that are digitally connected—for example, during a job interview or a quiz. The concerns around the proposed device as that which would bring the technology into such close proximity to the body that it had potential for surreptitious or secretive purposes were often offset by arguments that framed it as simply a tool of the body, with particular benefits for persons with disabilities (Tsukayama 2013).

Catherine Happer (2013) has described Google Glass as a device that would "mediate between the user and reality," and this aspect of its perceived potential cultural usage is part of the presentation of anxiety around the cyborgisation of the body that becomes dependent on technology. Of course, there is nothing necessarily new about a device that mediates between the corporeal everyday and the 'reality' of real space around our bodies—smartphones do this the moment we use maps to help determine our location and the best ways to walk to our desired rendezvous, or when we engage in a Skype conversation between two bodies on different sides of the planet. What is more startling, perhaps, about wearable technology worn as glasses is the fact that the screen is designed as something which intervenes between the eye and what the eye sees as the space around it. It is the figure of the screen that acts as a window between the eye and its surrounds rather than as a screen that displays information that is at stake here, participating in the representation of the contemporary body as—itself—'biomediated' in ways which do not necessarily understand the mediation technologies as being fully within one's control (Clough 2008, p. 2).

If 'looking' is, effectively, an element of performative identity whereby it is one of the ways in which we articulate ourselves in accord with particular codes and conventions—the looks we give, the things we look at, the things we are expected to avoid seeing, how we stare or avoid staring, ways of appreciating or sizing-up those around us, flirting with the eyes, communicative engagement with others through a glance—then how that sense of seeing and how we appear to be doing that seeing changes when mediated in this particular, peculiar way. The connection between the eye, sight and the space and objects around are altered through the immediacy of that mediation in ways which can materialise our corporeal selves differently, those being ways which are too new to understand in advance.

The fact that questions arose about Google Glass and that it was ultimately withdrawn is indicative of how anxieties emerge about the engagement between the body and digital communication tools. One way to look at this is to consider the body and the technology as an 'assemblage' whereby there has always been a relationship, but where that relationship between technology and the body steps outside accepted norms—ones that are difficult to know in advance—they generate anxiety over identity. Who are we talking to if our coffee partner is also reading their messages? Can we trust the person on the train sitting opposite us that they are not taking very surreptitious photos of us? Who am I if I am so connected physically that messages are not a beep in my pocket that I *choose* to check but appear in front of my eyes while I'm off on a walk? Thus, while the relationship or assemblage between the mobile phone and the body was one built around contact, presence and proximity to communication tools, Google Glass was one which was perceived as reducing agency to decide *when* and *how* we communicate—even if it did have settings and controls that prevented interruptions. The question was not about how much control any party would have, but the fact that this advancement in technology began to blur how we comport our bodies in public and private spaces as part of our identities.

3.4.2 Bodily practices and technologies

The shifts in the relationship between the body and the tools and technologies of digital communication change the practices of how we use our bodies, particularly in relation to new innovations in design, interface and the creative uses of technologies. They produce new habits of the body and new norms. Norms emerge as forms of etiquette, but they are also contested as well as being deeply felt and are the site of substantial attachment (hence, for example, the anger one person expresses when someone else touches their screen because to their old-school views, the screen should never be touched). For Norbert Elias (1991), the ways in which we perceive our embodiment and corporeality are related to everyday performative practices and habits, such as the wearing of clothes, behaviours related to eating and forms of politeness and decorum in dealing with others. In that sense, relationships with technology are embodied and form a particular kind of language of sign system. For Elias:

> The make-up, the social habitus of individuals, forms as it were, the soil from which grow the personal characteristics through which an individual differs from other members of his society. In this way something grows out of the common language which the individual shares with others and which is certainly a component of his social habitus—a more or less individual style, what might be called an unmistakable individual handwriting that grows out of the social script.
>
> (p. 182)

Suggesting that there is a shared language of bodily engagement with digital technologies is not, of course, to suggest that it is singular and dominating. Rather, it is to argue that there are languages of that relationship that help establish the acceptable norms of how we use digital technologies. One example is that the bio-mediated device that I own can be touched by me, but to touch another person's smartphone is considered a breach of those shared norms. This, in turn, establishes norms over how close *my* body should come to *your* mobile device or tablet or laptop, and the norms work differently from, perhaps, how my body might interact with your car keys, your plate at a restaurant or your curtains in your lounge room.

Cultural systems of etiquette in relation to our own and others' devices do not, of course, emerge and then remain concrete. They develop and change over time and differ in particular contexts. For example, instances of 'frape' (the untactful abbreviation for 'Facebook Rape,' in which a person changes another person's Facebook settings, profile, pictures, relationship status and so on in order to cause a momentary humiliation, generally occurring when one has left a laptop open and unlocked momentarily among friends) are, contextually, comic and a scene of amusement among the group. Indeed while the victim of 'frape' might indeed be annoyed at the inconvenience or the risk of being genuinely humiliated among a broader social group, cultural etiquette insists that the subject hide that annoyance and laugh off the fact that friends touched his or her device without permission. In other words, expectations, rituals and norms in relation to touch and device can be complex, changing, context dependent and build on a sense of play as much as the protection of one's technology, one's information and one's relationship with digital space and self-representation.

Those rituals and norms, however, are part of the *assemblage* of engagement between corporeality and technology. To unpack a little further how an assemblage works, we can draw on Elizabeth Grosz's understanding of the relationship between the body and the city in which the body moves. For Grosz (1995), there are two problematic models of the body and the city. In the first, the city is seen as a *reflection* of the body in which bodies are understood mythically to predate the city, and the city is designed around the needs and practices of our bodies, as if those bodies are timeless (p. 105). This view tends towards a one-way relationship between bodies and cities in which the city is always the *effect* of the needs of the body. To put this perspective into the digital technology setting, it would be the same to suggest that our technologies are developed precisely for our needs which remain unchanged over time.

The second model of bodies and cities to which Grosz objected involves the association of cities and states, whereby the historical city–state had sometimes been described as having been designed on the basis of the body, for example, that it has a 'head' (its prince or leader), a set of arms (its military) and a body (its people, and buildings) and bowels (its sewage infrastructure), veins (its roads and walkways) and so on (pp. 105–106). This model is perhaps less applicable than the first to how we think about digital technology and communication networks, although the idea of communicative flows in a network is sometimes represented by the arterial flows of blood in our bodies—and the relationship between blood as the life force of human corporeality and communication as that which binds together a network, group or society is a useful one.

Grosz's solution to the problem of the two common models of bodies and cities above was to view the relationship between the two as neither the first (the human body *causes* the city) nor the second (the city represents the body) but instead as assemblages of the body–city:

> What I am suggesting is a model of the relations between bodies and cities that see them, not as megalithic total entities, but as assemblages or collections of parts, capable of crossing the thresholds between substances to form linkages, machines, provisional and often temporary sub-or micro-groupings. This model is practical, based on the productivity of bodies and cities in defining and establishing each other. It is not a holistic view, one that would stress the unity and integration of city and body, their 'ecological balance.' Rather, their interrelations involve a fundamentally disunified series of systems, a series of disparate flows, energies, events, or entities, bringing together or drawing apart their more or less temporary alignments.
>
> (p. 108)

If we replace the concept of city in this quote with the 'language' of contemporary digital technologies, we might say it is therefore possible to think of bodies and technologies as interfacing, connected and mutually determining. That is, digital technologies give our bodies particular practices, ways of thinking and ways of being material, and at the same time, our bodies interface with those technologies that do things as our bodily practices change.

To give a personal example, a few years ago I began introducing Google Home and Google Speakers to my house along with smart light globes and smart switches to control lights and lamps. The practice was one which involved an adjustment to the body—a difficult learning experience not to reach for the switch every time one enters a dark room but to speak a command to the Google Home network. What forms, however, is an assemblage between the body and the technology—an adjustment to the practices of the body such that it eventually becomes normative to speak the lights on. At the same time, however, the technological network of Google adapts to its assemblage with my body: the machine-learning algorithm becomes predictive, maps my vocal patterns so that it is more likely to understand my instructions and is adapted to the needs of the human beings in the household. The network of devices grew as it became more useful to incorporate new devices and new nodes in other rooms. Neither the bodily practices nor the technology direct the other—rather, in working together both experience changes and the bodily practices of everyday life in the household adapt to that assemblage such that the inhabitants of the house now do different things with their bodies (including particularly spoken commands that were less thinkable a decade ago).

Linkages, communicative flows, collective actions and activities over global spaces that come to resemble machines, temporary sites of group work, in a disunified series of systems and flows become not only normative in the everyday engagement of embodied subjects with others but produce meanings in ways which mutually define bodies and technologies. Here, the assemblage between bodies and technologies is significant in that it is the site at which we locate the conceptual and the practical adaptations, whether that is wearing technology, speaking to it, manipulating it, incorporating routines around the network or the networking developing routines around my body. This body–technology assemblage, then, becomes one of the ways in which digital technology plays a role in constituting identity—how we perform our identities is always a process, but that process includes adaptations that incorporate new technologies into those daily routines that make us 'what we are.'

3.4.3 Body information: the body as a project

Another way in which we can understand the body–technology assemblage is in the role digital technologies play in 'bettering' the body. Substantial scholarship over the past decade has explored the role of technologies in everyday body improvement practices in the space of health, exercise, mental health, body function tracking and prevention of illness. In this context, digital technologies can be seen as an outcome of a long-standing cultural shift in which the body came to be seen as a 'project' for constant improvement. Chris Shilling (2003) noted that contemporary culture since the 1980s introduced the idea of the body as being subject to conscious, intentional and reflexive betterment. This was to view the body not as static, or progressively ageing in a linear pattern, but as a 'project' upon which work must be undertaken. Widespread social, public service and individualised discourses of dieting; the de-valuation of bodily fat; and the promotion of exercise, toning, muscle-building and heart health improvement helped to produce new ideas of the body that were not in circulation as 'ideals' a century ago: the ideal body as hard, muscular, sleek and toned (Woodward 2002, p. 118). In this context, the body came to be seen not merely as the inferior object in a mind/body dualism but as something to be 'acted upon' in order to treat it as both an aesthetic object and to disavow the undisciplined body. This is not, of course, to suggest that such views of the 'fit' body are universally held and hegemonic; there are a number of minority articulations that embrace obesity as a choice and there is a known racialisation of bodies in terms of what kinds are permitted to be weightier than others, both perceptually and in practice (Walcott et al. 2003, p. 232). The substantial population health and community interest in obesity and other fitness concerns is not necessarily separable from some of the formations through which digital technologies are utilised in the context of body improvement. This is the body both subject to technologies for the purposes of betterment as a technique and as an outcome, as well as being produced and materialised as a body that incorporates technologies of fitness as assemblage.

The contemporary body is, for Bryan Turner (2008), one which is instrumentalised within a dynamic that, on the one hand, seeks to enhance performance, labour capabilities and longevity and, on the other, does so in order to produce increased pleasure through consumption and sex (p. 98). Indeed, pleasure has come to infiltrate several elements of the performativity of corporeal bodies in both space and communication (Urry 2007, p. 48) which includes entertainment, sport, physicality and movement. The model of masculine professional sporting bodies can, perhaps, be thought of as having come in to everyday body projects by extending the sports discourse in which the subject sought to produce a particular kind of 'fit' body in order to maximise pleasure, with that was off-field enjoyment, the joy of winning or the pleasure in achieving a goal (Cover 2015). The nineteenth-century British codification of much team-based sports was part of a culture in which bodies were subject to two attitudinal poles:

- a puritanical and stoic pole that emphasised the health and fitness of the body through intensive and regular discipline, and
- a Dionysian pleasure-seeking formation that, although diametrically opposed to the puritanical and more often 'hidden' in the social activities of the post-sports social activities, emphasised pleasure, partying, drinking and excess—alongside the other pleasures of fitness (Dunning and Waddington 2003).

In the same way, the contemporary, public discourses that emphasise fitness for maximised pleasure are part of the framework that manufactures the new attitude to the body as its own project.

In this context, it can be argued that the use of online, digital communication mirrors the two poles of the body project: discipline and pleasure. Digital communication tools provide sources of information that support the development of the body, and wearable fitness technologies are now widely used to enhance the tracking that—previously—was only undertaken by very serious and well-funded professionals. At the same time, however, the digital setting is the site of a particular kind of pleasure around the body project: the posting of images, the confirmation received from others at how fit and healthy a person appears on Instagram, the pleasure of a bodily exhibitionism and the interaction with others who are also engaged in their own body projects in forums and social media.

The tools of digital communication, then, become not merely the site of ready-access for information, but the framework through which subjects now have access to competing information and to a range of tools in which to conduct the project of body management. The capacity not only to find scales and measurements for the normative production of selfhood but also the compulsion to do so in order to produce the normative body as a practice of identity is enhanced through the combination of online information made broadly available as expertise and the wearable technologies and other devices that enable the measurement against those norms. This is where digital communication comes to serve as the fruition—or at least the next step—in providing the cultural conditions for the body as a project.

At one level, what occurs here is the shift of the normalisation of the body from the realm of institutional discipline, surveillance and normalisation (of the sort many of us experienced in school sports and physical education programmes) into that of 'biopolitics.' Michel Foucault (1994) defined biopolitics as a technology of power that emerged in the nineteenth century that shifted from the disciplinary focus on the individual body to the body of the population as a whole: "the endeavor, begun in the eighteenth century, to rationalize the problems presented to governmental practice by the phenomena characteristic of a group of living human beings constituted as a population: health, sanitation, birthrate, longevity, race …" (p. 73). Biopolitics is, for Foucault, a form or 'technology' of power that addresses and acts upon whole populations through regulatory practices that seek to ensure an economic, cultural and political status quo in order to aid the free enterprise culture of neoliberal society and ensure the life and health of the wider population. As Foucault (2004) put it:

> like disciplinary mechanisms, these mechanisms are designed to maximize and extract forces, but they work in very different ways. Unlike disciplines, they no longer train individuals by working at the level of the body itself … It is therefore not a matter of taking the individual at the level of individuality but, on the contrary, of using overall mechanisms and acting in such a way as to achieve overall states of equilibration or regularity.
>
> (p. 246)

Both operating alongside with and distinguishing itself from the power formation of disciplinarity expressed through surveillance, supervision, inspections and the production of docile bodies (Foucault 2007, p. 4), biopolitics governs through investigation, assessment and examination at the level of the demographic and statistical; it intervenes and regulates where necessary for equilibrium and balance and social modification, thereby producing a subject which is in flux, flexible and available for commodification.

It is in the gathering of statistical information that permits biopolitical governance to make or recommend adjustments that we see the body–technology assemblage act upon identity. Wearable technologies and other body-tracking systems gather information from very large numbers of users (crowd-sourcing big data) and use that to finesse and enhance the recommendations for health by making ever-more sophisticated articulations of distributional norms, curves of normality and categories of what 'counts' as a healthy body. Those norms are used to compel conformity among the population such that to belong to the normative range of the population—and thereby have a coherent, intelligible, recognisable and conforming identity—we treat our bodies as a project to improve, maintain and sustain. In this sense, technology does not just work for our individual body project goals but for the production of a normativity identity. In this respect, digital technologies and devices taken together as a *complex* are the biopolitical tools *par excellence* in that they not only produce and circulate ranges and scales of the normative body, but they provide the tools (at hand, in hand and readily worn) for the persistent measurement, self-vigilance, self-monitoring, diligence and tracking of the body's progress and thereby the means by which we conform to identity norms.

3.4.4 The concept of the seam

The final element of the body–technology assemblage I would like to raise is a concept I have discussed elsewhere (Cover 2016). I've argued that our relationship or assemblage with digital technology might be understood as a constant movement towards the 'seam' between technology and corporeal life. Although I have argued above that the idea of a distinction between the real (or embodied) and the digital (or virtual or cyberspace) is not only outdated, but was very problematic to begin with, we can critique from another angle—the way in which these are not separate spaces but settings conditioned by an ever-closer *movement* towards each other in assemblage.

The notion of a conceptual separation between the real and the digital is upheld by narratives, stories and articulations that see it as collapsed when in the process of digital communicative or interactive engagement such as gaming or online communication, as I have described above. The separation of 'spaces' leads to problematic uses of the idea of immersion, whereby a user, game player or web surfer is seen to reduce the 'importance' of the corporeal body while being cognitively immersed in the imaginative world of the game. As Lahti (2003) has described, thinking about the relationship between text, digital game play and identity through a concept of penetration,

> much of the development of video games has been driven by a desire for a corporeal immersion with technology, a will to envelop the player in technology and the environment of the game space. That development has coincided with and been supported by developments in perspective and the optical point-of-view structures of games, which have increasingly emphasized the axis of depth, luring the player into invading the world behind the computer screen.
>
> (p. 159)

It is definitely true that the idea of becoming further immersed in digital settings has driven the technological advancements and marketing of digital technologies. In some ways, we see this with our entertainment technology that comes closer and becomes more immersive: the development of the 'home theatre' suite of devices (audio, video, recording, play, connectivity) over the past two decades involves constant improvements that see us closer and—importantly—*more surrounded* by those digital technologies—larger screens, 5.1 and 6.1 surround sound, more sophisticated and body-compatible remote controls, the use of subwoofers that allow us to feel as well as hear and so on.

At the same time, digital workspace becomes more immersive in the sense of surrounding the body with larger and more curved monitors, lending the illusion of greater immersion in digital settings. Likewise, gaming chairs have been designed that literally *surround* a user, with monitors, controls all around, foot pedals and sometimes arranged in ways which 'lock in' a user much as a pilot is strapped into a military combat plane's cockpit. The VR helmet is, of course, one of the points of fruition of a shift towards immersion, although the interest, popularity and research and development endeavours on VR devices have come and gone over the years, the increasing and waning interest in VR can be recognised as a flirtation with finding the most workable immersive experience for our bodies. Finally, the recent substantial investment in the so-called metaverse in which predictions of VR technologies and machine-operated augmented reality (AR) processing are perceived as one of the possible futures of digital engagement (Newton 2021) in which the spaces we inhabit will be engaged with as an immersive digital environment.

Although many of these developments are often described through the older real/virtual dichotomy, a better way of thinking about them retains the centrality of corporeal, embodied life and understands digital technologies as that to which we move closer in assemblage to a recognisable 'seam' between the 'real' and the 'digital.' The notion of a 'seam,' then, can be described as the site at which the body 'rubs up' against digital technologies but at no stage should be recognised as a mind entering those spaces and leaving the body behind (as in cybercultural accounts of digital spaces). Why? The problem with those older ideas is that they represent digital communication *as if* there is something behind the screen. Rather, it is the screen itself that matters here. The trend towards an increased closeness with the screen—without needing to articulate absurd ideas of crossing it—is discernible in the history of technological innovation towards immersion I have been describing above. This is a seam which cannot be crossed, but one for which there is a productive, corporeal and libidinal desire to rub up against, to come close and to do so in a way which *simultaneously* imagines our immersion or even our merger with it (as cyborg, wearing it, part of it and technology as part of us).

Despite the ubiquitous normative uses of digital technologies, it remains that the perception of two spaces is at play, and this governs those technological developments to provide not an actual crossing of the seam but an artificial *perception* that we do so in ways which allows us to adapt, enhance or develop our bodily identities. The space on the other side of the screen can only ever be figured as mythical, entirely constructed by our desires to project ourselves towards and beyond the seam in an immersion that can never really, corporeally happen. Space is always constructed in movement—indeed, for Grosz (1995), space is constituted only in the ability to move within it:

> It is our positioning within space, both as the point of perspectival access to space, and also as an object for others in space, that gives the subject a coherent identity and an ability to manipulate things, including its own body parts, in space. However, space does not become comprehensible to the subject by its being the space of movement; rather, it becomes space through movement, and as such, it acquires specific properties from the subject's constitutive functioning in it.
>
> (p. 92)

While this applies to physical space—or space that is perceived as physical—it also helps us to make sense of why we have culturally built the mythical idea of a space beyond the screen, a screen which serves as the seam that separates two spaces. Because interactivity is produced through manipulations of text, image, game character, idea or others in ways that require that we see these as objects and, thereby, as objects that are moved in our interaction and are available for movement, digital information comes to be understood as 'locatable' within a conceptualisation of space. That we are positioned not *in* that space but alongside it, at the seam, with tools useful to manipulate objects in that space (much as we might rake up leave from the pool with our leaf-catcher on a long rod; much as we drive a car and manipulate it through streets looking through a windscreen without ever being exposed to the space, smells or sounds of the road), our identities are constituted with bodies that are materialised through our positioning as coherent by virtue of, as Grosz described it above, our ability to manipulate things. Movement of things constitutes this alternative space and, in turn, we are constituted by the capacity to make those movements. This does not, of course, dissolve the seam but makes the seam itself the site of the most important contemporary engagement with communication, culture and selfhood.

The increasing closeness between the space in which corporeal bodies move and the space we perceive as that beyond the screen and the interface for networked communication is, then, historical, adaptable and quickly changing. Most important here is that it is not necessarily the case that such a seam is a conceptualisation that will have usefulness into the far or even near future. The former executive chairman of Google, Eric Schmidt, once suggested that the Internet itself is disappearing. Speaking at a 2015 World Economic Forum meeting in Davos, Switzerland, he argued that the ubiquity of connected devices in everyday corporeal space—the Internet of Things—has made the idea of 'going online' meaningless, as one is already always online: "There will be so many sensors, so many devices, that you won't even sense it, it will be all around you … It will be part of your presence all the time" (Carter 2015). What Schmidt meant by this was not that the Internet no longer exists, but that its ubiquity in *surrounding* us bodily makes it difficult to distinguish the Internet or digital setting from the space in which we move and articulate our corporeal selves.

To extend the metaphorical myth of immersion in water somewhat further, having our bodies surrounded by digital devices that are ubiquitously connected is a little like being in a very humid environment in which everything feels wet all the time, and putting one's hand into water does not have the potency of the distinction between dry and wet—only of various gradations of wetness. This does not mean, however, that we are suddenly always crossed-over into water. Likewise, we do not become digitised ourselves, but our uses of digital communication move in-and-out of various gradations as we find ourselves so utterly immersed we do not necessarily consciously make sense of any distinction between our corporeal lived everyday and our acts of digital communication. In this sense, we might say that the performance of our identities is one conditioned not by whether we are online or offline or extending ourselves into online spaces or being influenced by what is encountered in digital communication. Rather, we perform our identities in ways that are constituted by the surrounds of digital life as acts that move us closer to that seam—even when we disavow communication, disconnect for a time and attempt to isolate ourselves for a period.

3.5 Conclusion

If we are to understand our identities as performative, as conditioned by the languages and cultures that precede and surround us, then we need to think about how the performance of our identities through our bodies has also been conditioned by our relationship with our communicative technologies. In this chapter, I have argued that we do well to get away from older ideas of the real/virtual and mind/body dichotomies, as well as speculative ideas about leaving the body behind and existing as only 'mind' in digital networks. Such creative use in science fiction and cyberculture theories was useful for providing critical alternatives but does not provide a good reflection of how everyday people actually use digital media in embodied ways.

This chapter has worked through several key concepts about bodies, identity and digital communication: the fact that no digital communication is ever disembodied, the significance of the increasing representation of the body on-screen that is distinct from earlier, text-based Internet use and the extension of our bodies into digital settings through the manipulation of avatars in game play. I have also addressed some of the ways in which our bodily practices are—today—increased governed by our relationship with digital communication technologies, including those that we wear, those that develop or enhance our bodily practices, those that establish norms around the fit or healthy body (as a project) and how the concepts of the body–technology 'assemblage' and the 'movement towards the seam' play a powerful conceptual role in helping us understand not only how our identities are formed in the context of digital communication, but how the body remains central to those identity performances online.

Key points

- The real/virtual body distinction tends to drive much discussion about digital communication, and this is risky because it inaccurately describes digital identities as disembodied.
- Bodies and bodily senses, touch and action are central to identity, communication and the use of digital media.
- After the advent of Web 2.0 bodies came to be overrepresented on digital screens in the form of image and video, in contrast to earlier versions of the Internet that were primarily based in interactivity with written texts. Although a significant shift, it also has pitfalls such as the circulation of stereotypes.
- There are several emerging theories that help us understand the relationship between bodies and digital technologies in ways that are formative of new identity practices, including theories of body–technology assemblage and movement towards a theoretical 'seam' between bodies and digital-conceptual spaces.

References

Benford, S., Bowers, J., Fahlén, L.E., Greenhalgh, C. and Snowdon, D., 1997. Embodiments, avatars, clones and agents for multi-user, multi-sensory virtual worlds. *Multimedia Systems,* 5 (2), 93–104.

Bourdieu, P., 1990. *The Logic of Practice.* Oxford: Polity.

Butler, J., 1990. *Gender Trouble: Feminism and the Subversion of Identity.* London: Routledge.

Butler, J., 1993. *Bodies That Matter: On the Discursive Limits of 'Sex.'* London: Routledge.

Butler, J., 1997. *The Psychic Life of Power: Theories in Subjection.* Stanford, CA: Stanford University Press.

Carter, R., 2015. Internet will 'disappear,' Google boss Eric Schmidt tells Davos. *Sydney Morning Herald,* 23 January. Available from: www.smh.com.au/technology/internet-will-disappear-goo gle-boss-eric-schmidt-tells-davos-20150123-12wsxs.html [Accessed 3 June 2022].

Clough, P.T., 2008. The affective turn: political economy, biomedia and bodies. *Theory, Culture & Society,* 25 (1), 1–22.

Cover, R., 2003. The naked subject: nudity, context and sexualisation in contemporary culture. *Body & Society,* 9 (3), 53–72.

Cover, R., 2015. *Vulnerability and Exposure: Footballer Scandals, Masculine Identity and Ethics.* Crawley, WA: UWA Publishing.

Cover, R., 2016. *Digital Identities: Creating and Communicating the Online Self.* London: Elsevier.

Descartes, R., 1968. *Discourse on Method and the Meditation,* trans. F.E. Sutcliffe. Harmondsworth: Penguin.

Dunning, E. and Waddington, I., 2003. Sport as a drug and drugs in sport: some exploratory comments. *International Review for the Sociology of Sport,* 38 (3), 351–368.

Elias, N., 1991. *The Society of Individuals.* Oxford: Blackwell.

Filiciak, M., 2003. Hyperidentities: postmodern identity patterns in massively multiplayer online role-playing games. *In:* M.J.P. Wolf and B. Perron, eds. *The Video Game Theory Reader.* New York: Routledge, 87–101.

Foucault, M., 1994. *Ethics, Subjectivity and Truth,* ed. P. Rabinow, trans. R. Hurley et al. New York: New York Press.

Foucault, M., 1977. *Discipline and Punish: The Birth of the Prison,* trans. A. Sheridan. London: Penguin.

Foucault, M., 2004. *Society Must Be Defended: Lectures at the Collège de France, 1975–76,* ed. M. Bertani and A. Fontana, trans. D. Macey. London: Penguin.

Foucault, M., 2007. *Security, Territory, Population: Lectures at the Collège de France, 1977–78,* ed. M. Senellart, trans. G. Burchell. Hampshire: Palgrave Macmillan.

Green, L., 2002. *Communication, Technology and Society.* St. Leonards, NSW: Allen & Unwin.

Grodal, T., 2003. Stories for eye, ear, and muscles: video games, media, and embodied experiences. *In:* M.J.P. Wolf and B. Perron, eds. *The Video Game Theory Reader.* New York: Routledge, 129–155.

Grosz, E., 1994. *Volatile Bodies: Toward a Corporeal Feminism.* St. Leonards, NSW: Allen & Unwin.

Grosz, E., 1995. *Space, Time and Perversion: The Politics of Bodies.* London: Routledge.

Happer, C., 2013. Google Glass: augmenting minds or helping us sleepwalk? *The Conversation,* 28 January. Available from: https://theconversation.com/google-glass-augmenting-minds-or-help ing-us-sleepwalk-11784 [Accessed 31 May 2022].

Haraway, D., 1991. *Simians, Cyborgs and Women: The Reinvention of Nature.* London: Routledge.

Huizinga, J., 1949. *Homo Ludens: A Study of the Play-Element in Culture.* London: Routledge & Kegan Paul.

Lahti, M., 2003. As we become machines: corporealized pleasures in video games. *In:* M.J.P. Wolf and B. Perron, eds. *The Video Game Theory Reader.* New York: Routledge, 157–170.

Lingis, A., 1994. *Foreign Bodies.* New York: Routledge.

Miller, V., 2011. *Understanding Digital Culture.* London: Sage.

Nakamura, L., 2008. *Digitizing Race: Visual Cultures of the Internet.* Minneapolis, MN: University of Minnesota Press.

Newton, C., 2021. Mark Zuckerberg is betting Facebook's future on the metaverse. *The Verge,* 22 July. Available from: www.theverge.com/22588022/mark-zuckerberg-facebook-ceo-metave rse-interview [Accessed 18 November 2021].

Olivarez-Giles, N., 2012. Google to launch 'Terminator-style' smart glasses: report. *Sydney Morning Herald,* 23 February. Available from: www.smh.com.au/technology/google-to-launch-terminat orstyle-smart-glasses-report-20120223-1tozi.html [Accessed 4 June 2022].

Rosello, M., 1998. *Declining the Stereotype: Ethnicity and Representation in French Cultures.* Hanover, NH: University Press of New England.

Ruston, S.W., 2012. Calling ahead: cinematic imaginations of mobile media's critical affordances. *In:* N. Arcenaux and A. Kavoori, eds. *The Mobile Media Reader.* New York: Peter Lang, 23–39.

Shilling, C., 2003. *The Body and Social Theory.* London: Sage.

Sydney Morning Herald, 2006. Dance Pad lets your feet do the typing. *Sydney Morning Herald,* 2 March. Available from: www.smh.com.au/national/dance-pad-lets-your-feet-do-the-typing-20060302-gdn2n2.html [Accessed 4 June 2022].

Tsukayama, H., 2013. Google Glass gives independence to people with disabilities. *The Age,* 9 August. Available from: www.theage.com.au/technology/google-glass-gives-independence-to-people-with-disabilities-20130809-2rlif.html [Accessed 2 June 2022].

Turner, B.S., 2008. *The Body and Society: Explorations in Social Theory.* London: Sage.

Urry, J., 2007. *Mobilities.* Cambridge: Polity.

Walcott, D.D., Pratt, H.D. and Patel, D.R., 2003. Adolescents and eating disorders: gender, racial, ethnic, sociocultural, and socioeconomic issues. *Journal of Adolescent Research,* 18 (3), 223–243.

Wiley, J., 1999. Nobody is doing it: cybersexuality. *In:* J. Price and M. Shildrick, eds. *Feminist Theory and the Body.* Edinburgh: Edinburgh University Press, 134–139.

Woodward, K., 2002. *Understanding Identity.* London: Arnold.

Young, I.M., 1990. *Throwing Like a Girl and Other Essays in Feminist Philosophy and Social Theory.* Bloomington, IN: Indiana University Press.

4 Simulacras

The evolution of the deepfake

4.1 Introduction

Having explored several different angles of the relationship between identities, bodies and digital communication practices across the past three chapters, this chapter begins the discussion of the various *implications* of digital culture for how we perform, practise, represent and know our identities that comprises the remainder of this book. I would like to start with an area which has been the cause of much excitement, alarm and anxiety in very recent years: the creative potentials and pitfalls of deepfake videos as they emerge in an era of disinformation, misinformation and misleading content.

In its current, contemporary form, disinformation, misinformation and fake news emerged as a cultural concept in the mid-2010s, framed not only as a social issue but as a 'crisis' calling for solutions. There has, of course, been a long-standing concept of false communication, lies, propaganda and media bias, extending back centuries and related often to the key emergent media and communication forms of the day. However, the circulation today of fake news as online material—either as deliberate disinformation or accidentally believed and shared as misinformation—is widely recognised as having a serious and problematic impact on trust in digital communication which, for us, means trust in how our identities are represented. Disinformation, fake news and misleading content is also clearly affecting aspects of how we live as human beings, including its impact on accurate health information, particularly in relation to the COVID-19 pandemic. Finally, it has had an impact on how we perform social belonging, particularly in relation to its capacity to disrupt one key node of belonging—the electoral process and political communication in the United States of America, Europe, Australia, South America and East Asia.

Although fake news, disinformation and misinformation is a complex, wide area of emergent digital and platform activity (see Cover et al. 2022) and has an impact on identity because of the way in which it changes the trust relationship between readers, users and content online, one of its forms that is interesting for us to explore here is the 'deepfake' video. The deepfake is a technologically enhanced false video and audio text that draws on genuinely recorded and existing images, but reconfigures and re-juxtaposes them to produce 'fake' video and audio material that *appears* to be credible, even to the most discerning viewer. Significantly, the software and mobile apps that use machine learning to enable quality deepfakes are widely available and very simple to use. In that context, the advent of deepfake video has changed one of the ways in which digital communication is used, by allowing unskilled people to produce computer-generated content of high quality, fostering an exciting new form of creativity that is substantially different

DOI: 10.4324/9781003296652-4

from previous years' engagement with video content. At the same time, of course, any creative capability is available for surreptitious, malicious and harmful use, including for the purposes of creating believable disinformation. As one form of digital disinformation, the deepfake affects how we perceive authenticity of visual representations of identity, primarily because it has the capacity to perform identity fraud.

Although it is tempting to discuss deepfakes only through the lens of disinformation, it is important to bear in mind that the creative potential is powerful and that *most* people are not motivated to use technology to produce false or deliberately misleading content. It is therefore more valuable to take a step back from condemnation to consider how they emerged within digital cultures and the range of potential uses. Deepfake technology sits at the intersection between the digital practices of interactivity and co-creativity, on the one hand, and the contemporary framework of postmodern hyperreality, on the other hand, including what is described in more detail below as the culture of 'simulacra' (Baudrillard 1988). Just like other forms of digital interactivity, the deepfake belongs to and extends the boundaries of 'fake news,' posing a greater threat to the quality and control of evidence, information and communicative norms and thereby to the reliability of the normative discourses through which identities are made intelligible, coherent and recognisable; yet it also extends and expands the capabilities of creative interactivity. Its implications for the performance and authenticity of identity representations are only beginning to emerge. This chapter provides an overview of deepfake video, how it emerged as a topic of anxiety and concern in recent public debate and its origins as a form of simulacra that has implications for the veracity and authenticity of identity.

4.2 Deepfake as a topic of concern

Deepfakes are videos in which a subject's face or body has been digitally altered to make them look like someone else—usually a famous person. One notable example is the @deeptomcruise TikTok account, which has posted dozens of deepfake videos impersonating Tom Cruise, and attracted some 3.6 million followers. In another example, Meta CEO Mark Zuckerberg seems to be confessing to conspiratorial data sharing. More recently, there have been a number of deepfakes featuring actors such as Robert Pattinson and Keanu Reeves without their permission or knowledge. Although deepfakes are often used creatively or for fun, they're increasingly being deployed in disinformation campaigns, for identity fraud and to discredit public figures and celebrities.

The term 'deepfake' emerged in the past half-decade to describe a significant new tool that draws on advancements in computer processing power to create and make available false and misleading visual material for both powerful creative or artistic purposes and for surreptitious use in creating and 'proving' disinformation. Most commonly, deepfakes draw on machine learning and modern capabilities for processing information to allow users to insert the face, body and visual information about a real-world person (sometimes from a still image) into a recording of someone else, also known as face-swapping (Fried 2019). This enables them to replicate voice and mimic movements in a way that looks 'real,' for example, representing former US Secretary of State Hillary Clinton giving a speech she never gave, looking credible and saying things that may persuade people she holds views she does not. With very simple tools, I could record a video of myself looking like I am violently assaulting a third party and then use a deepfake app to put your face in pace of mine, taking the image from your LinkedIn account. I might then use that to blackmail you, cause you to lose your job or just damage the public perception of your identity forever.

The use of this technology has therefore resulted in public debate on its implications for representing truth and authenticity, particularly in relation to electoral politics and to how it might contribute to a wider culture of disinformation (Cover et al. 2022). In the context of everyday creative practices, then, the ability to produce and share credible-seeming video footage involves substantial developments in cultural concepts of representation: complexifying the ability to categorise and distinguish information from entertainment, footage from animation, factual content from fictional content and original footage from remixed or adapted audio–video. We might therefore say that the emergence of the deepfake is the fruition of several, sometimes-competing culturally embedded desires and social trends in co-creative interactivity and postmodern creative practice.

Despite deepfake technology being built on pre-existing practices and a longer history of digital creativity, it is typically perceived in public sphere and the scholarly discourse *as if* it is an entirely unanticipated technology, external to cultural practice and impacting on it either *positively* (in the case of film industry) or *negatively* (in the case of identity fraud and questions over the veracity of representation). By way of example, one report from investigative cluster *Deeptrace* which researches cybersecurity detection technologies, described the advent of the deepfake as an "unsettling" phenomenon, quickly changing the landscape of pornography, security and institutional authority (Ajder et al. 2019). Others have described deepfake technology as bringing about an "infocalypse" (Lenters 2021), as heralding a dystopian communication ecology (Yadlin-Segal and Oppenheim 2020), or as an part of a wider unwelcome application of artificial decision-making technologies in everyday life (Pavis 2021).

Although deepfakes are a very new digital technology, there is already some early research that assesses the technical aspects of deepfakes (Fleming and Bruce 2021), some of which explores deepfake implications for cybersecurity and foreign relations (Westerlund 2019), and some scholarship on the role that might be played artificial decision-making tools, machine learning and other technical options for detecting deepfakes (Mirsky and Lee 2021). Additionally, there has been some assessment of the threats and opportunities deepfake technologies provide for existing creative industries (e.g., Kietzmann et al. 2021). The cultural and social concerns raised by scholars take into consideration key issues such as deepfake's capabilities for contributing to the existing problem of disinformation (Diakopoulos and Johnson 2021), the potential for deepfakes to distort public knowledge and public memory of events (Murphy and Flynn 2021), and—very importantly—the particular implications of deepfakes for people in relation to image-based sexual abuse such as the faking of revenge pornography that can destroy a person's reputation if they cannot prove that a shared video was false (van der Nagel 2020). Additionally, some research has begun to explore how we might consider and develop ethical responses to deepfakes in ways which don't seek to shut them down completely, although that has been the knee-jerk reaction so far (Le 2020).

At the same time, there has been some considerable public opinion writing on the deepfake phenomenon that positions it as an unexpected technology *external* to contemporary culture *as if* it were some alien technology that is disrupting our existing communication norms. The idea that deepfake technologies are disruptive is usually framed either as:

- a positive utility for creative industries, such as the realistic depiction of deceased actors sometimes referred to as 'resurrection' technology (Lees et al. 2021); or
- through alarmism over the implications for information veracity in electoral communication, consumer rights and for intellectual property, representational integrity and policy.

In line with other developments in digital policy over the past half-decade that seek to find better ways to regulate digital platforms and what are sometimes seen as the excesses of contemporary technologies (Flew 2021), there is growing public and scholarly discourse that calls for the securitisation of this new technology through state regulation (Taylor 2021).

Rather than viewing deepfake technology as external to culture and thereby warranting regulation in the form of censorship or content removal that shifts the deepfake from being recognised as harmful to being made illegal (Flew 2021, pp. 225–226), it may well be better to argue that the deepfake can only be understood as a 'cultural artefact' and 'creative practice' that emerges from *within culture*. This is to see it, like all digital technologies, as a response to specific cultural desires and demands for co-creativity and within our postmodern culture of simulation, hyperreality and play. It is therefore better to see the problems associated with deepfake technologies as requiring more imaginative responses than simply regulating or banning it. In disavowing the alarmism and the understandings that see it as dangerous, we are better off asking what the recent emergence of the deepfake tells us about how we understand creative critique, textuality, representation, authenticity and identity in light of the broader cultural shifts that constitute the formation and uptake of deepfake technology and practices. To that end, we need to *start* by understanding deepfake technology as an emanation of culture and history rather than an 'alien' or 'technologically determinist' phenomenon that disrupts it. Secondly, we need to make sense of the means by which *diverse and competing uses* contribute to the situation in which it is perceived as a social issue warranting intervention. And we need to make sense of how the calls for regulating it or preventing its use have been deployed in ways which disregard the present culture of digital creativity.

To analyse the deepfake phenomenon in this way is not to disavow the serious, problematic uses and misuses of a technology that has at times been weaponised as a form of disinformation and image abuse (including particularly women and minorities and those in the public sphere through pornographication and false attribution). Nor is it to proscribe a decidable position 'for or against' deepfake technology. Rather, it is to critique its conceptualisation to strengthen the possible ethical responses by understanding culture's constitutive relationship with emergent technologies.

4.3 Deepfake as a technology of identity (fraud)

Some of the ramifications of the widespread availability of technologies and applications that allow everyday users to develop deepfake video content were spelled out in a letter by US lawmakers to the US Director of National Intelligence:

> Hyper-realistic digital forgeries use sophisticated machine learning techniques to produce convincing depictions of individuals doing or saying things they never did, without their consent or knowledge. By blurring the line between fact and fiction,

deep fake technology could undermine public trust in recorded images and videos as objective depictions of reality.

(cited in Chakhoyan 2018)

Andrew Chakhoyan (2018) suggests that deepfake videos can increase the political polarisation that has marked many of our contemporary democracies, and that was particularly evident during the 2016 presidential election in the United States of America. He cites as an example a Buzzfeed video from 2018 in which footage of Barack Obama was manipulated to make it appear as though he was making ludicrous statements. This video was designed to illustrate how deepfaking works, but it's not unimaginable that the same deepfake it could be used to demonise Democrat politicians and polarise the public even further (Chakhoyan 2018).

A common everyday popular cultural use has been for the purposes of ostensible and obvious parody, pastiche and humour, retrofitting popular cinema from the past with new celebrity actor faces, such as Tom Cruise inserted into *American Psycho* (Holliday 2021) or the production of 'Cage Rage' viral videos in which Nicholas Cage's likeness is sutured onto other texts to make an emotive point (Pulver 2018). While these deepfakes are all created for the purpose of humour that is obvious to audiences who recognise and find entertainment value in these representations—alongside the entertainment found in films that are marketed deliberately as including 'resurrected' actors—such uses can also be said to open questions about identity and identity fraud:

- Should Tom Cruise or Nicholas Cage be paid for the use of their likeness?
- How will the public know that either Cruise or Cage acted in these videos, including decades into the future?
- Will humorous Cruise and Cage deepfakes lead to more problematic ones which represent them as holding unpalatable political views?
- What occurs for the identity of a celebrity when a deepfake pornographic video is created, as has been the case more for women public figures?

Indeed, we have numerous examples of deepfake texts which perpetrate a kind of identity fraud by making 'real-looking' content that could easily be believed that a person (usually a public figure) has stated or done something they did not do. Examples include deepfakes of US House of Representatives Speaker Nancy Pelosi appearing to be intoxicated while giving a speech (Towers-Clark 2019)—a very simple form of deepfake that caused the audio of her voice to sound slurred. The utility of this for anti-Democrat politics is obvious. Some of the alarming examples of deeply damaging deepfakes include content of Meghan, the Duchess of Sussex appearing to be performing in a pornographic film by placing her face seamlessly on the body of a porn actor in such a way that actually generated a widespread belief among her detractors that she had a secret history of starring in pornography (Carmen 2019).

Others have made use of a combination of existing images and new, for example, footage of former President Barack Obama or Facebook co-founder Mark Zuckerberg giving a speech, but using software that expertly mimics the voice such that they are speaking words they never actually spoke and thereby represents them as saying something they would never necessarily say (Gilbey 2019). Key here is the range of communicated and surreptitious manufacturing of scenes that did not occur; the way texts which lead an audience to knowingly or unknowing see them as 'authentic'; and broad range of uses across entertainment, humour, political satire, defamation, unwarranted sexualisation or revenge porn.

To put this in the context of identity, we should begin by defining 'identity fraud.' We usually understand identity fraud to be the use of another person's private information to deceive a third party, and it has typically related to the use of forged identity documents or credentials and the unauthorised use of logins or passwords; to access a victim's banking accounts, financial details, personal information or correspondence such as email; or to gain physical access to secure buildings, workplaces or homes. A subset of identity fraud is known as criminal impersonation, whereby a person uses (without authority) data about a victim to convince a third party that it is the victim acting. A simple example is, of course, impersonating someone in an email sent either from that person's account without authority or from an account that 'appears' to be that person's, e.g., an account set up with a similar name.

The existence of identity fraud as a contemporary issue points to the significance of documents, images, logins, passwords and other mechanisms of giving 'credentials' to how we prove our identities—that we are who we say we are. Although losing a passport does not cause us to begin questioning our identity, it does change how we are able to perform and articulate our identification. As importantly, it has an effect on our belonging and social participation: not being able to move seamlessly through an immigration queue at the airport, being treated differently from others or with suspicion and intense scrutiny is—for many—an anxiety-producing experience. It is probably safe to say that losing control of our communication tools (email, social networking accounts, online forum logins) is even more anxiety-provoking, particularly if it means that a person has sent communication or posted content that is not our own, purporting to be us—this is far more serious for identity.

Why? Because if our identities are merely constituted in our articulations and performances, including what we communicate, then for that communication to come from someone else without our permission or authority changes how we are perceived by others. Obviously, the extent to which this affects us depends on the situation and our own, personal desires for agency—a joke image posted to Instagram by a house-mate when one leaves a tablet unattended is possibly amusing; some far-right content posted in that person's name may leave a false trace (forever) that they are a Nazi sympathiser.

This takes us, then, to the question of the deepfake. With a technology that is so convincingly capable of showing video footage of someone else doing something (say, attending a far-right political meeting) with *your* face and *your* voice is deeply concerning for the relationship between identity and digital communication. In this context, deepfakes *can be* a powerful tool for identity theft and identity fraud. There have been a number of cases already of deepfakes used as a form of identity fraud for financial gain, including a case of artificial intelligence (AI) software credibly mimicking an employee's boss' voice to 'authorise' a £200,000 transfer to a cybercriminal (Hendrikse 2019). Concerns have also been raised about the use of deepfakes in phishing scams, gaining access to organisational databases containing significant personal data, AI-driven voice-cloning used to replicate voice-activated security systems, imposter scams that prey on the elderly and so on (Bateman 2020). Although the digital technology of the deepfake is new, the practices and goals of such scams and identity fraud are, of course, much older and simply take advantage of a new technology to impersonate their victims.

Indeed, digital image manipulation itself has, of course, been part of everyday media and cultural practice since the widespread accessibility of audiovisual editing tools, the requisite computer processing power since the mid-1990s and the capacity to share non-professional creative work online since the advent of YouTube and other social media in the mid-2000s. However sophisticated the skills of the user, most everyday manipulation or remixing fell short of generating moving images and sound that could convince a relatively discerning viewer that it was recorded footage. In the past half-decade, however, the increased capacities of machine learning and AI, and the automation of sophisticated but simple-to-use apps, has made the technology of audiovisual image manipulation very accessible. In that sense, computer-generated footage that 'appears real' (i.e., appears as if it were traditionally recorded without post-production manipulation) is now widely available.

This has another implication for identity practices that, in fact, falls outside of the identity fraud and identity theft framework. If identity is performative, as we have been discussing over the previous chapters, then our communication is one of the facets of embodied, corporeal performance that retroactively stabilises a sense of selfhood (Butler 1990). Digital image manipulation has, for many years, allowed us to represent ourselves in ways that are not necessarily truthful (I could insert my image before shots of the Colosseum in Rome to fake an Italian holiday or could use Photoshop to convincingly suggest I was a very good friend of President Joe Biden). Deepfake technology now allows even more convincing identity representation that is untruthful—you may not believe a deepfake showing my winning gold at the Olympics (because that's easily verified), but you might be convinced if I represented myself falsely accepting a major award. Or, you may recognise straight away that a photograph of myself with the Queen of the United Kingdom is probably photoshopped (because photoshopping images has been available for many years now), but you may be convinced by video footage of a meeting with the Queen (because deepfake technology is new, and many do not yet understand how powerful the technology behind it has become). While such uses of the technology are likely to come close to perpetrating fraud, there are many similar 'mistruths' that may be produced that are not necessarily fraudulent but certainly open questions as to the veracity of any video footage anyone posts online—a substantial cultural shift since video footage has usually been regarded as a more credible proof that something occurred than an eye-witness account, a written statement or a still image.

At the same time, of course, it is possible for a person to utilise deepfake technology in entirely practical ways that do not necessarily become fraudulent or a falsification. For example, deepfake might allow me to record some lectures that are given *as if* I were present in the lecture theatre, even though I was at home in a dirty t-shirt only recording my voice. While it would be untrue that I was in a crowded lecture theatre, this is not necessarily *fraudulent* but an opportunity to *enhance* the visual look and feel of an otherwise boring lecture. Here is where it matters for representation: my self-identity as a professor is built on an array of activities that perform and affirm this identity, and lecturing is one part of that. In what ways, then, can we understand the use of a deepfake to enhance that performance? Is it representative of an identity? Does it perform my selfhood? Does intent matter? Is enhancement a falsification or bending the truth? What does it say about other aspects of my identity and how I articulated it in online settings? If I fool the audience with a deepfake lecture does it actually matter? These are key questions for a future of highly convincing digital video representation of the self, and they are not the kinds of questions that necessarily (yet) have an answer.

4.4 Deepfake as a cultural technology

Deepfakes have been described as the product of AI and machine-learning applications that "merge, combine, replace, and superimpose images and video clips to create fake videos that appear authentic" (Westerlund 2019, p. 39), a definition which implies a more benign desire for simple technology that helps the creative process of computer-generated footage. The typical creative use by professional screen creative artists is to create scenes that appear to have an actor in a particular space or doing a particular action which fit seamlessly into the remainder of a recorded film (Alexander 2017), including the depiction of deceased actors whose images are taken from elsewhere applied to another body such that they look and sound like they have been authentically recorded. Deepfake technology has also been used in the art, museum and gallery sectors to depict authentic-seeming persons to audiences (Mihailova 2021). All of which implies its emergence not for surreptitious or manipulative purposes but as a technology that fulfils a creative, cultural need.

Significant in making sense of the deepfake from within a scholarly framework attentive to history and identity, however, involves understanding it as actively constituted in—rather than a departure from—older technologies, practices and ways of perceiving textual integrity. In discussing the technological development of the television, Raymond Williams (1990)—whom we discussed briefly in Chapter 3—provided a very useful framework for comprehending the cultural emergence of contemporary communication and media technologies. Williams was critical of technological-determinist theories that viewed the invention of a technology as an accident or an individual invention, unrelated to existing needs, desires and demands, that then goes on have an impact on society, change institutions and practices and produce other unforeseen consequences (pp. 10–11). He offered an approach that sought to restore *intention* to the understanding of technological development, such that new technologies are not seen as an accident or the work of an individual 'inventor' who discovers a technology that subsequently causes widespread social change but as "actively looked for and developed with certain purposes in mind" which includes primarily "known social needs, purposes and practices to which the technology is not marginal but central" (p. 13).

In the example of the television, he pointed out that there is no single event or moment of television's 'invention.' Rather, it developed over more than a century of deliberate research, investment, trial and related construction of the technical artefact, building on existing technologies (radio and film) and extant communication practices (news-making, theatre, broadcast). Important, however, is not only the history of a technological development but the purpose for which a new technology responds to multiple, intersecting cultural needs. In the case of the television, these included the need for mass visual communication (p. 17), the expansionist desires of industrial capital (p. 19) and the demand for entertainment that crossed into the domestic space of the emerging nuclear family household (pp. 20–21). Without a set of cultural demands already at play, no serious investment in the research, development, labour, infrastructure and marketing would have been feasible.

In the case of the deepfake, a similar pattern of development can be seen: building on existing audiovisual manipulation practices and the application of computing techniques operating in other spheres (machine learning), an investment in research and development responds to various cultural needs, desires and demands experienced socially. That is, deepfake applications were not an accidental discovery, nor the brainchild of, say, a young app developer working from a bedroom in her parents' home (although these are always part of the emanation of the cultural desire or demand for the technology and part of a common narrative of development). Rather, deepfake technology has been developed over time in response to a perceived cultural need, desire or demand for the capability to generate footage that is as good as (or better than) recorded footage. Early work on visual facial reanimation in combination with sound from elsewhere dates back at least as far as the late 1990s (Bregler et al. 1997). The research that went into the underlying platform technologies, such as neural auto-encoding, and generative adaptation algorithms are part of that wider developmental picture, as has been the entire digital video effects (DiVX) industry supporting major film and television production for over 15 years (Hashim et al. 2015; Debussman 2021).

In the development of user-friendly apps, these build upon and respond to practices of digital video editing and image manipulation that had already transitioned from skill-based professional practices to everyday uses to fulfil a wide array of desires, with substantial increases in computer processing power making possible what was already foreseen and recognisable. Commercial development of deepfake applications such as FakeApp, the open-source FaceSwap and the mobile application. Impressions were developed and made available in 2018, 2019 and 2020, respectively. In other words, a considerable investment of human and other resources was undertaken by institutions over a protracted period towards the deliberate and knowing development of software that enables the computer generation of believable audio–video content depicting a person who was not recorded but placed into a recording or other setting, doing or saying things they had not said. And it does so to respond to pre-existing demands, including those within a film industry keen to invest in improved digital video effects (Naruniec et al. 2020) and wider cultural desires for textual play, humour, creativity, as well as cultural practices we might otherwise wish were divorced from everyday sociality such as surreptitious fakery and disinformation.

In this context, we might see the everyday use of deepfake technology as constituted in two underlying cultural shifts: (i) the postmodern recognition of textuality through bricolage, pastiche, hyperreality and audience engagement frameworks of polysemy that have their origins in early twentieth-century practices and becoming practices of creative production and readership across the century (Fiske 1989); and (ii) the desire to engage in co-creativity through digital interactivity that marked all stages of the Internet and later platform use (Cover 2006). That is, in addition to the most obvious industrial demands, deep-seated cultural shifts come together to create the grounding in which the deepfake is developed as a cultural technology. In the context of the first, the desire for *hyperreality* as a normative part of everyday media engagement in which we no longer expect authenticity, 'reality' or see the 'real' as being superior to the 'digital' (Zizek 2002) underpins a wider loss of faith in—and desire for—'real' video footage, understood instead as increasingly mythical and even as constraining of creativity. In eroding the boundary between the authentic and simulation, contemporary postmodern culture not only produces the possibility of seeing the deepfake as a creative, textual form rather than a deceptive fakery but embraces the potential to explore alternative ways in which the ethics of representation and veracity circulate in everyday contexts.

The deepfake can therefore be thought of as building on the existing postmodern practices of 'remix,' taken up, for example, by screen media fans in the late 1990s who utilised video footage from television shows and films, reordered scenes, combined them with alternative layers of audio from other sources, to generate new works that had new textuality and new meanings (Cover 2010). Despite industry copyright concerns, remix texts were a transformative art that did not seek to compete with existing texts but to utilise creative practices and available technologies for creative purposes via manipulation, mash-up, convergence and intermedia layering, juxtaposing and packaging them into each other to produce an ostensibly intertextual experience (Lessig 2008), as part of the ongoing practice of consumer co-creation of audio and video texts (Cover 2006). The same formation of remix underlies the creation of humour deepfakes such as the 'Cage Rage' and Tom Cruise misplacement videos described above.

Secondly, deepfake needs to be recognised as a cultural technology constituted in— and responding to—broad-based desires for interactive, co-creative engagement with extant texts and artefacts. I have discussed the significance of interactivity as a key component of digital communication in Chapter 2. Indeed, I have suggested that the idea of interactivity with texts and other users, and the user-generation of content, is one of the most pivotal shifts in digital communication in ways which genuinely has a profound impact on identity. Although interactivity was introduced in the 1990s as a way of describing the advent of networked communication and the encouragement of participatory engagement with online texts, it was also a form which responded to much *older* audience demands for a right to engage, collaborate, co-create and participate in creative texts (Cover 2006).

In that sense, deepfake technology needs to be recognised as emerging from the interactivity that was understood to be a democratic engagement with practices of editing, adapting, changing and re-figuring extant material. In just the same way that editing a wiki page or remixing a video clip is interactive in the co-creative, participatory sense, so too is using an AI-enabled application that processes face-swapping, that convincingly shows a speaker saying words they hadn't spoken and that otherwise engages in intertextual capabilities of the digital era. Deepfake technology, then, is not the attempt to *disrupt* this contemporary cultural scene of creative engagement. Rather, it is in its very constitution, operationalised by the fact that digital interactivity and participation in tandem with postmodern dissolution of textual authenticity enable the generation of content of all kinds (recorded footage; manipulated video) and the capacity of it to be shared for diverse reasons and motivations.

This, however, opens a very big question for us. If deepfake technology is developed from *within* culture and is by no means unexpected or 'alien' to our communication but instead responds to some deep-seated demands to extend our participation in creativity, why is it a topic of such anxiety, of demands for regulation and of concern about truth? Again, we can draw on some of the cultural studies thinking of Raymond Williams to help answer this. In Williams' (1977) work on the relationship between culture and society in the late 1970s, he introduced a very important concept of "structure of feeling," describing the public consciousness of a particular historical moment in regard to a particular group or setting within a cultural milieu. It is helpful to think about this idea of a structure of feeling in terms of another set of concepts he introduced to describe culture: the distinctions between the *residual*, the *dominant* and the *emergent* (pp. 122–125), whereby all are part of the broad structure of feeling of a culture but function in somewhat different ways. In this context, in the second decade of the twenty-first century, we might argue that there is an existing 'residual' culture of communication.

For Williams, the residual is not 'archaic' or wholly of the past—we might imagine communicating by carving symbols on stones or the use of semaphore as archaic, possibly existing still for artistic purposes but absolutely non-functional in a contemporary society.

The residual, however, describes certain meanings, values, experiences and ways of being that operate today but cannot be expressed or understood in terms of dominant culture. We might consider a residual form of communication to be the use of the landline: in many parts of the world, mobile devices have replaced the use of landlines communicating across copper wires in the private, domestic home. However, they still exist as a form of communication, some people prefer them to the use of a mobile, but they are broadly residual: they play a role, they are recalled, we talk about landlines, but they are no longer the dominant form of real-time voice communication in our contemporary, mobile-saturated world.

Residual forms continue into the contemporary era, for Williams (1977), because the dominant 'replacement technologies' cannot go too far too quickly in excluding the residual in case it is challenged by it, and it returns to dominance—there is always that risk (p. 123). For example, if landlines were all cut off in the year 2000, the very large numbers of people who had still not quite got used to thinking about the cell phone as the principal mechanism of voice communication might revolt. Or businesses would be disrupted for a time and face substantial costs if they needed to move too quickly away from the use of fax machines. While we will eventually see the residual *become* archaic, it must remain part of the available technologies so as not to upset the 'dominance of the dominant.'

Raymond Williams spent less time defining how the dominant cultural structure is constituted, although we might consider this to be the culture of digital interactive engagement that includes the use of platforms, the practice of still image manipulation, the use of smartphones, engaging with television and film through online channels and so on. Although some people still refer to digital communication as "new media," it is more appropriate to understand it as part of the matrix of dominant communication forms, technologies and cultural practices available to a contemporary society today. Communication technologies and practices that developed from the 1990s (Web 1.0) and in the early 2000s (Web 2.0) added to the existing forms such as radio and television, transformed or adapted some of them, did not replace others that remain dominant, for example, reading books, and form the dominant communication practices of this particular historical moment.

Both the residual and the dominant differ from the emergent, which Williams (1977) described as being marked by new articulations that arise not as processes isolated from the dominant but from new configurations of knowledge, meanings, values, practices and relationships. That which is emergent is not necessarily fully oppositional to the dominant but may include "elements of some new phase of the dominant culture" as well as those which are depicted as "substantially alternative" (p. 123). In other words, a new emergent process does come about in isolation, but *through* the dominant in ways which also leave it open to reincorporation as *part* of the dominant (p. 124) or sometimes it is depicted as an oppositional *threat* to the dominant and thereby excluded or suppressed (p. 126).

In the case of deepfake technology, we might understand it as an emergent technological process and cultural practice. It is, as I have been describing above, not alien or external to culture but part of the interactive digital framework through which we communicate today. It emerges in ways that are partly foreseen and demanded (the possibilities of new creativity and textual play) but also in ways which are not fully foreseen in advance (its use in identity fraud, disinformation and false or misleading representation of public figures). In this sense, it is not (yet) quite part of the dominant digital culture and hence becomes an object of anxiety, seen as a *threat* or *change*, bringing new ways of playing with texts and new challenges to how we perform identity, verify identity and align identity with authenticity and truth. It is also why it becomes an object of regulation, as I discuss in more detail towards the end of this chapter.

I have been describing the present form of deepfake technology as both something which has cultural precedent (coming from deep-seated cultural desires for participatory control of texts) and, at the same time, as emergent (coming from the margins to do things that might upset the dominant attitudes to communication). Despite these cultural origins, it does not mean deepfake technology is not a cause of stress and anxiety in ways which impinge on current practices of identity. Rather, the emerging capacity of digital technologies to produce authentic-seeming audiovisual footage has become a topic of public debate and the object of alarm and social concern (Robinson 2018). Part of that concern relates, rightly, to the surreptitious or malevolent use of the deepfake to perform violence on others. This includes the finding that more than 90% of deepfake videos circulating online have been identified as pornographic in nature, with the majority fictitiously representing non-pornographic actors and singers engaged in fake sex acts (Wang 2019). There are also indications that deepfakes are used in domestic life as a form of sexual image abuse such as in revenge pornography (van der Nagel 2020). The relationship between a new technology and its perceived infiltration by pornography has, typically, been related to causing moral panic (Kipnis 1996).

Likewise, public concern has arisen over the use of deepfake for other non-entertainment purposes such as accelerating political unrest in Gabon and Malaysia (Ajder et al. 2019, pp. 10, 13); the use of deception to defraud businesses and everyday users, including through synthetic voice simulation, false smear campaigns among neighbourhood adversaries (Bellware 2021) and electoral manipulation (CBS News 2019); the deliberate defaming of celebrities and public figures, including through face-swap fake pornographication (Collins 2018; Maddocks 2020; Ohman 2020), causing international misunderstandings of the kind that may lead to violent reactions (Karr 2019); and the capacity to be used as visual evidence for fake news, disinformation and misleading narratives (Maras and Alexandrou 2019).

To understand why an emerging technology that has so much creative potential and is developed to respond to our desires for digital effects enhancement, interactive textual play and the generation of new creative works becomes a cause of anxiety involves more than simply slamming it as dangerous for political processes or as concerning for identity fraud. Rather, we might say that the cause of anxiety over the deepfake is not in its threats to democratic institutions, its potential for defamatory content generation or its destabilisation of Enlightenment-era regimes of truth. Rather, anxiety and a sense of 'crisis' emerges from the social recognition of the *multiplicity of uses*, each having differing relationships with creative ethics, representational practices, liberal and postmodern norms. That is, anxiety emerges in the *unknowability* of how it might be used, rather than the technology itself. It opens questions as to how we should weigh up (i) the creative potential for films and arts with (ii) the malevolent use of the technology for disinformation and identity fraud. Are there limits? Who should have access to it? In what other, unforeseen ways might it be misused?

Deepfake enters public sphere debate by being framed as a kind of 'rupture' from past practices, even though it emerges from those older practices of interactivity and photoshopping. The unknowability that is opened by a cultural rupture is, as Maurizio Lazzarato (2013, p. 20) has suggested, a subject of anxiety since rupture emerges from both within history and from that which is outside history. Lazzarato understands crisis and rupture, in fact, to be a *permanent* mode of contemporary history, politics, economics and sociality since at least the 1970s (such that any new technology is introduced both as fetish and as crisis). The social anxiety over the development of deepfake technology is just one such rupture in the ever-changing framework of digital practices—both an emergent technology to celebrate and an emergent technology that threatens the dominant social practices in which we rely on recorded footage for 'truth.' The impossibility of a culture that desires such technology to position itself in regard to its own cultural production produces a *transformative* rupture, obliging debate in order to apprehend, circumscribe and frame the deepfake.

The crisis or cultural rupture of the deepfake emerges, then, in the perception of a push-and-pull between different modalities of cultural production: a creative pursuit designed to showcase technological film-making skill and to demonstrate that skill by announcing publicly how such a work was made—part of the wider genre of behind-the-scenes and how-to that has accompanied major visual creative endeavours for several decades. Yet, the evidence that it is aligned with purposes *other* than entertainment, fascination, enjoyment of the 'trick' or alternative practices in which the pleasure of the deepfake is an audiences' 'knowingness,' the fact deepfake technology has been used for malicious purposes to masquerade as 'real' has resulted in it being positioned as a rupture. This thereby obscures its very constitution in wider cultural demands for hyperreality and co-creative interactivity. In that respect, although it emerges from within culture to challenge aspects of the dominant, its existence has implications for how we think about technologies that convey and represent identity.

4.5 Identity and simulacra

Having discussed some of the ways in which deepfake becomes a topic of concern and the way it is used for identity fraud, but recognising that it is also an emergent technology that emerges from culture rather than outside it in ways which create anxieties about communication, I want to turn in this section to seeing how we might make sense of it as part of some wider cultural changes for identity and how we perceive and understand reality. One useful concept for thinking about deepfake technology as part of a wider 'package' of shifts in how we communicate, how we value certain media texts and how we relate to them in identity terms is the concept of *simulacra*. A simulacrum refers to a representation that has a likeness or resemblance to something else but is not *exactly* that something else. In the strictest sense, a photograph of a person is a simulacrum because it does not reproduce the person but represents them in a two-dimensional image.

The term *simulacra* was further developed by theorist Jean Baudrillard to refer to imagery with "nothing behind them" and is understood as the kind of imagery that stands in place of truth and *becomes its own truth* (Baudrillard 1988, p. 169). This occurs, for example, when photographic evidence is treated as greater 'proof' that something occurred than an eye-witness account, despite all the problems with photography serving as evidence (e.g., what falls outside the frame, the time taken, the ability to manipulate, etc.). It falls into part of what theorists think about as 'hyperreality'—something that is beyond the real but comes not only to stand in for it but to be seen as superior to it. In a very simple way, the advent of the zoom meeting during the COVID-19 pandemic was often the simulacra of a face-to-face meeting in which we go through the motions *as if* present. It serves as a form of hyperreality, however, when it comes to be felt as superior to the face-to-face meeting which can occur for a whole range of reasons—the ability to record, the ability to auto-caption and so on. Alternatively, when we appreciate that a film with computer-generated imagery (CGI) footage is better and 'more realistic' than a film that used, say, puppets or costumes to represent aliens, we are part of the hyperreal culture that puts simulacra up to a new level.

In other words, hyperreality and simulacra become a cultural logic not in the long-anticipated places of virtual reality and digital gaming but across the whole spectrum of digital communication. In a postmodern culture, we can also see the advent of the hyperreal through what French Situationist thinker Guy Debord described as the 'society of the spectacle.' Debord saw spectacle, at the early stages of consumer capitalism, as the replacement of the perceptible, referential world with images not only coming to be felt as superior to that 'real world' but as losing their function to represent it. Just as the contemporary cultural practice of the selfie involves not just an enhancement of the self but a re-figuration that bears less-and-less resemblance to the self (Kwon and Kwon 2015, p. 305), the circulation of deepfake video content involves not just a sneaky motivation to trick viewers but an *artistic* practice of creating content that mimics recorded footage while bearing no actual reference to real events or recordings.

This contrasts, then, with older, dominant forms of communication such as film and television, recorded press conferences and so on, all of which were developed *prior* to the postmodernisation of communication and the advent of hyperreal simulacra. The primacy of the recorded footage as 'truth' was key to it being stylised as informational communication. Deepfake content, on the other hand, works in the postmodern 2020s because creators are unashamed to produce content that no longer represents reality but replaces it. It is the difference, identified by Manuel Anselmi (2018) between the manipulation of communication and a cultural form that artfully ignores an ideal of truth as a strategy and a cultural operation of production.

There is much to celebrate about the technological capacities of simulacra in the form of digital advancements for creative industries. Film and television have long taken advantage of ongoing advancements in computer processing to produce digital effects that enhance storytelling (Alexander 2017). Arguably, such advancements not only represent the artistic practices of hyperreality, bricolage and pastiche in positive and productive ways; they enable creative producers to overcome obstacles such as the death of an actor who can later be sutured using deepfake technologies into unfilmed scenes, or replacing an actor, producing more effective doubles without the use of green screen and body doubles and placing actors into scenes which would otherwise be dangerous or threatening (Debussman 2021).

This hyperreality is culturally demanded within the late capitalist postmodern framework that, as Slavoj Zizek (2002) described it, warrants content that is "*unreal*, substanceless, deprived of material inertia" (p. 13). That is, it is a loss of the myth of *authenticity* that constrained creativity as representative rather than as liberated. (Authenticity is not, of course, completely lost, as I discuss more in Chapter 8 where I describe TikTok's cultural use of an 'authenticity aesthetic.') In obliterating the boundary between the authentic and simulation, contemporary postmodern culture not only produces the idea of the deepfake as a powerful creative form but embraces the potential to explore alternative ways of being, communicating and engaging (Filiciak 2003, p. 98). The postmodern culture of production and pastiche enables at one level the acceptability of the fakery in deepfake content. It is, then, an emergent cultural formation which demands the tools not only for *more* spectacle and simulacra that trumps the previously dominant value of 'real footage.' The tools that allow the everyday subject to participate in building the hyperreal become demanded as part of interactivity, to increase our own creative engagement—even if some of us will use that for surreptitious, illicit or mischievous purposes. Aside from what we might personally feel about authenticity, and in a contrastive struggle with Enlightenment-era demands for the authentic, the normal, the real and truthful, the participation in the production of the hyperreal underlies the contemporary condition of human communication and engagement.

So what does a digital culture that embraces simulacra do for identity? According to the theorist Fredric Jameson (1985), simulacra and hyperreality are often expressed in the form of 'pastiche' which he describes as an imitation or mimicry of the real within a postmodern culture that no longer connects the sign (words and symbols) with the referent (the real-world thing to which the sign refers). The circulation of postmodern pastiche or simulacra has substantial implications for identity, according to Jameson. While an Enlightenment-era sense of identity as unitary, fixed and with agency has been part of the dominant liberal-humanist culture of subjectivity as I described in Chapter 1, it becomes for Jameson a schizophrenic experience in a world in which the sign is no longer connected to the referent or in which we see the simulation as superior to the real. By referring to schizophrenia, Jameson is not talking about the psychiatric illness but a way in which identity fragments because it does not have a 'real' on which to hold nor a language system of sign referent to keep it grounded. The unknowability of simulacra—or, in this case, the deepfake—upsets our sense of the real in such a way as to take our identities out of continuity with ourselves over time. This is not, necessarily, to say that this is the *universal* experience of identity in an age of deepfake technology, not is it to suggest that new approaches to identity that undo the dominant demands for identity authenticity and coherence are necessarily bad things. Rather, what it indicates is a different way in which to live in the world, and one for which we do not yet know the effects or impact of changes in terms of how we ground ourselves as subjects.

4.6 Regulating the deepfake

In this final section, I want to discuss some of the reasons why the anxiety that deepfake technology produces for identity becomes subject to regulation. If deepfake is already positioned as a 'social concern' and may indeed disrupt our identity practices, it becomes conceived as an object of regulation (including criminalisation). This is despite its origins in earlier, dominant practices of interactivity and textual play. Importantly, the idea that deepfakes should be regulated is occurring alongside a wider 'mood' for regulation of digital platforms, companies and providers. Where earlier digital culture until about 2016 was marked by the laissez-faire freedoms given to Silicon Valley companies (where they enjoyed particularly strong protection from intervention in the United States), a move to regulate digital culture is underway, and deepfakes will undoubtedly be part of that shift.

Indeed, the platformisation of the Internet of Web 2.0 social media and the socio-political concerns which have emerged such as privacy concerns, sale to third parties of user data, hate speech and the proliferation of disinformation (Cover et al. 2022) have resulted in what Terry Flew (2021) has identified as a sea change in policy whereby trust in individual users and civil society to manage online interactions is replaced by emergent frameworks in which the nation-state is seen to have a necessary role in regulating digital communication (pp. 104–105). This should not, as Flew points out, be understood only as restrictive or coercive, since there have always been regulatory measures that are enabling and facilitative, including those that encourage good communicative behaviours (p. 106).

Regulatory intervention over the deepfake has taken a number of different forms, early in its introduction and use. The first is *legislative*, whereby early alarmist calls for legislation were made across scholarship (e.g., Harris 2019) and public opinion (e.g., Davidson 2019), often arguing that legislation is required to prevent the use of machine-learning video production or to require creators to provide a verifiable imprimatur that indicated it was not 'real.' The US state of California, for example, has enacted legislation to make it illegal to post or distribute any video content that deliberately manipulates the face or speech of a political candidate 60 days prior to an election. Although this is important symbolic legislation to indicate concerns over electoral implications, doubts have been expressed as to the real capacity to police such videos given the likelihood of the anonymity or invisibility of the creative source (Karr 2019). Given the known difficulties involved in intervening when legislation is jurisdictional but problematic digital content circulates across borders, calls for cross-jurisdictional strategies towards systemic legislation have been made (Pavis 2021). In some jurisdictions, however, regulation through censorship has been found to be impossible—in the United States, for example, it is felt that requiring deepfake videos to be removed may be unconstitutional on the basis that the United States' Supreme Court ruled in 2012 that the first amendment prohibits regulating content simply because it is untrue or unrepresentative (Sunstein 2021).

A second regulatory form is grounded in a discourse of *technological or human intervention*. Although labour-intensive, human moderation practices substantially increased across social media sites, with mixed results in effectiveness as stemming problematic content (Beckett et al. 2019). Research is being undertaken on technology to authenticate deepfake videos, although this is very much in its early stages with some indication that detection software will have difficulties keeping up with continued advances in deepfake production (Maras and Alexandrou 2019, p. 260). While technological advances that can help identify recorded footage from face-swapped videos would be valuable in encouraging an engagement with textuality, the past two decades have indicated that most attempts to intervene in digital texts or their circulation are located within a push-and-pull struggle between intervention software and 'work arounds' that free those texts for further circulation or manipulation (Cover 2006). This form of regulation places the responsibility for detection, moderation, removal and banning on platforms themselves, often relying on user terms and policy as enablers (Farish 2020). Here, the notion that the deepfake is—or may be—an objectionable text that should be subject moderation and intervention is grounded in a liberal-humanist discourse that makes monolithic a myth of textual 'authenticity' and assumes that a 'clean' Internet is one built on the veracity of recorded footage rather than the circulation of the deepfake. Regulation here focuses on the text or content, rather than the motivations, intentions and practices of users or the cultural antecedents that enabled deepfake technology.

Given the harms of the greater proportion of deepfake videos in circulation, regulation in some form is necessary and unavoidable, and digital regulatory regimes have moved beyond simplistic dualist approaches to freedom of expression versus censorship (Balkin 2018). A cultural perspective on regulating deepfakes needs, however, to be attentive to two factors that focus not on the text but on (i) the vulnerabilisation of users by apprehending some deepfakes as injurious and (ii) the culture of the digital ecology in which textual play is integral and fulfils a deep-seated cultural demand. Firstly, a focus on injury helps disavow any residual debate on regulation away from dualist free speech versus censorship arguments and consider not what a deepfake is, but the ways in which it may make some subjects—typically those it depicts—vulnerable to injury. Although audiences are widely recognised in cultural studies as active and empowered in the interpretation of meaning and the assessment of content (Fiske 1989; Radway 1988), and that may include the capacity to recognise the deepfake, a portion of users engagement is undertaken within a cultivated ignorance and rejection of critical engagement (Gilson 2011).

This is to suggest, then, that the violence or injury of *instances* of deepfake texts is located in the positioning of some audiences *not* to recognise, research, fact-check or take into account the labour of verification. The injury of the deepfake, then, is one to the subject of the video but also to target audiences whose vulnerability to being 'duped' is reinforced. An ethical approach calls upon regulatory measures that actively encourage critical engagement with textuality itself, rather than a sole focus on the deepfake text and its curtailment. Secondly, while regulation shapes and frames use, textuality and reading practices, it is important to account for the longer cultural history of communication, polysemy and co-creativity that grounds contemporary digital culture and the digital ecology. Regulation, therefore, must not risk injury to that digital culture which produced the means of deepfake in the first instance and recognise that some forms of regulation may, as Judith Butler (2009, p. 119) has shown, entail a violence towards the "living relationship" between texts, subjects and readers, including the relationships that encourage ethical creative practices. Indeed, as Taylor (2021) notes in relation to how deepfakes are 'securitised,' what makes them objectives of securitisation is not their inherent content but their relationship with actors.

4.7 Conclusion

When taken from the perspective of some of the cultural factors described above, deepfake technology is regularly oversimplified and thereby positioned as both an 'alien' technology separate from everyday contemporary culture and as an object of social concern warranting regulation. Understanding the emergence of deepfake technology as culturally constituted rather than formed as if through some external process helps us to think about some of its implications for identity practices, whether that is opening up new ways of representing and articulating our identities through play with texts, new opportunities to reflect on identity by embracing the disruption to older identity practices that emerge in a culture of postmodern hyperreality and simulacra and new ways in which we may be subject to identity fraud.

Key points

- Deepfakes are videos which use algorithms and machine learning to swap a face and/or voice into recorded footage which produces a text that can easily convince a viewer that the person was really recorded.
- Deepfakes have potential for both the creative industries and for the surreptitious production of disinformation, including particularly identity fraud, political disinformation, revenge pornography and harms to celebrities' reputations.
- Deepfakes are often discussed as an 'alien' threat to truth and factual content but can better be said to be the product of long-standing cultural desires for textual manipulation.
- As a form of simulacra and hyperreality, deepfakes create anxieties over identity and representation because they are part of a substantial, wider change in communication.

References

Ajder, H., Patrini, G., Cavalli, F. and Cullen, L., 2019. *The State of Deepfakes: Landscape, Threats, and Impact*. Available from: https://regmedia.co.uk/2019/10/08/deepfake_report.pdf [Accessed 11 December 2020].

Alexander, B., 2017. *The New Digital Storytelling: Creating Narratives with New Media*. Santa Barbara, CA: Praeger.

Anselmi, M., 2018. *Populism: An Introduction*. New York: Routledge.

Balkin, J.M., 2018. Free speech is a triangle. *Columbia Law Review,* 118 (7), 2011–2056.

Bateman, J., 2020. Deepfakes and synthetic media in the financial system: assessing threat scenarios. *Carnegie Endowment for International Peace*. Available from: www.jstor.org/stable/pdf/resrep25 783.10.pdf [Accessed 4 January 2020].

Baudrillard, J., 1988. Simulacra and simulations. *In:* M. Poster, ed. *Jean Baudrillard: Selected Writings*. Cambridge: Polity Press, 166–184.

Beckett, J., Martin, F. and Paech, V., 2019. Revenge of the moderators: Facebook's online workers are sick of being treated like bots. *The Conversation,* 16 October. Available from: https://theconversation.com/revenge-of-the-moderators-facebooks-online-workers-are-sick-of-being-treated-like-bots-125127 [Accessed 7 January 2020].

Bellware, K., 2021. Cheer mom used deepfake nudes and threats to harass daughter's teammates, police say. *Washington Post,* 14 March. Available from: www.washingtonpost.com/nation/2021/03/13/cheer-mom-deepfake-teammates/ [Accessed 16 March 2021].

Bregler, C., Covell, M. and Slaney, M., 1997. Video rewrite: Driving visual speech with audio. *Proceedings of the 24th Annual Conference on Computer Graphics and Interactive Techniques*. Available from: www2.eecs.berkeley.edu/Research/Projects/CS/vision/human/bregler-sig97.pdf [Accessed 2 January 2022].

Butler, J., 1990. *Gender Trouble: Feminism and the Subversion of Identity*. London: Routledge.

Butler, J., 2009. The sensibility of critique: response to Asad and Mahmood. *In:* T. Asad, W. Brown, J. Butler, and S. Mahmood, eds. *Is Critique Secular? Blasphemy, Injury and Free Speech*. Berkeley, CA: University of California Press, 101–136.

Carmen, 2019. Meghan Markle sex tape allegedly being shopped! WATCH THIS! *Carmen,* 2 April. Available from: https://b95forlife.iheart.com/featured/carmen/content/2019-04-01-meghan-markle-sex-tape-allegedly-being-shopped-watch-this/ [Accessed 2 January 2022].

CBS News, 2019. Doctored Nancy Pelosi video highlights threat of 'deepfake' tech. *CBS News,* 24 May. Available from: www.cbsnews.com/news/doctored-nancy-pelosi-video-highlights-threat-of-deepfake-tech-2019-05-25/ [Accessed 2 January 2022].

Chakhoyan, D., 2018. Deep fakes could threaten democracy. What are they and what can be done? *World Economic Forum*. Available from: www.weforum.org/agenda/2018/11/deep-fakes-may-destroy-democracy-can-they-be-stopped/ [Accessed 12 January 2022].

Collins, B., 2018. Russia-linked account pushed fake Hillary Clinton sex video. *NBC News,* 11 April. Available from: www.nbcnews.com/tech/security/russia-linked-account-pushed-fake-hillary-clinton-sex-video-n864871 [Accessed 4 January 2022].

Cover, R., 2006. Audience inter/active: interactive media, narrative control and reconceiving audience history. *New Media & Society,* 8 (1), 213–232.

Cover, R., 2010. More than a watcher: *Buffy* fans, amateur music videos, romantic slash and intermedia. *In:* P. Attinello, J.K. Halfyard and V. Knights, eds. *Music, Sound and Silence in Buffy the Vampire Slayer*. London: Ashgate, 131–148.

Cover, R., Haw, A. and Thompson, J.D., 2022. *Fake News in Digital Cultures: Technology, Populism and Digital Misinformation*. London: Emerald Publishing.

Davidson, J., 2019. Australian law behind the times on deepfake videos. *Australian Financial Review,* 8 July. Available from: www.afr.com/technology/australian-law-behind-the-times-on-deepfake-videos-20190703-p523pi [Accessed 3 May 2022].

Debussman Jr, B., 2021. Deepfake is the future of content creation. *BBC News*, 8 March. Available from: www.bbc.com/news/business-56278411 [Accessed 2 May 2022].

Diakopoulos, N. and Johnson, D., 2021. Anticipating and addressing the ethical implications of deepfakes in the context of elections. *New Media & Society*, 23 (7), 2072–2098.

Farish, K., 2020. The legal implications and challenges of deepfakes. *Lexis PSL*, 2 September. Available from: www.lexisnexis.com/uk/lexispsl/disputeresolution/document/412012/60RH-PX63-CGXG-054B-00000-00/The%20legal%20implications%20and%20challenges%20of%20deepfakes [Accessed 3 May 2022].

Filiciak, M., 2003. Hyperidentities: postmodern identity patterns in massively multiplayer online role-playing games. *In:* M.J.P. Wolf and B. Perron, eds. *The Video Game Theory Reader*. New York and London: Routledge, 87–101.

Fiske, J., 1989. *Understanding Popular Culture*. London: Unwin Hyman.

Fleming, G., and Bruce, P.C., 2021. *Responsible Data Science: Transparency and Fairness in Algorithms*. Indianapolis, IN: John Wiley & Sons.

Flew, T., 2021. *Regulating Platforms*. Cambridge: Polity.

Fried, P., 2019. Deepfake. *Pennsylvania Literary Journal*, 11 (2), 234, 269.

Gilbey, R., 2019. A 'deep fake' app will make us film stars—but will we regret our narcissism? *The Guardian*, 5 September. Available from: www.theguardian.com/technology/2019/sep/04/a-deep-fake-app-will-make-us-film-stars-but-will-we-regret-our-narcissism [Accessed 1 May 2022].

Gilson, E., 2011. Vulnerability, ignorance, and oppression. *Hypatia*, 26 (2), 308–332.

Harris, D., 2019. Deepfakes: false pornography is here and the law cannot protect you. *Duke Law & Technology Review*, 17, 99–128.

Hashim, H., Mohamad Salleh, M.A. and Mohamad, E., 2015. Usage analysis of visual digital (DVFx) special effects on short films and genre. *Malaysian Journal of Communication*, 31 (2), 99–115.

Hendrikse, R., 2019. How deepfakes could become a threat to your identity. *Forbes*, 20 December. Available from: www.forbes.com/sites/renehendrikse/2019/12/20/how-deepfakes-could-become-a-threat-to-your-identity/?sh=124b7bca1063 [Accessed 22 December 2019].

Holliday, C., 2021. Rewriting the stars: surface tensions and gender troubles in the online media production of digital deepfakes. *Convergence: The International Journal of Research into New Media Technologies*, 27 (4), 899–918.

Jameson, F., 1985. Postmodernism and consumer society. *In:* H. Foster, ed. *Postmodern Culture*. London: Pluto Press, 111–125.

Karr, C., 2019. Enforcing California's 'deepfake' ban could prove challenging. *Epoch Times*, 18 October. Available from: www.theepochtimes.com/enforcing-californias-deepfake-ban-could-prove-challenging3115476.html [Accessed 1 May 2022].

Kietzmann, J., Mills, A.J. and Plangger, K., 2021. Deepfakes: perspectives on the future 'reality' of advertising and branding. *International Journal of Advertising*, 40 (3), 473–485.

Kipnis, L., 1996. *Bound and Gagged: Pornography and the Politics of Fantasy in America*. New York: Grove Press.

Kwon, Y.J. and Kwon, K.-N., 2015. Consuming the objectified self: the quest for authentic self. *Asian Social Science*, 11(2), 301–312.

Lazzarato, M., 2013. *Governing by Debt*, J.D. Jordan, trans. South Pasadena, CA: Semiotext(e).

Le, V., 2020. The deepfakes to come: a Turing cop's nightmare. *Identities*, 17 (2–3), 1–11.

Lees, D., Bashford-Rogers, T. and Keppel-Palmer, M., 2021. The digital resurrection of Margaret Thatcher: creative, technological and legal dilemmas in the use of deepfakes in screen drama. *Convergence: The International Journal of Research into New Media Technologies*, 27 (4), 954–973.

Lenters, M., 2021. Deepfakes: danger to democracy or creativity for all? *Innovating Origins*, 30 March. Available from: https://innovationorigins.com/deepfakes-danger-to-democracy-or-creativity-for-all/ [Accessed 12 May 2022].

Lessig, L., 2008. *Remix: Making Art and Commerce Thrive in the Hybrid Economy*. London: Bloomsbury.

Maddocks, S., 2020. 'A deepfake porn plot intended to silence me': exploring continuities between pornographic and 'political' deep fakes. *Porn Studies,* 7 (4), 415–423.

Maras, M.H. and Alexandrou, A., 2019. Determining authenticity of video evidence in the age of artificial intelligence and in the wake of deepfake videos. *The International Journal of Evidence & Proof,* 23 (3), 255–262.

Mihailova, M., 2021. To dally with Dalí: deepfake (inter)faces in the art museum. *Convergence: The International Journal of Research into New Media Technologies,* 27 (4), 882–898.

Mirsky, Y., and Lee, W., 2021. The creation and detection of deepfakes: a survey. *ACM Computing Surveys,* 54 (1), 1–41.

Murphy, G. and Flynn, E., 2021. Deepfake false memories. *Memory.* DOI: 10.1080/09658211.2021.1919715

Naruniec, J., Helminger, L., Schroers, C. and Weber, R.M., 2020. High-resolution neural face swapping for visual effects. *Eurographics Symposium on Rendering,* 39 (4). Available from: https://studios.disneyresearch.com/wp-content/uploads/2020/06/High-Resolution-Neural-Face-Swapping-for-Visual-Effects.pdf [Accessed 1 May 2022].

Ohman, C., 2020. Introducing the pervert's dilemma: a contribution to the critique of deepfake pornography. *Ethics and Information Technology,* 22 (2), 133–140.

Pavis, M., 2021. Rebalancing our regulatory response to deepfakes with performers' rights. *Convergence: The International Journal of Research into New Media Technologies,* 27 (4), 974–998.

Pulver, A., 2018. Nicolas Cage expresses 'frustration' with Cage Rage internet meme. *The Guardian,* 19 September. Available from: www.theguardian.com/film/2018/sep/19/nicolas-cage-rage-internet-meme-mandy [Accessed 2 January 2022].

Radway, J., 1988. Reception study: ethnography and the problems of dispersed audiences and nomadic subjects. *Cultural Studies,* 2 (4), 359–376.

Robinson, J., 2018. The legal nightmare that is FakeApp. *Medium,* 6 February. Available from: https://medium.com/@astukari/the-legal-nightmare-that-is-fakeapp-321afc0565e3 [Accessed 2 January 2022].

Sunstein, C.R., 2021. Can the government regulate deepfakes? *The Wall Street Journal,* 7 January. Available from: www.wsj.com/articles/can-the-government-regulate-deepfakes-11610038590 [Accessed 2 January 2022].

Taylor, B.C., 2021. Defending the state from digital deceit: the reflexive securitization of deepfake. *Critical Studies in Media Communication,* 38 (1), 1–17.

Towers-Clark, C., 2019. Mona Lisa and Nancy Pelosi: the implications of deepfakes. *Forbes,* 31 May. Available from: www.forbes.com/sites/charlestowersclark/2019/05/31/mona-lisa-and-nancy-pelosi-the-implications-of-deepfakes/?sh=336ed8214357 [Accessed 2 January 2021].

van der Nagel, E., 2020. Verifying images: deepfakes, control, and consent. *Porn Studies,* 7 (4), 424–429.

Wang, C., 2019. Deepfakes, revenge porn and the impact on women. *Forbes,* 1 November. Available from: www.forbes.com/sites/chenxiwang/2019/11/01/deepfakes-revenge-porn-and-the-impact-on-women/?sh=6092fe8a1f53 [Accessed 2 November 2019].

Westerlund, M., 2019. The emergence of deepfake technology: A review. *Technology Innovation Management Review,* 9 (11), 39–52.

Williams, R., 1977. *Marxism and Literature.* Oxford: Oxford University Press.

Williams, R., 1990. The technology and the society. *In:* D, Bennett, ed. *Popular Fiction: Technology, Ideology, Production, Reading.* London: Routledge, 9–22.

Yadlin-Segal, A., and Oppenheim, Y., 2020. Whose dystopia is it anyway? Deepfakes and social media regulation. *Convergence: The International Journal of Research into New Media Technologies,* 27 (1), 1–16.

Zizek, S., 2002. *Welcome to the Desert of the Real! Five Essays on September 11 and Related Dates.* London: Verso.

5 Geographies

Globalisation and re-nationalisation of digital communication

5.1 Introduction

Digital communication is usually thought about as something that is very much part of the 'globalisation' that took place in the late twentieth and the early twenty-first centuries. Although globalisation is another one of those buzzwords that has often lost any concrete meaning, we can make sense of it as a set of cultural practices with a long history that includes many of the following:

- processes of European colonisation;
- international trade as a key component of how we receive goods and services, where they are made and how parts from different regions of the world are brought together;
- the use of labour outside the country for a country's products and services;
- the establishment of faster and cheaper international transport systems and the introduction of air travel for leisure and recreation;
- the historical development of telegraphic cables enabling eventually the international telephone;
- the development of satellite technology that enabled the real-time broadcast of footage from around the world;
- shifts in neoliberal capital enterprise production methods that increased the number beyond the nation-state;
- the post-Second World War increase in transnational migration and the growth of diasporic communities.

Digital, networked communication has, of course, occurred alongside many of those processes, both enabling the embedding of global practices and communication flows and, in many ways, always developed as a response to deeper desires for a more global, post-national world. Obviously, the early Internet revolutionised how we communicate internationally with the development of email, allowing for the first time written communication to be read instantly by a person on the other side of the planet. Increased processing power and broadband connectivity made videoconferencing possible for everyday people, substantially changing how we conduct workplace meetings across international settings or communicate with family and friends on the other side of the world. Likewise, the increasing capacity for quality automatic translation of textual content, and translated closed captioning of audio and video, has furthered the project of globalisation through digital media whereby it is easier now for those with only one language to access texts, ideas and discourses from other linguistic regions.

DOI: 10.4324/9781003296652-5

How increased networking and uneven access (sometimes referred to as the international 'digital divide') has had an impact on identity has been little studied from the perspective of online selves. While we think about our use of digital communication as broadly 'borderless,' it is also important to pay attention to two factors that are constitutive of how we perform our identities:

1. The way in which global communication practices changes our sense of place, space and time and the role of location and geography in giving meaning to our identities;
2. Emerging regulatory practices within nation-states that—often rightly—seek to address the problems of platform-based communication by setting up non-international protocols for communication, censorship, filtering and reporting regimes.

This chapter introduces some of the key ways in which digital communication and identity can be understood, firstly, from the globalisation push of digital media and, secondly, from the practices that reassert the idea of the nation and national identity. As many of the shifts between global and national occur in ways governed by history, society and changing political contexts, and since the emerging practices of nation-state regulation of digital content is very new, this is one of those areas in which we can speculate a great deal to make sense of how identity might be informed by communication geographies but not one on which it is easy (yet) to make concrete statements.

5.2 Digital communication as a globalising technology

A useful place to start thinking about the digital geographies of identity is in terms of the intersection between globalisation and digital communication. Globalisation has a number of different meanings: broadly speaking today, it tends to refer to the vast movement of information across the globe that has developed alongside increased migration and mobility (Urry 2007). It also refers to a number of cultural changes that occur in relation to the global spread of corporate neoliberalism as a mode of exchange, commodification and valuation, subsequent to the fall of the Soviet bloc and the power of its anti-capitalist discourse. Paul James (2006) notes that globalisation can best be understood as "the extension of social practices across world-space where the notion of 'world-space' is itself defined in the historically variable terms in which it has been practiced and understood" (p. 42), thereby pointing to how globalisation is not a singular specific condition or event, but a layered, uneven process that has not eradicated older models of nationhood, locality or regionalism but operated alongside them.

In terms of the development of the digital, globalisation has often been articulated through the Canadian theorist Marshall McLuhan's (1962) notion of the "global village"—in which all participants on the planet can engage with each other in the form of a local community as if members of the globe know and research each other as face-to-face locals. McLuhan's idea of the global village was, in the 1960s, primarily in reference to the idea that people will move closer and closer towards personal interactions on a global scale so that the whole of the world feels like it is part of a singular village in which people know and interact regularly with each other. In many respects, the development of the Internet did produce some of the interaction and transnational engagement McLuhan envisaged. In other respects, of course, this did not quite produce a *unified* world with shared understandings but international communities of people communicating with each other but often polarised and not necessarily engaged with those who did not share their views.

The idea of a global village is, then, a fairly utopian one which foregrounds an idea of a unified world and global peace—not the experience of the world in the 2020s where both online hostility or hate speech and war are current features of our international and transnational existence. Nevertheless, digital communication did play a role in integrating parts of the world into what Manuel Castells (2000) referred to as "global networks of instrumentality" and an "array of virtual communities" (pp. 21–22). He felt that these global networks were bringing together sites of difference and thereby increasing the capacity for networks of peers and families that criss-cross the geographic space of the globe to talk together. Importantly, he also felt that networks helped permit different practices, ideas, uses and concepts of space and time that have an impact on identity in the sense of how we perceive our place in the world and who we can talk to or relate to in real time.

If we want to think about globalisation and the development of global digital cultures as processes, we need to differentiate some of the different phases of globalisation that occurred in different historical periods, while bearing in mind that earlier phases are often drawn on to describe how later phases have unfolded and therefore how we make sense of earlier forms of globalisation through the more recent concepts. Terry Flew (2013) identified three phases of globalisation which are described as:

1. an *early modern* phase from the fourteenth to the eighteenth centuries which saw the emergence of the modern nation-state, territorial expansion, territorial empires and colonialism linked to trade;
2. a *modern* phase from the early nineteenth century to the end of the Second World War, which was marked by foreign trade and international investment, substantial international movement of people and migration and the consolidation of colonial empires; and
3. a *contemporary* phase since 1945 which is framed by the settlement of a global system of states, decolonisation of non-European regions and an intensification of economic globalisation in all its forms, including trade, investment and production (p. 20).

We might be tempted to add to this the vast increase in the *amount* of communication on a global scale, from the internationalisation of simplified international calling on the telephone to international sharing of television with both recorded and, later, live broadcast and ultimately the Internet. All of these have, of course, made available more information than previous generations experienced and might be related to what is sometimes referred to as 'information overload.'

Contrasting Flew's differing frameworks of globalisation with each other opens up the need to think about digital communication as one facet among the competing formations through which information about the world is made available. This affects how we participate in the practices of identity that emerge from our *relations with others*. For example, if one facet of identity was governed in previous centuries by neighbourhoods whereby those we interact with were more likely to be those who lived nearby, we can note the marked difference today whereby we may not speak to our neighbours, and more of our interactions may well be with people in other countries using Zoom, mobile phones, email, social media and so on. (Today, I spoke to only seven people—six of them were in a different hemisphere from where I have been living.) This is not to say that there has been some kind of levelling out, a universal peace or an embrace of concepts of sameness across the globe. What it means is that exposure to the 'otherness' of people living else-where is linked to how identity practices have changed in line with some of the more recent processes of globalisation.

At the same time, however, it is important to remember that this is not only about the ability to communicate or access information online about other people and places—although the ability to look at neighbourhood images on Google Maps of a country one has never been to that is thousands of kilometres away is a shift in exposure. Rather, what it means is that we have added frameworks through which we 'locate' ourselves in geo-graphic terms and in the contexts of relations with others that impact on how we think about identities through place, space and time.

As with many other developments and changes that impinge on identity, the develop-ment of globalisation and global communication technologies are not things that were done to people that thereby changes us. Rather, they are constituted in culture itself as part of and alongside wider social, political and economic changes. For Australian scholar Ien Ang (2011), globalisation is a kind of social mood in which the world is re-conceived as broadly complex in ways that drives both positive and negative developments and change (p. 779). In this sense, then, globalisation is always a multiple but uneven process and not something that everyone experiences in the same way. For some writers, the experience of globalisation and global networked communication is to be understood as a compression of the world's 'time' and 'space' that produces an intensification of know-ledge about the world and makes events that occur elsewhere more meaningful for our-selves than they were for, say, our great-grandparents (Barker 1999, p. 34).

No matter how one describes the causes of the late twentieth-century forms of glo-balisation, most writers take note of the significance of the production and circulation by media of images, concepts, texts and thoughts from some parts of the world to other parts of the world in ways which adjust a sense geography. This, of course, has an impact on the relationship between place, time and identity. In an era of digital connectivity, globalisa-tion thus is framed by the *rapidity* of the circulation of media and image in ways which call upon us to rethink how place defines our selfhood. John Urry (2007) has argued that rapid movement of image and text presents a sense of global *complexity* although warns that we should not see this necessarily as the kind of information overload that is often thought about as 'chaos' (p. 27). For some writers, this rapidity is also a kind of warfare, both phys-ical and symbolic, stemming from the demands of transnational corporate enterprises that regularly seek labour and market opportunities beyond national boundaries within what is sometimes seen as a push towards an "aggressive global society" (Carver 1998, p. 18). At other times, this rapidity is represented through concepts of nostalgia that hail the slower pace of local information and local ways of living as simpler and healthier.

Globalisation is, within this perspective, understood, on the one hand, to produce new and sometimes productive or positive transformations of the relationship between the local and the global (Woodward 2002, p. 55). At the same time, of course, aspects of global corporatism and the movement of capital have produced or exacerbated insecurities and inequities between different parts of the world (Poynting et al. 2004, p. 82). In that respect, how we experience global communication as something which impinges on identity is most certainly not experienced in the same way—there is no 'levelling out' of difference within a global culture that is marked by distinctions of power, wealth and access (Jensen 2004) and expansionist frameworks of some parts of the world (Hardt and Negri 2000) as well as older legacies of colonialism that were part of earlier globalisation frameworks (James 2006).

Media and cultural scholar John Hartley (1998) defines global and popular media together to show the certain inequitable globalisational power frameworks are operationalised by the circulation of contemporary popular entertainment media rather than an expansion of the democratic public sphere. The increasing ease of popular media to circulate around the globe through digital networks often works closely with the circulation of transnational capital, influence and military intervention—as has been seen in the twenty-first century in the cases of the United States of America, China and Russia. Perspectives such as these tend to see globalisation through concepts of reducing the distance between different, competing cultural frameworks in ways which produce new kinds of dominance, whereby 'soft power' through cultural expansion is an *extension* of older forms of military intervention and colonisation rather than merely the circulation of media texts for consumption.

Other ways of defining globalisation as a cultural and conceptual re-figuring of local, regional, national and global relationalities include thinking about the ways in which the conditions of globalisation impinge directly on the body. Lauren Berlant (2007), for example, suggested that the catchphrase term "globesity" (referring to the assumption that obesity has been a global problem of humanity) links the global practice of westernisation of traditionally non-Western regions of the world with health concerns around fitness and bodies. Here, globalisation is written on the body through the uneven distribution of privilege and poverty, of agency and control and of development and underdevelopment (p. 758).

Mark Poster (2001) made a similar remark in suggesting the body is, itself, rewritten through the conditions of globalisation as both a global capitalism/imperialism and a new way of doing community. Globalisation, in this sense, draws together human bodies and the technologies of communication and machinery. In this sense, the relationship between globalisation and digital communication is much more than simply a way of accessing texts more easily and quickly around the world. Rather, it acts upon bodies in changing concepts of space, time and speed to produce new ways of understanding the body in the context of geographies (Sharma 2011, p. 439). Globalisation is therefore very much tied up with new cartographies of identity that bring selfhood and digital communication together in ways which rewrite the perception of identity.

5.3 Beyond the local/global dichotomy

At one level, globalisation operates as a set of concepts that bear on how we perform our identities in the context of our relationalities with others across the world. This has helpfully counterpointed and critiqued the sometimes problematic framework of national identity which is always in some respects in service to nationalism and practices of social exclusion (Anderson 1983). Both of the concepts of the nation and the globe circulate through master narratives and storytelling that has an impact on other narratives and practices, including identifications. The narrative of nations and nationality have often been reproduced over time through the circulation of symbols and their force peaks and wanes over time and in accord with a range of other contextual factors, including economic, international relations, electoral politics and populism (David and Munoz-Basols 2011, p. xvii). The centrality of the nation-state as the principal form of governance since the nineteenth century competes now with alternative narratives of global thinking, whether that is the needs of global corporate trade and consumption or the urgencies of thinking globally to tackle human-induced climate change (McNevin 2007; Poster 2001). This has altered the efficacy with which national identifications used to be formed. Nationality is, then, one practice of identification among several others in everyday life and is often related to the circulation of norms and expectations in local areas.

It is important, however, not to assume that the global and the national are "two mutually exclusive entities," as these formations occur "at multiple, mutually entwined scales" whether territorial or social in form (Ang 2011, p. 783). The role of the nation-state in the public imaginary remains strong despite global thinking, substantial migration and mobility and the shifts in communication practices that disrupt national identifications (Ang 1993; Butler and Spivak 2007). The fact that many aspects of contemporary globalisation have, in fact, supported and solidified some nation-states' hold on power over trade and geographies has resulted in digital communication as sometimes being seen as the 'safe' form of globalisation. This is partly because it is seen as *individually* beneficial to people in liberal-humanist frameworks who are perceived as being able to 'better themselves' through exposure to other cultural forms without the physical encounter of the other in one's imagined 'home' space of the nation (Cover 2015). Popular culture, diasporic film, digital communication and online tourism are positioned as globalisational—entertaining, pedagogical and stemming ignorance, but this does not mean that global discourse comes to *replace* the nation. Rather, they (a) compete with the nation by adding an additional framework for identification and belonging on top of it and (b) spread the framework of national identity norms on a wider scale. In other words, there is some risk in celebrating the idea that nationalism has been overcome by a global cosmopolitanism simply because people more easily interact online on an international scale. Rather, the role of globalisation is, as I discuss in more detail below, more complex because it is framed by identity knowledges that deploy multiple concepts of global and local spaces and global and local time.

To summarise so far: the idea of a national/global dichotomy is a false one because globalism does not undo national identity—instead, it adds further components to how we perceive ourselves in the context of place and geographies. It is also subject to a competing dichotomy which is also a problematic one: the global/local distinction. Local is not always the same as national and never has been—local attitudes, concepts, rivalries, identifications, nostalgia and community formations have traditionally been positioned as capable of being at odds with the national; likewise regional identifications that put into question the monoliths of national and global affiliation complexifies the local. Discourses of globalisation create new relationships between the concepts of the local and the global in ways which operate across the two (Woodward 2002, p. 55).

However, the concepts of the global and local constitute each other—that is, a sense of the local is different today in a post-globalisation world than it was a hundred years ago (Barker 1999, pp. 41–42). While broadcast televisual media altered the balance between local communities and global affiliations or sensibilities (Cooper 2002, p. 135), and while digital communication has consolidated those changes by providing a conceptual and technological framework that links up different sites, towns and cities in ways that mirrors the network flows across nodes and hubs (Castells 2000, p. 445), the notion of the local is still one that is very meaningful in everyday life, even if there are times and contexts in which it is subordinated to the global—say, in the context of the economic impact on the local global trade, or the need to think about climate change from global perspectives in order to address it more adequately than we can do by preserving the local environment (Gibson-Graham 2003, p. 50).

Responses to the complexity of global and local identities have included the emergence in the late twentieth century of journalistic-style terms such as 'glocalisation' to help account for the overlap in different perspectives of geography and place. Despite the simplification of such terms, it remains true that both local and global forces interact with each other to form particular ways of thinking about space and selfhood, although the complexity is undoubtedly at the heart of some of the anxieties that are expressed over local places being altered by global concepts (Perera 2007, p. 5), whether that's the force of climate change arguments, the presence of migrants or the Americanisation of local entertainment media. That is, while popular culture, media and digital communication bring transnational and global information into the site of the local, it remains that the ways in which such material, experiences, commodities and concepts are interpreted, understood or have their meanings productively activated occur only through the lens of the local and the regional, both of which may become reframed through a nostalgic romanticisation of *home* as one of the competing (and mostly mythical) 'sources' of identity (Woodward 2002, pp. 49–50). Thus, when an identity framework emerges and circulates around the globe as a particular way of thinking about ourselves and belonging in the world, that information is tailored through the experiences a subject has gained in the local environment of place.

5.4 Globalisation and identity

Having discussed how digital communication can be understood as a technology and practice that is, on the one hand, the result of recent historical phases of globalisation and, on the other hand, something which extends and sustains certain aspects of globalisation, and having made some remarks about the complex intersections of global, national and local, it is worth turning attention to how these play a role in the relationship between geographies and identity.

In Chapter 1, I outlined some of the different approaches to making sense of identity, subjectivity and selfhood and argued that Judith Butler's (1990) approach to identity performativity, in which we are compelled to articulate our identities in accord with a range of norms and practices that precede us in language and culture, provides the most useful conceptual tools for understanding the relationship between identity and digital communication. Butler drew on earlier psychoanalytic and poststructuralist understandings of identity to shift away from the liberal-humanist idea of personal identity as the source of a person's actions, speech, thoughts, attitudes and behaviours and—instead—to demonstrate how those actions, constrained and regimented by diverse social norms, retroactively constitute identity as an effect of those actions.

In this sense, identity is a process we undergo to fulfil the social obligations of performing selfhood with coherence, intelligibility and recognisability in order to belong. In that context, concepts of the local, national, global and other normative ways of perceiving place, space, time and geographies are part of the cultural framework that shapes our identity performances—not necessarily always in conscious or apparent ways but nevertheless a key backdrop to how are operationalised as identities in the world. And how those various aspects of geographies change and shift over time in our lives has an impact on the limits and possibilities of personal identity.

How we are 'placed' in a world that is perceived as a globe depends on a range of factors, including consumption tastes, mobility, movement, where we live, how we are conditioned to make choices about place and—particularly—how we engage in the range of digital communication tools and capabilities that enable global communication networks. This is not, of course, to suggest that in the context of globalisation, we suddenly become equal, undifferentiated individual 'human beings' as the principal framework of identity. Such a thing would be a very nice, liberal-humanist and utopian ideal, but globalisation has not, as I showed above, completely eschewed the identity frameworks of the local and the global. In that sense, there has been no flattening out of "the very differences on which any identity depends" as Eagleton has put it (2005, p. 85). Nevertheless, there are some universalising aspects that circulate through globalisational knowledge frameworks that impinge on how we perform our identities (Radhakrishnan 1996, p. xxvii) and that circulate during instances of global thinking—engaging, for example, in online protest actions over human-induced climate change may well be one instance in which we perceive a kind of universality as part of our identity as bodies living on a shared planet. At the same time, a person participating from the Kiribati in the Pacific Ocean—which is threatened by climate change-induced sea-level rises—may feel markedly different in the experience of global identity, as the immediacy of the threat to the local that may well be meaningful in their identity that is performed through a marked difference from those living in less-threatened regions of the world. In other words, global thinking does not operate hegemonically to produce sameness of identity, despite some of the criticisms of global popular culture (Barker 1999, p. 43).

One element of the globalising force of westernised identity frameworks is the resultant formation of *diversity* as the conceptual means by which local identities and global difference are thought in a world in which globalisation is experienced through digital communication and mobility as nodes that constitute the relationship between populations and identity (Cover 2020a). This framework is the default model by which multiculturalism is expressed as a means of conditional integration and social cohesion rather than a performance of unconditional welcome to others, whether permanent or temporary migrants residing in the country. More than population cohesiveness and integration, multicultural claims of diversity retain a core, liberal-humanist element of assimilation which, as Greg Noble (2011) has pointed out, is a logic that "has not been supplanted but operates as a larger frame" for understanding relationality between peoples in cultural and multicultural terms (p. 836). Indeed, the tolerance-based *condition* of multiculturalism can be said to be built primarily on assimilation: that is, those who arrive and settle in one part of the globe (within a nationalist identity framework) are tolerated on condition that they assimilate into the imagined core national identity and the local ritual practices of identity. While doing so, they may retain certain cultural practices usually related to the consumption of food, the performance of festivals and other traditions that are effectively 'residues' of older cultural forms in countries of origin.

This is what Ghassan Hage (2000) noted as the kind of "white multiculturalism" practised in many Western countries that claim to be part of the wider project of globalisation. Here, 'safe' cultural practices such as food, restaurants and festivals are tolerated, while the core Western (usually Anglo-Celtic) culture remains unaffected. Diversity is thus re-signified as a tool of *conditional inclusivity* rather than an ethical framework for belonging. It is what scholar Sara Ahmed (2007) identified as a form of gesture that upholds the status quo in many settings rather than permit ethical change. This upholds an older, liberal-humanist idea of identity in which ethnicity and race are seen as opportunities for othering rather than in the complex histories, cultures and social settings that enable uneven experiences including, as the Black Lives Matter movement has shown so clearly, the right to remain alive.

When we put this in the context of the relationship between identity and digital communication, the 'right' to participate in settings such as online platforms is equally framed by practices that may not be genuinely, ethically embracing of diversity and inclusivity. For example, platforms that preference the English or Chinese languages over others typically practise a form of exclusion based on the language of users perceived by identity groups, location and belonging. The hate speech that marks so much online activity in platforms and forums is another framework by which the globalisational dream of digital communication and McLuhan's so-called Global Village are not necessarily realised in the present form of digital culture but become settings of heightened anti-diversity and exclusion (Cover 2022). Digital culture has a non-monolithic *tendency* to reify a westernised framework of identity that is built on categorisation, exclusion and difference (Foucault 1977, pp. 232–233); a form of imperialism masquerading as global tolerance (Spivak 1999).

Finally, we might also pay attention to the ways in which search engines have been known to give primacy to certain sites that emerge from certain regions of the globe, often ignoring the knowledge frameworks that may exist outside of these geographies. Sometimes this depends entirely on the cookies on a local device; at other times, it is understood (although the proprietary algorithms are not fully known outside most search engine companies) to depend on the national IP address or the user. At other times on the geo-locational site from which the user accessed the search is pivotal to the circulation of information that forecloses on opportunities for sharing knowledge frameworks around the globe.

Together, these aspects of digital culture have a tendency to normativise identity practices, particularly through the circulation and consumption of norms that operate in the shadows of online diversity claims (Korten 1999, p. 62), serving as the means by which identity is produced in both local and global terms. While liberal-humanist identity frameworks will, regularly, sideline notions of class demarcations and inequalities, aspects of globalisational digital culture are implicated in the exacerbation of class-based inequalities. For example CEOs of corporations, leading industrialists and entrepreneurs, venture capitalists and senior executives, all have substantial privileges and identities expressed through non-localised mobilities and operate as 'global citizens' (Hall et al. 2013, p. 12). In contrast, a global poor retain a more localised set of identities, even if that locality is not a place of origin but a site of temporary refuge while waiting for resettlement. Digital access becomes part of the framework through which such inequalities are lived. In this context, class returns through the forms of digital globalisation that were seen as having promise for the eradication of difference and inequality, and in this sense, inequality becomes the marker of identity as lived through digital global culture.

5.5 Global and digital space

If the multiple experiences of 'place' and 'space' play a constitutive role in how we perform our identities because we exist in relationships with places and spaces—including those we do not personally traverse—then it makes sense to consider some of the ways in which our perceptions of space have changed in a digital era.

In a seminal work for understanding the cultural perceptions of communication and media technologies, Joshua Meyrowitz (1997) notes that the specialness of place is transformed by electronic communication as a result of the ways in which it dissociates *physical place* and *social space* (p. 49). That is, because communication and interactive engagement with others can occur in spaces that are vastly separate (such as on a social media page with friends and connections in different hemispheres), the sense of space between vast geographic and global frameworks operates through multiple 'registers.' This implies, for the performativity of identity, multiple relationships between different concepts of physical space (home, local, the distance between ourselves and those places we engage with online through, say, a Zoom call) as well as multiple social spaces (various online communities, our use of global platforms, our engagement with various media).

If all identity is relational from the beginning, meaning our performance of self-hood always occurs in relation to others (even when alone), and if the spatiality of those others is seen as significant (because we are all 'located' variously in these physical and social settings), then part of contemporary identity means the need to navigate the complex array of space and spatialities that we experience in everyday life. The transnational organisation of information through concepts of both physical and conceptual networks (Castells 2000) works in a way that calls upon us to shift our relationship with space regularly throughout the average lived day. In this context, the way in which we cite culturally given norms in order to produce over time a sense of coherent and intelligible identity occurs in the context of different spatial relationships.

If the 'compression' of space is the felt experience of living in a world of global networks, the spatial aspects of globalisation present us with new, ever-changing frameworks not only for navigating and performing identity in ever-more complex ways but for reflecting on how our identities are performed across local, regional and global spaces, many of which are experienced as 'real' and others which have the sense of being 'less real' albeit equally as meaningful. A useful concept for thinking about these 'unreal' spaces of digital communication is the space of 'heterotopia.' Heterotopias are conceptual spaces of difference, each with their own geographies and forms of disciplinary power, functioning separate from but in relation to the spaces around them (Munt 2002, p. 16). For Foucault (1986), heterotopic spaces are not 'utopias,' which have no real placeness about them at all. Rather, heterotopias have a placeness that is connected with all the spaces surrounding them and yet are also simultaneously unreal, much as the mirror has a place in the room but reflects a subject in ways which are unreal yet familiar (p. 24). In the same way, much of our digital communication across distance presents spaces that are experienced differently but not in ways that are disconnected from where we are.

For example, when we engage in a Zoom, Skype or Teams meeting with a group of people across the world, we do so in ways which locate us from the beginning in our local space (the office, the home, the lounge, the bedroom or, when on a mobile device, the street, the café, etc.). At the same time, we have a screen presence, very often one we see and witness like a mirror. There is a sense of presence of others in our space, on our screens that are in homes or workplaces and a knowledge that the same occurs elsewhere. So what we have is a form of identity play and performance that is from the very beginning of that call multiple and mutual. All spaces—conceptual, physical, geographic, heterotopic—are developed through adaptations and ideas that may have an affect but are constituted by pre-existing cultural desires and demands. They do not develop if there has not been "in the play and strategy of human relations something which tended in that direction" (Foucault 1993, p. 169).

Importantly, heterotopias can be spaces *for* subjects whose identities are expressed through norms as well as alternative frameworks of difference (Foucault 1986, p. 25). In that sense, we can view the conceptual space of digital communication as being a space in which we perform our identities with certain kinds of otherness that we cannot perform in other settings. That is, how we act and behave in one meeting is determined by the norms of those spatial arrangements—and it is in the juxtaposition of these different spaces (global, national, local, online, offline) that opens possibilities for seeing identity as far more fragmented or requiring the labour of identity 'navigation' across the multiplicity of these spaces, topias and heterotopias. This can be anxiety-provoking or productive of change, depending on the circumstances and, of course, the spaces.

5.6 The re-nationalisation of digital communication

Despite the above arguments about how digital communication works hand in hand with post-national globalisation in interesting ways, recent years have seen a push against frameworks in which digital settings are seen as synonymous with certain kinds of global cultures and ways of behaving and identifying. This has occurred primarily through a mood towards regulation that occurs at the level of the nation-state in ways which set up different practices for how people engage online in different settings. Indeed, Terry Flew (2021) described this as a "resurgence of tech nationalism" (p. vii). Much of this has been a response to the perceived power of platforms which themselves were derived from a post-national setting in Silicon Valley, USA, whereby United States' laws enabled many digital operators to self-regulate and sought to prevent their expansion from being curtailed by regulation and national controls. I will describe some of the ways in which this impinges on identity practices in Section 5.7, but here it is helpful to work through some of the ways in which the figure of the nation-state persists and reasserts itself despite the globalising trends of digital media.

In some parts of the world, a national digital culture is nothing new. For example, the People's Republic of China used legislative and administrative controls to prevent their own citizens from accessing various foreign websites and domains. These have had significant implications not just in terms of censoring information that might flow more freely elsewhere but in promoting domestic companies for goods and services over international ones and in keeping out content described as 'sensitive,' that is, content which might be critical of the Chinese government. In many ways, the Chinese internal Internet is promoted and perceived as Chinese 'sovereignty' that should not be seen in any way as post-national (Denyer 2016). As with much of the local/global conceptual and practical interchange, Chinese users have, of course, often found workarounds to the firewall that permit substantial access to international sites and platforms. Nevertheless, for the vast majority of users, the experience of digital communication is one that is overwhelmingly marked by the national and nationalism in China.

For different reasons, several other countries have begun to develop frameworks that seek to put a national spin on digital communication. These again are not always new—many countries have had laws which prevent the sharing of abusive material, particularly where it relates to child protection and different countries have different practices related to how defamation occurring through online carriage services is dealt with. In this sense, there has since at least the last years of the twentieth century been constraints to digital communication that mean what we do online depends on the national setting in which we are accessing, uploading or engaging.

Notably, attempts to shape digital behaviour by asserting some form of national sovereignty or national restrictiveness through legislative and administrative controls are well meaning in seeking to protect citizens from harms (including aspects of digital hostility and hate speech, which I address in Chapter 6). However, they also have a tendency to overreach by not necessarily promoting democratic engagement with digital practices but being more censorious than older, more traditional media regulatory systems (Flew 2021, pp. 240–241). Undoubtedly, some of this is a reaction to the absence of editorial gatekeeping practices that were part of newspapers, broadcast radio and television and book publishing in the era in which they remained the most dominant media and communication forms.

There is also some question as to how effective nation-state regulation of digital communication can be when there is genuinely an incident that warrants the protection of a citizen. For example, as Nicole Vincent (2017) has pointed out, jurisdictional differences often prevent cybercrimes from being adequately pursued. For example, a cybercrime that is perpetrated by a user in Russia, using a platform that is owned by a company in the United States and victimising a person in New Zealand is very difficult to police, even if all three national settings have laws against those crimes. The average user is not always well resourced to find a legal remedy to a crime or incident that can traverse so many jurisdictions. This is not, of course, to suggest that a laissez-faire free-for-all that operates beyond nations is a better framework for digital communication. Rather, it is to say that not only is digital governance complex but that only the most simplistic approaches to digital communication would see it as truly globalised and divorced from nation-state forms.

5.7 National identity and regulation?

As we know, one significant facet of identity performance involves the nation. The degree, however, to which the nation or nationalism figures as part of our everyday identities is widely variable. When we hear people at a Trump rally, for example, chanting "USA! USA!" we can see a particular theatrics of intensive nationalism at play, one which is alarmingly reminiscent of the nationalism that marked Hitler's Nuremberg Rallies in Germany prior to the Second World War. One needs to ask, of course, how much of this is produced in the context of mob-like behaviour in a physical setting, and how much of it is developed prior to attendance through the consumption of nationalistic discourse online. Either way, in the relational setting of people who identify with each other, the signifier of the nation is at times dominant and certainly has become more dominant in settings marked by national populisms, so-called anti-globalisation and anti-elitism (Cover 2020b). This, of course, tends to polarise people into national-populist and cosmopolitan liberal perspectives and through communities and affiliations with those political perspectives we all form identities in which the 'shadow' of the nation and nationalism remain part of our practices of belonging.

The notes above on the increasing shift towards digital regulation by nation-states leads us to ask a significant question about nations and nationalism: does nation-state regulation of digital communication exacerbate nationalism and its production of national identity? Or does its potential use in curtailing, say, racist hate speech indicate a desire to move away from the radical nationalism that circulates in some online settings where the free expression of hatred of migrants and extremist responses to non-white groups have circulated freely in alarming ways? This is not one of those questions that can be answered in advance, and the hold of nationalism is something that is very debatable and changes for all sorts of social, cultural and historical reasons, not just how we communicate online (even though that is very important). I would like to consider in this final section some of the ways we can think about whether nation-state regulation of digital communication might or might not play a role in promoting national identity.

If we bear in mind that all subjects are multiply-constituted, and that such constitution occurs through a range of attachments, sites and contexts, then we must remember there can be sites at which there is mutual recognition while regulatory regimes may refuse to recognise and indeed such mutual recognitions in one site may provide the resources for a subject to 'cope' with being unrecognisable and thereby non-belonging in another site. This is important in the context of national belonging, which itself has multiple meanings and operates in different ways at different times but tends to be dominated by the overly constructed notion of *national identity*. Nation-states are a site of considerable attachment for many subjects and thus are dominant in how identities are constituted at particular times. The nation-state requires the development and management of a sense of common belonging in order for the historically recent idea of the nation to proceed into an ongoing future (Taylor 2011, p. 45). In Benedict Anderson's (1983) framework, the nation-state is *imagined* into existence to comply with the demands of nationalism. This imaginary national community in which people who don't know each other feel a sense of affiliation and belonging through a shared national identity was initially developed through certain ritual practices such as consumption of national newspapers. Through the persistent ritual that frames off the national from the global, people forge particular attachments, and in many cases, these can be—as with many other types of community—particular symbols and constructs put into wide circulation, frequently within media practices operating within the public sphere (Cohen 1985).

Yet what constitutes belonging and identity in terms of that nation is more complex than simply the existence *of* a group of individuals. The very term 'nation' is derived from the term *nascere* meaning "to be born" (Minca 2006, p. 393). Although national identity as one mode of population belonging is always performative and constituted in the repetition of practices of belonging that are conditioned by reframing the population as a 'national population,' the figure of birth haunts definitions and concerns over who belongs to *which* population, at what time and in what conditions. The right to participate in the sovereign nation as a way of performing identity and population membership is one which returns retroactively to birth as the primary norm of that belonging. Birth is the alibi for such belonging, by which it is possible for a subject to turn to the claim to birth in order to justify and give coherence to belonging to the nation as a particular and highly limited form of population belonging. Birth within a nation also becomes the justification for exclusionary actions, such as the exclusion of some migrants from being permitted to feel a full sense of belonging (McAllan 2011, pp. 11–12).

Governance of the nation-state is central in this context, for it is the state which services "the matrix of the obligations and prerogatives of citizenship. It is that which forms the conditions under which we are juridically bound" (Butler and Spivak 2007, p. 3). Administrative governance of populations breaches the birth-nation-belonging continuum such that migration is uneasily permitted when particular conditions that would *tolerate* a form of belonging are permitted. The administrative element here is one which concerns itself with spatial definitions of the nation, protecting borders from 'unauthorised' crossings and enveloping the meaning of population in terms of territory and spatiality by linking these with an idea of national character (Saxton 2003, pp. 111–112). It remains the formation which determines belonging here in terms of national populations by administering, regulating and regimenting particular kinds of border crossing.

It is here that the question of national regulatory practices over digital communication comes into play. There are, of course, many regulatory practices that are enacted by nation-states to prevent certain kinds of online communication (sharing of child abuse images; certain kinds of hate speech; defamatory content). The potential for a shift here, however, is as nation-state regulations come to bear down on individual digital practices, there is the possibility of identification, affiliation and a sense of belonging to a national digital communication network that is marked by its differences from other nations. Whether or not that effectively increases the facet of identity that is based on national belonging is, of course, completely unknown. As with other digital media restrictions and, for example, the nationalised strictures on digital communication in China (the so-called Great Firewall), users may find workarounds that maintain the 'global' experience of digital communication over the discourse of national regimentation of digital culture. This is a wait-and-see moment.

Indeed, whether the governmental and administrative frameworks of a nation will always have much bearing on national identity is debatable, and that may be the case on the possible reshaping of a global Internet into fractured nationally regulated practices. The discourses that constitute the relationship between subjectivity and national population belonging are not just those that circulate in governance, policy and administration—despite the investment of governance in border policing, promoting population norms and forms of regulation. Other levels of experience play a significant role in how belonging to a population is produced and performed. Greg Noble (2002), for example, has criticised approaches derived from Anderson for their overreliance on the idea of the nation as an ideational category communicated in contemporary media. He argues that public rituals of national attachment are not necessarily the source of national identity, nor are there adequate reasons given for why people choose to partici-pate in such national events.

Instead, he points to the force of everyday aspects in forging national identity: "Our capacity to identify with the nation comes not simply from these events per se, but from the somewhat submerged, half-conscious and ubiquitous experience of nation throughout our everyday lives which makes those moments of national identification possible" (Noble 2002, p. 53). Analysing the everyday furnishing, décor and decoration choices made in the private home by a range of people, Noble demonstrates the ways in which the attachment to the nation occurs through submerged and non-voluntary dec-oration choices, rather than through the ritual annual events of nationhood or the pro-motion of the nation in media and other public discourse. Rightly, the sites of nationhood are not those obvious points of national identification.

In that context, it might be better to say that the capacity for nation-state regula-tion of digital communication to have an effect on identity will depend on the extent to which such regulation is experienced as part of the *everyday digital culture*. It may well be the case that it is merely a backdrop whereby legislation and regulation come into play only when there is a high-profile instance of abuse or a legal case—and it otherwise might turn out to be mostly irrelevant to how everyday people communi-cate online. The extent to which digital communication remains post-national will, of course, depend on a number of factors, such as the mood by which under-regulation is tolerated, the force of nationalist-populism and whether it remains with us for long and the ability of those who seek a post-national world to put forward convincing arguments. At this stage, it is safe to say that the globalisational form of digital commu-nication is with us to stay, but that various geographic, political and social counterpoints (local, national) continue to exert a force on that, and that these are not always wholly negative or nostalgic.

5.8 Conclusion

This chapter has taken a perspective on the relationship between digital communication and identity that is attentive to geographic concepts of place and space. The early Internet of the 1990s and subsequent forms of digital networks and platforms have often been described in the conceptual language of globalisation, which is a key cultural framework that has powerfully changed how people perceive themselves in the context of place and the world over time. In its most recent phases, it has a number of positive values (promoting human-induced climate change awareness; revaluing how people from outside one's home country are perceived) and negative values (a consumption, labour, corporate ownership, trade and international finance system that creates greater inequities for some parts of the globe). However we value different aspects of globalisation, it is impossible to perform identity in this world external to its conceptual influence on the perception of space and place.

Despite the power of globalisation as a discourse, there has been a move towards regulation of digital communication by nation-states in many parts of the world. As I outline above, although this is not as new as it seems by the recent move to address some of the crimes and victimisations that circulate through online media, this too impinges upon the possibility of performing digital identities in ways which are enabled equitably around the world. The involvement of nation-states in regulatory forms is not, in itself, a bad thing, given the needs to address cybercrime and the circulation of extremist hate speech and violence. However, in doing so, the figure of the nation—which traditionally has been a formation for the categorisation and performance of normative identities—re-emerges in a new form. While it is too soon to say whether it substantially changes the globalisational force of digital networking and platform use, it remains an important one to watch if we want to understand how digital communication enables particular ways of doing identity into the future.

Key points

- In some respects, digital communication emerges due to a cultural feeling or desire to break free from the communicative constraints of localness and national media systems.
- Globalisation is a key framework by which contemporary cultures make sense of themselves, and it is impossible to perform an identity without feeling the force of globalisation.
- Digital communication has established some frameworks by which space is rethought in more global terms, although the local and the national continue to play a role in how both communication and identification operate.
- There is an increasing mood for regulation of digital communication occurring at the level of the nation-state. While this is neither a positive nor a negative thing, it too impinges upon identificatory practices, and we will need to see over the next few years whether it has an effective impact on our use of digital networks.

References

Ahmed, S., 2007. The language of diversity. *Ethnic and Racial Studies,* 30 (2), 235–256.
Anderson, B., 1983. *Imagined Communities: Reflections on the Origins and Spread of Nationalism.* London: Verso.

Ang, I., 1993. Migrations of Chineseness: ethnicity in the postmodern world. *In:* D. Bennett, ed. *Cultural Studies: Pluralism and Theory.* Melbourne: University of Melbourne, 32–44.

Ang, I., 2011. Navigating complexity: from cultural critique to cultural intelligence. *Continuum: Journal of Media & Cultural Studies,* 25 (6), 779–794.

Barker, C., 1999. *Television, Globalization and Cultural Identities.* Buckingham: Open University Press.

Berlant, L., 2007. Slow death (sovereignty, obesity, lateral agency). *Critical Inquiry,* 33 (4), 754–780.

Butler, J., 1990. *Gender Trouble: Feminism and the Subversion of Identity.* London: Routledge.

Butler, J. and Spivak, G.C., 2007. *Who Sings the Nation-State? Language, Politics, Belonging.* London: Seagull Books.

Carver, T., 1998. *The Postmodern Marx.* Manchester: Manchester University Press.

Castells, M., 2000. *The Rise of the Network Society.* Oxford: Blackwell.

Cohen, A.P., 1985. *The Symbolic Construction of Community.* London: Ellis Horwood & Tavistock Publications.

Cooper, S., 2002. *Technoculture and Critical Theory: In the Service of the Machine?* London: Routledge.

Cover, R., 2015. Mobility, belonging and bodies: understanding attitudes of anxiety towards temporary migrants in Australia. *Continuum: Journal of Media & Cultural Studies,* 29 (1), 32–44.

Cover, R., 2020a. *Population, Mobility and Belonging: Understanding Population Concepts in Media, Culture and Society.* London & New York: Routledge.

Cover, R., 2020b. Vulnerability and the discourse of 'forgotten people': populism, population and cultural change. *Continuum: Journal of Media & Cultural Studies,* 34 (5), 749–762.

Cover, R., 2022. Digital hostility: contemporary crisis, disrupted belonging and self-care practices. *Media International Australia,* 184 (1), 79–91.

David, M. and Munoz-Basols, J., 2011. Introduction: defining and re-defining diaspora: an unstable concept. *In:* M. David and J. Munoz-Basols, eds. *Defining and Re-Defining Diaspora: From Theory to Reality.* Oxford: Inter-Disciplinary Press, xi–xxiv.

Denyer, S., 2016. China's scary lesson to the world: censoring the Internet works. *Washington Post,* 23 May. Available from: www.washingtonpost.com/world/asia_pacific/chinas-scary-lesson-to-the-world-censoring-the-internet-works/2016/05/23/413afe78-fff3-11e5-8bb1-f124a43f84d c_story.html [Accessed 1 June 2022].

Eagleton, T., 2005. *Holy Terror.* Oxford: Oxford University Press.

Flew, T., 2013. *Global Creative Industries.* Cambridge: Polity.

Flew, T., 2021. *Regulating Platforms.* Cambridge: Polity.

Foucault, M., 1977. *Language, Counter-Memory, Practice: Selected Essays and Interviews,* ed. D.F. Bouchard, trans. S. Simon. Ithaca, NY: Cornell University Press.

Foucault, M., 1986. Of other spaces (J. Misowiec, Trans.). *Diacritics,* 16 (1), 22–27.

Foucault, M., 1993. Space, power and knowledge. *In:* S. During, ed. *The Cultural Studies Reader.* London: Routledge, 161–169.

Gibson-Graham, J.K., 2003. An ethics of the local. *Rethinking Marxism,* 15 (1), 49–74.

Hage, G., 2000. *White Nation: Fantasies of White Supremacy in a Multicultural Society.* London: Routledge.

Hall, S., Massey, D. and Rustin, M., eds., 2013. *After Neoliberalism? The Kilburn Manifesto.* Available from: www.opendemocracy.net/en/opendemocracyuk/after-neoliberalism-introduction-to-kilburn-manifesto/ [Accessed 1 May 2022].

Hardt, M. and Negri, A., 2000. *Empire.* Cambridge, MA: Harvard University Press.

Hartley, J., 1998. 'When your child grows up too fast': Juvenation and the boundaries of the social in the news media. *Continuum: Journal of Media & Cultural Studies,* 12 (1), 9–30.

James, P., 2006. Globalisation and empires of mutual accord. *Arena Magazine,* 85, 41–45.

Jensen, R., 2004. *Citizens of the Empire: The Struggle to Claim our Humanity.* San Francisco, CA: City Lights.

Korten, D.C., 1999. *The Post-Corporate World: Life after Capitalism.* San Francisco, CA: Berrett-Koehler Publishers.

McAllan, F., 2011. Getting 'post racial' in the 'Australian' state: what remains overlooked in the premise 'getting beyond racism'? *Critical Race and Whiteness Studies,* 7, 1–21.

McLuhan, M., 1962. *The Gutenberg Galaxy: The Making of Typographic Man.* Toronto: University of Toronto Press.

McNevin, A., 2007. Irregular migrants, neoliberal geographies and spatial frontiers of 'the political.' *Review of International Studies,* 33 (4), 655–674.

Meyrowitz, J., 1997. The separation of social space from physical place. *In:* T. O'Sullivan and Y. Jewkes, eds. *The Media Studies Reader.* London: Edward Arnold, 45–52.

Minca, C., 2006. Giorgio Agamben and the new biopolitical *nomos. Geografiska Annaler: Series B, Human Geography,* 88 (4), 387–403.

Munt, S., 2002. Framing intelligibility, identity, and selfhood: a reconsideration of spatio-temporal models. *Reconstruction,* 2 (3). Available from: www.reconstruction.ws/023/munt.htm [Accessed 29 December 2002].

Noble, G., 2002. Comfortable and relaxed: furnishing the home and nation. *Continuum: Journal of Media & Cultural Studies,* 16 (1), 53–66.

Noble, G., 2011. 'Bumping into alterity': Transacting cultural complexities. *Continuum: Journal of Media & Cultural Studies,* 25 (6), 827–840.

Perera, S., 2007. 'Aussie luck': the border politics of citizenship post Cronulla Beach. *ACRAWSA e-Journal,* 3 (1), 1–16.

Poster, M., 2001. Citizens, digital media and globalization. *Mots Pluriels,* 18 (August), 1–11.

Poynting, S., Noble, G., Tabar, P. and Collins, J., 2004. *Bin Laden in the Suburbs: Criminalising the Arab Other.* Sydney: Sydney Institute of Criminology.

Radhakrishnan, R., 1996. *Diasporic Mediations: Between Home and Location.* Minneapolis, MN: University of Minnesota Press.

Saxton, A., 2003. 'I certainly don't want people like that here': the discursive construction of 'asylum seekers.' *Media International Australia,* 109, 109–120.

Sharma, S., 2011. The biopolitical economy of time. *Journal of Communication Inquiry,* 35 (4), 439–444.

Spivak, G.C., 1999. *A Critique of Postcolonial Reason: Toward a History of the Vanishing Present.* Cambridge, MA: Harvard University Press.

Taylor, C., 2011. Why we need a radical redefinition of secularism. *In:* E. Mendieta and J. VanAntwerpen, eds. *The Power of Religion in the Public Sphere.* New York: Columbia University Press, 34–59.

Urry, J., 2007. *Mobilities.* Cambridge: Polity.

Vincent, N.A., 2017. Victims of cybercrime: definitions and challenges. *In:* E. Martellozzo and E.A. Jane, eds. *Cybercrime and Its Victims.* Abingdon: Routledge, 27–42.

Woodward, K., 2002. *Understanding Identity.* London: Arnold.

6 Hostilities

Trolling, hate speech and exclusion in digital settings

6.1 Introduction

There is no doubt in the 2020s that much contemporary digital media is marked, sadly, by hostile behaviour, hate speech and aggressive communication. Experiencing hostility, adversity, aggression and hate speech while communicating on platforms and in online forums has become commonplace for many users of digital communication and social media over the past decade. To give just one example of the extent of the problem, in Australia an estimated 14% of adults are understood to experience hate speech online, and we can reasonably assume that a substantially larger percentage of users are exposed to other forms of online hostility (eSafety Commissioner 2020). The growing evidence that many settings of digital communication are becoming toxic has sponsored legislation and policy initiatives (Flew 2021); concerns about well-being and mental health (Chalmers et al. 2016); calls for greater platform moderation (Gillespie 2018); and a range of civil society, cross-jurisdictional and industry agencies calling for greater regulation to protect the quality of online discourse (Berners-Lee 2019; Christchurch Call 2019).

The experience of hostility and hate speech online is an important issue for the safe practice of identity in digital settings. Current scholarship recognises a relationship between exposure to online hostility and harm to well-being, including emotional stress and mental health harms (it has become better understood in recent years that there is a correlation between online hostility and the experience of negative mental health issues (Lewis et al. 2017; Gorman 2019) and suicidality (Hinduja and Patchin 2010; Bauman et al. 2013) with a number of high-profile cases in which experiencing hostility in the form of a Twitter pile-on preceded suicides (Thompson and Cover 2021). Among moderators, online community managers and others who are involved in policing hate speech on platforms, there is also some growing evidence of harm, including two high-profile court cases currently facing Meta (Facebook) resulting from online moderators developing post-traumatic stress disorder (PTSD) from overexposure to other people's hate speech. In that respect, online hostility has recently shifted in public sphere debate as being seen initially as a matter of unpleasantness or incivility towards being viewed as one of serious health and mental health policy.

At the same time, recent evidence indicates that, in exasperation with a lack of regulation and poor moderation practices that fail to keep up with abuse, some users protect themselves by disconnecting and disengaging from online settings (Light 2014). Other users and digital workers have tried to manage their own support innovatively by setting up and developing mutual care networks among people who have experienced high rates of online aggression, hate speech and hostility (Black et al. 2022; Cover 2022). There is

DOI: 10.4324/9781003296652-6

a lot of further work that needs to be done to ensure people are appropriately protected when engaging online, and some of that involves the kind of regulation mentioned in Chapters 4 and 5, while some of it involves substantial cultural change to our practices if we are to express ourselves online safely.

This chapter describes how the high rates of digital hostility and hate speech might be understood to have an impact on digital identity. Over the previous chapters, I have discussed several of the ways in which digital communication operates as the everyday setting in which we express identities and participate in social belonging. What happens, however, when that everyday setting becomes toxic? For whom is it toxic, and what happens to our sense of self-identity, resilience and belonging when subject to shaming? What is different from being shamed by a person in the street as opposed to having a mass pile-on of people scolding us on Twitter for an ill-thought comment or for holding a particular viewpoint? In what ways does that make us feel like 'ungrievable' subjects who no longer belong?

I will start with working through a few ways we can define digital hostility as a collective term for a range of bad behaviours online, and how it can be perceived as a cultural issue for the 2020s. I would like to say a few things about how it has been seen to create new kinds of 'digital divide' that are no longer about who has *access* to digital technology but who is *allowed* and *not allowed* to participate online safely. To discuss the relationship between digital hostility and identity, we need to bear in mind the argument that social networks and online communication play a pivotal role in constituting and performing identity and that while debate and disagreement are always part of identity expression, digital hostility experiences are indicating ways in which identity can be disrupted or upset when the experience becomes toxic. I will therefore draw attention to how the negative impact on the intelligibility and coherence of identity occurs across two key experiences of digital hostility: the experience of the *mass online pile-on* in which the group or multitude comes to represent the public and the form that public shaming takes as a disruptive element for subjectivity and finally the experience of perceiving oneself as being positioned by a hostile group as an *ungrievable subject*. Although theories of online identity are multiple and widespread and can best be understood through sophisticated, poststructuralist approaches to the cultural constitution of subjectivity (Cover 2016), taking a performative perspective on identity is useful for making sense not only of how we articulate ourselves as people online, but how online spaces can destabilise identity by marking some lives as liveable and others as ungrievable or unworthy of life and non-violent engagement.

6.2 What is digital hostility?

'Digital hostility' is a useful concept for making sense of the collective array of contemporary practices of adversarial online behaviours and their effects on others that mark everyday digital culture. Digital culture is understood here as the everyday lived experience in which digital networks, spaces and forms of social engagement are a core element in communication, identity and livelihood more broadly. One of the key arguments here is that we need to think of digital hostility as *cultural* rather than *behavioural*, because to do so opens the possibility of understanding online adversarial behaviour, hate speech and harmful online acts towards other users as *everyday* experiences that are increasingly *normalised* parts of communication, rather than rare acts of a few 'bad apple' individuals (or 'trolls') that ruin things that are otherwise okay (Ringrose 2018; Haslop et al. 2021).

While there is important research on extremist sites and those message board platforms such as 4chan, 8chan and Gab (Munn 2019), which serve as relatively exclusive echo chambers for users holding extreme political and social views (Nagle 2017), the practice of adversity in the more 'everyday' sites of YouTube, Facebook, Twitter and Reddit as well as online news forums generates the circumstance in which an average, everyday user may unwittingly experience threatening, abusive behaviours and hate speech. In this context, the growth of online hostility can be understood as a *cultural condition* which constitutes the contemporary experience of communication and one mode of attitude or disposition towards others that takes advantage of the affordances of mass networked communication, relative anonymity, instantaneity and virality to circulate adversarial speech and images.

If we think about digital hostility as a cultural formation, then we can think not just about different kinds of experiences of hostility, but of the ways in which they cross over into each other. Some of the forms at play include the following:

Cyberbullying: This is usually thought of as the use of digital communication tools to enact bullying and harassment, such as repeatedly posting rumours, threats, negative remarks, insinuations of derogatory speech about the person, sometimes perpetrated by one person and sometimes by a group of people acting together (Smith et al. 2008). Concerns about cyberbullying emerged in the early 2000s, particularly when it was uncovered that younger people were being affected by it, often as an extension to other forms of bullying experience in, for example, school or workplaces. A number of jurisdictions around the world funded education campaigns about the harms of cyberbullying and enacted laws to penalise cyberbullying and cyber-abuse. It's useful to bear in mind that cyberbullying continues to be a major problem affecting people who are otherwise themselves simply trying to engage socially in online settings (Chalmers et al. 2016). However, the term is problematically used at times to cover all kinds of digital hostility, and this is unhelpful for two reasons: firstly, the concept of cyberbullying and its presumed remedies are build on older models of 'playground' bullying (McMahon 2014; Olweus and Limber 2018) which does not necessarily represent the extensive way in which the tools of digital communication are used innovatively by those seeking to harm others or where others unthinkingly abuse because it has become part of the culture. Secondly, as a concept it tends to focus on the identification of bullying by the offensiveness or harm of *individual* items of content as assessed as harmful by third parties, rather than the *effect* of large-scale exposure to hostile behaviours that—in themselves—may not be apparent when just looking at individual items of content.

Internet pile-on: The term 'Internet pile-on' describes the practice in which an individual is publicly criticised by digital users in numbers larger than an easily count-able group—often exceeding the thousands (Hamad 2019). It incorporates users taking advantage of social media to respond to the politics, faux pas, difference of opinion, unfashionable ideas or Twitter slip-ups of a user. The pile-on differs from cyberbullying because it takes online hostility into a new *register* marked not by the content produced by online bullies or the extensiveness of an offensive remark but by the *sheer numbers* of perpetrators in what can be described as the 'massification' of digital hate (Seymour 2019). In that sense, then, individual posts may be mild and therefore not identified as bullying and abuse *on their own*, but when taken together, the experience of a pile-on in *very large numbers* combined with the *instantaneity* of those posts occurring in a short time frame (Papacharissi 2015, p. 44) solidifies the statements through instant repetition into truth. Although resembling the exclusionary behaviour of 'the multitude' or 'mob' (Urry 2007), this is a new 'mode' of communicative abuse for which there is not yet a clear language by which to critique and address it. Nor is there clarity yet on how users experience, engage with and respond to it.

Doxxing: Doxxing (or doxing) is a term that describes the act of finding and releasing personal information about a user online in order to embarrass or harm them. Sometimes, it is understood as publicly identifying a person who is otherwise engaging online under a pseudonym or anonymity, although it has also been used to generate a spillover of hostility from online to offline by finding and releasing a user's private address, work-place details and so on that puts them at risk of in-person stalking or attack or makes them feel threatened and vulnerable to such attacks. For example, it has been used in the United States of America by anti-abortion activists to release the personal details and home address of abortion service providers to put them at risk of personal attack or injury (Cohen and Connon 2015). When used to provide personal information about a user—such as their workplace, employment history, family, sexual orientation and so on—that was otherwise not part of an online conversation, it harms the user by taking away a sense of control over their private information, releasing aspects of an identity that the user had not necessarily wished released or disrupting the self-representation of a curated profile.

Cross-platform trolling: Trolling was initially defined as the act of deliberately baiting people online to elicit an emotional response and was—early on—considered a form of pranking for the purposes of generating humour or shock (Marwick and Lewis 2017). Increasingly, it has been identified as the act of creating discord online by begin-ning quarrels, deliberately upsetting and persistently posting inflammatory content in order to unsettle other users (Jane 2015; Lumsden and Morgan 2017). Although the term has morphed to describe any bad behaviour online, much of it today is about baiting in order to hurt those whom the troll sees as politically opposed or coming from a distinct (often minority) social group (Cover 2022). Whether or not it is considered a 'mild' form of digital hostility, one of the difficulties with dealing with trolling and other forms of aggressive or upsetting online behaviour is that it regularly occurs in a cross-platform context (Phillips 2015). That is, a troll baits or unsettles a user on Facebook and, having done so, follows that user to Twitter, Reddit, Instagram and other sites. This makes it very difficult for that user to address, having to block, shut down or withdraw from multiple platforms and sites and experiencing online hostility in a form that resembles stalking (the perpetrator appearing everywhere they seem to be—making their online life unliveable no matter where they go). This also suggests difficulties for regulation by moderators who are charged with resolving complaints *per platform*, not the kinds of experiences that cross platforms. Adding to this concern is the fact that the trolling on one platform may be mild but when a user is trolled across multiple platforms and accounts the experience is markedly different—but very difficult to address using the available tools of moderation, reporting, complaints and legal action.

Shaming, call-out culture and cancellation culture: Over the past half-decade, 'call-out' culture has become a significant part of addressing social issues, primarily in online spaces and often involving forms of hostility, trolling and pile-ons (Bartlett et al. 2019). Shaming can—in itself—be positive because it can generate and foster better ethics among those who are shamed (Probyn 2005), for example, when a perpetrator has committed acts regarded by the community as egregious such as appearing in 'black face' or 'fat shaming' and is called out by other users. Digital bombardment from overwhelm-ingly large numbers calling for permanent 'cancellation' of a subject's online or public life (KhosraviNik and Esposito 2018), however, not only buries the ethical argument (Hamad and Liddle 2017) but puts a user one who is trying to 'educate' at risk of harm. The impact of call-outs and calls for cancellation are not yet well understood and warrant continued investigation and research.

Extremism and hate speech: A growing body of research has demonstrated how hate speech and disinformation have been deployed by extremist groups in online spaces to attack their political opponents and minorities in the community (Burgess and Baym 2020; Davis 2021). Hate speech is usually defined as content that targets minorities and disenfranchised identity groups in a harmful way, typically related to axes of discrimination such as race, ethnicity, gender or sexual identity, age or disability (Bilewicz and Soral 2020). Definitions of hate speech have been determined by criminal law, with findings that this does not match with how everyday users perceive hate (Brown 2017). Extremist speech, which is sometimes linked with terrorist activity and gun-related violence, takes hate speech to a new level (Waldek et al. 2021), not only harming individuals and groups who are from minority or disenfranchised background with their content but encouraging others and building online and offline communities of others who hold extremist views, creating widespread risks not only for other users but for the community as a whole. Perpetrators have become more efficient at using hate speech in harmful but coded ways that avoid penalisation by social media moderators.

Across these forms of digital hostility, what has shifted from older models of cyberbullying, flame wars and other adversities is the *massification* of hate as a cultural form and the *normalisation* of hostile, aggressive and adversarial behaviour online (Ringrose 2018; Cover 2022). This form of group rather than individual violence actively reduces the capacity of a subject to respond, to defend a position or to develop a conversation that demands recognition. In some cases, the hostile speech not only *represents* a multitude but cannot be conceived as articulations of an individual, being the work of paid troll farms, bots and other automated programmes with no distinct person as author of the hate speech (Golbeck 2018).

In that sense, it is helpful to think of digital hostility as a continuum. This is because the definitional difficulties over different forms of online hostility have been unhelpful in apprehending or preventing these forms because experiences often exceed definitions. That is, while it is generally accepted that there is a distinction between hostile online behaviour and heated online disagreements (Jane 2015), the difficulties are increasingly recognised as hurdles for automated detection of potentially harmful speech and behaviour online (Burnap and Williams 2015), or they result in instances of *victim blaming* for toxic communication that falls short of legislated definitions of hate speech (Lumsden and Morgan 2017; Haslop et al. 2021). A lack of terminological agreement and difficulties knowing how everyday users perceive and recognise hostility had made it difficult for platforms, regulators and policymakers to know where to 'draw the line' (Suzor 2019).

However, although the definitional difficulties may limit the opportunity to build widespread public, stakeholder, governance and international (cross-jurisdictional) support for intervention, prevention and care solutions that work, at the same time the lack of clarity may indeed help us by opening up the possibility of defining other online acts under the umbrella of digital hostility. It is therefore useful to understand user experience of hostility in terms of a continuum in which some forms of digital hostility are treated as more normative than others, but across the continuum, there is a likelihood for many users to experience or be exposed to racial hate speech (Cleland 2017), extremism (Davis 2021), trolling (Beckett 2017), 'pile-ons' and other forms that may be minimally offensive but harmful when experienced as shaming by thousands of other users (Hamad 2019), in addition to the harms done to the digital ecology by a culture and experience that increasingly feels toxic (Seymour 2019).

6.3 Digital hostility as a cultural issue for the 2020s

If we want to understand the impact of digital hostility on the relationship between identity and digital communication, then we need to account for the way in which hostility is not some 'alien phenomenon' that came and infected an otherwise peaceful, liberal and well-meaning digital culture but emerges as part of it. Hostility experienced in online communication has, indeed, been a significant part of digital culture since the early Internet. The 1990s Web 1.0 era of interactivity through chatrooms, newsgroups and email listservs were noted for their polarising arguments sometimes referred to as 'flame wars.' Cyberbullying that spilled from the school or workplace into the domestic and private space of online engagement became significant social issues in the early 2000s. And, as I noted above, we have witnessed new forms of online hostility, hate speech and problematic behaviour, including the experience of mass Twitter pile-ons, public shaming, cross-platform trolling, doxxing and violent extremist language.

It has been argued that mass online hostility and hate speech has become widely normalised as part of digital culture (Ringrose 2018) and implicitly endorsed by platforms (Marwick and Lewis 2017), resulting in evidence of a reticence among users to report hostile online behaviour or hate speech (Haslop et al. 2021, pp. 1427–1428). This reticence indicates the extent to which hostile and harmful behaviour has become part of the 'norm' of online engagement. Referring to it as a norm not only means that it is an expectation but that users are 'disciplined' both into perceiving it as part of the practice of communicating online and—for some—feeling that it is okay to be insulting, offensive, hurtful.

Normalisation cultures changes and adapt, and through practices of normalisation, behaviours that were previously considered unacceptable gradually become taken for granted and accepted as natural.

The normalisation of incivility and harmful behaviour online is one aspect of the way in which it becomes part of digital culture. Another, however, is to consider how it comes out of digital culture itself. Just as we discussed some of the ways in which identity practices emerged from the interactivity of digital communication in previous chapters, it can be noted here that the present online form of hostile and aggressive behaviour, harmful content and hate speech are (in part) the outcome of earlier aspects of digital culture:

- **Anonymity**—early Internet practices tended to be more anonymous than today, particularly in chatrooms and online forums (Kennedy 2006). Today, there is an increasing emphasis on non-anonymity on social media, with several platforms (including Facebook) having installed 'real names policies.' Nevertheless, the use of workarounds, false names and the wider perception of anonymity facilitates some aspects of online hostility, including particularly cyberbullying (Peebles 2014). In this respect, one core aspect of the historical development of online communication is a key factor in enabling an uncivil or hostile communication environment.
- **Lack of gatekeeping**—traditional media forms such as print, radio and television involved practices of gatekeeping that often prevented uncivil or harmful behaviours from being published or broadcast, such as a television network refusing to broadcast

material that was considered offensive (Boyd-Barrett 1995). Gatekeeping practices online exist, but they are more marginal. Digital workers, often precariously employed, undertake everyday moderation for platforms and have sometimes been referred to as the "custodians of the Internet" (Gillespie 2018), meaning those charged with maintaining civil and legal behaviour and compliance with platform terms. It is widely recognised, however, that not only are the large numbers of moderators employed around the world unable to keep up with the workload, but that practices are inconsistent and they themselves are at risk of harm from persistent and regular exposure to hostility and hate speech (Roberts 2019). In this respect, while moderators mirror some of the more traditional gatekeeping practices, they are not positioned with the authority—or significant numbers—to prevent the normalisation of hostility online. Indeed, it is more useful to see the introduction of moderators, community managers and other digital workers performing gatekeeping roles as something new to combat the facilitation of hostile behaviours that emerged from the very design of digital communication as a site beyond gatekeeping.

- **Perception of distance**—this refers not only to geographic distance from a person who is being bullied or harmed but also the way in which non-real-time and non-facial aspects adjust the ability of an abuser to see the reaction or hurt on the face of the other in the act of doing or saying something harmful. The inherent capabilities of digital, networked communication are built around communicating 'at distance' and in both real-time and non-real-time frameworks. While there is nothing about this or other aspects of digital communication that turn people into bullies, it remains that a communicative framework in which the harms one might perpetrate cannot be witnessed on the face of the other is an aspect that enables digital culture to become more toxic than other, more traditional forms of real-time and face-to-face communication.

Despite digital hostility emerging from—and facilitated by—digital culture itself, there is a tendency in public debate and policy work on the issue to ignore its cultural roots and to maintain the idea that there are individual 'bad actors' who either work alone or in groups to harm another. The individualist approach to hostility online is not, in itself, surprising. We live in a contemporary, global society that is more-or-less usually marked by liberal-humanist approaches to law and behaviour, and these include at their core the primacy of the individual with agency to control their own behaviour. Such approaches often ignore how behavioural aspects become norms, and how people are disciplined by histories, institutions and practices to perform in particular ways, including ways that we might perceive as aggressive or harmful.

At the same time, some approaches to addressing victimisation online also perceive it as a matter of individuals—assigning responsibility to victims to manage their experience of online adversity, including often by recommending they withdraw from settings of heated public debate or hate speech or take time away from digital communication (Ordoñez and Nekmat 2019, p. 2500). Such approaches tend to elide the productive possibilities that emerge from understanding digital hostility as a culturally induced phenomenon, including its capacity to draw on extant practices of political polarisation (Bruns 2019, pp. 104–105), racism (Ringrose 2018), misogyny (Jane 2015) and homophobia (Thompson and Cover 2021). Individualised and technological-determinist approaches have limited capacity to account for the impact of 'massified' adversarial phenomena and the impact these have on identity and selfhood.

Niche literatures that help us begin to see online hostility in new, more appropriate registers are, however, beginning to emerge. These include nascent scholarship on the relationship between cultural misogyny and online harassment (Jane 2015; Banet-Weiser and Miltner 2016), the significance of mob mentality in the hostile pile-on (Thompson and Cover 2021), the advent of 'zoom bombing' during COVID-19 work from home as an emergent form of trolling (Tran 2021), the extent to which online hate speech can be equated with offline or face-to-face hate speech (Brown 2017) and the use of online hostility by far-right groups to undermine information quality (Fielitz and Marcks 2019). Together, this new literature is indicative of a desire to move beyond individualising approaches to both the experience and perpetration of digital hostility, of accounts that equate all hostility with cyberbullying practices and of seeking knowledge beyond the more pedestrian approaches that see online hostility as the fault of a 'few bad apples' (Dekker 2006) or, in the contemporary vernacular, in which "Haters Gonna Hate."

By perceiving the problem of digital hostility as a cultural one and not simply a matter of individual bad behaviour helps us break from those narrow, individualising models so that we can address the problem of harmful online behaviours as a matter for cultural practices of social engagement. This, in turn, opens the possibility of developing an understanding of the impact of hostility on identity coherence and social belonging and of social pedagogies grounded in ethics of non-violent use of online spaces. That is, the contemporary form of digital hostility as it has emerged over the past half-decade is a complex digital phenomenon in which hostility, threats and hate have become part of the normative cultural practice of digital media use, often taking an increasingly 'massified' form by a 'multitude' engaged in 'pile on' behaviour and mass shaming (Olweus and Limber 2018) and which can no longer be addressed through discourses of small-group or individual cyberbullying or content that can be determined to be insulting or aggressive speech acts.

A culturally focused approach opens the possibility, further, of developing ethical frameworks beyond individualist perspectives that can underpin the development of workable solutions, remedies and interventions. For example, when acts of digital hostility are seen not merely as individual or small-group repeated instances of harmful speech but as involving the relatively new phenomenon of 'massified' adversity, the disruption to identity and the labour of identity self-management occur together within a register different from those which can be addressed in an individualist conceptual framework. Significant here is that attention to the cultural–digital–identity triad prompts a new *ethical* approach that is attentive to the impact on identity and the related health and well-being risks of identity disruption. While, at its most extensive, ethical perspectives can serve as a social pedagogy to prompt norms of non-violent and non-exclusionary social behaviour, a culturally grounded ethics can also help key stakeholders, policymakers and service providers make sense of the urgency by which intervention in digital hostility is required.

6.4 Digital divides: misogyny and racism online

Before giving more detail on how digital hostility is implicated in the disruption of identity practices in digital communication settings in Section 6.5, it is useful to make a few remarks on how identity frameworks are used to create new forms of digital divide that make the experience of communicating online different for different groups of people.

The idea of a digital divide goes back to the early years of this century when concerns about access to digital technologies and infrastructure were beginning to be raised (Park

2017). These included particularly the global differences in access to digital, networked and mobile technologies across different regions of the world, as well as socioeconomic differences in some (primarily Western) countries whereby some groups, schools and regions enjoyed the financial access to digital networks in ways from which others were excluded. It also came to be recognised in the early 2000s that lack of earlier access or home access to digital technologies was creating a divide in the abilities and skills among school and higher education students (Attewell 2003; Friedman and Deek 2003). And, finally, it came to include those for whom disability meant reduced access to the interfaces that enabled digital communication (Hegarty et al. 2000).

More recently, however, Craig Haslop and colleagues (2021) have re-figured the concept of a digital divide to account for those who are excluded from certain ways of engaging online due to gender and the presence of high rates of misogyny in online settings. Misogyny came to be more widely recognised as a problem for digital culture in the wake of the 'GameGate' scandal which began in mid-2014, in which a widespread campaign of harassment of women gamers and the presence of feminist and progressive aspects of contemporary games was perpetrated by a widespread group of malcontents, arguably transforming into severe levels of hate speech on a grand scale (Flew 2021, p. 91).

GamerGate was not, of course, the first instance of widespread hate speech directed towards women online. As Emma Jane (2017), for example, has indicated, misogyny has for a much longer period been an element of online interactions experienced by women, even though it does not always form a core part of the public sphere debate about digital hostility and cyberbullying, which more often has focused on the impact of children and young adults. Jane asks a very important point about how we can start to perceive digital hostility directed towards women: is the articulation of misogynistic vitriol an "Internet phenomenon or are they the types of things men have always said or thought about women in private?" The same could be asked of racial hate speech. While institutional racism and race-based violence and stalking are very old and ongoing social problems, it is a considerable and well-recognised problem of digital hostility and hate speech (Daniels 2009)—is there something about digital communication that enables this form of digital hostility?

One aspect, of course, is that misogyny and racism are not new or re-emergent in online settings, in the same way that discrimination and hate speech in the forms of anti-disability, homophobia and other injurious speech about minorities is not new. What occurs, however, relates to an older laissez-faire approach to the Internet and digital communication which left most (not all) content not only broadly unregulated but represented digital communication as a site of radical free speech. Freedom of expression is, of course, enshrined in the constitution of the United States of America and, while many other countries do not have legislative protections for speech, the concept has often spilled out globally as an assumption that it is 'okay' to say what one thinks and that it is defensible on the basis of an assumed freedom of expression regardless of the injurious nature of the speech or the harms it produces. Free speech arguments are, of course, being questioned in emergent aspects of contemporary culture in response to online hostility. Thankfully, this questioning is helping to critique the boundaries of what is acceptable to say.

6.5 Identity and digital hostility

Although I have represented digital culture as marked by injurious and harmful behaviours and content, this is not, of course, to suggest that *all* everyday experiences of digital communication are settings of hate speech, threats, adversity and other forms of violent communication. Indeed, to suggest this would be to ignore the fact that users can be engaged in multiple forms of expression, intent and styles of communication, ranging from the adversarial to "purposeful discussion" (Murthy and Sharma 2018), and can be motivated by creative and ethical engagement (Burgess and Baym 2020). It is also to ignore the narrowcast framework of digital interactive communication (Cover 2006) with users operating through a matrix of interconnected, disconnected and discrete sites, all of which play a role in the production of interpretation, attitude and ethics, alongside operating as the complex setting in which identity is performed.

When faced with hostility and hate speech, however, the smooth play of performative identity is put at risk, undone or upset. To put the everydayness of mass online hostility into an identity perspective involves acknowledging from the beginning that the subjectivity of a user is not something which is brought to an online platform conceived only as a benign channel. Rather, identity and belonging are actively formed, constituted and shaped by online communication as much as any other cultural, social or communicative setting. Poststructuralist perspectives on identity, belonging and relationality have provided meaningful ways to understand how communication shapes, disciplines and normalises identity practices (Cover 2016). As we know from earlier chapters, Judith Butler's (1990) account of identity performativity is helpful for making sense of the utility of digital communication for identity performance because it allows us to perceive acts of online communication among the range of other corporeal, identity 'performances' that constitute the self.

For Butler, identity is 'performed' through the articulation of norms, cited from discourse, and that performance or communication retroactively lends the illusion of a coherent, unified and authorial self, with a sense of agency, social participation and belonging. In that sense, digital communication is not merely a tool through which a user communicates but an increasingly valuable cultural and discursive setting through which identity is actively performed, whether through older models of biographical profile development in which users "select a more or less complex representation of themselves" (Livingstone 2008, p. 403) or the more actively social and relational performances of online conversation, posting, tagging, tweeting, friending, unfriending and other real-time and asynchronous online engagement (Baym et al. 2007). In these communicative settings, the coherent, stable and unified subject is always an *effect* of those performances (Butler 1993, p. 12), lending the illusion of an inner identity core, or a user with complete agency and individuality behind the posts (Butler 1990).

As we know, all identity is constructed and contingent, and it is performed as a *process* towards unity, intelligibility and coherence in order to respond to the cultural demand that enables social participation and belonging (Butler 1997, p. 27). Because digital communication offers the tools for that process but does so in a highly interactive setting, our identity performances are subject to mutual surveillance, self-surveillance, revision, policing, normalisation and narrativisation of identity across both profile management, audio, visual and textual posts, conversations and cross-platform dialogue (boyd 2008, p. 128; Cover 2012). Given the extent to which online communication is central to everyday lives and is increasingly inseparable from other aspects of social life and liveability (Green 2008, p. 7), the experience of hostility, hate, exclusion, relegation and adversity in those settings upsets the *process* of identity.

It is, of course, important to bear in mind that digital settings and platforms are not at all sites of pure connectivity and social engagement but are themselves precarious networks built on arrangements of competing connectivities, fluidities, withdrawals, theatrics and engagements (Light 2014). Their significance, however, to social life in ways which are constitutive of identity call upon us for continued access and harmonious engagement in order to maintain the stability of our identities. When that 'connection' is lost or a subject is forced out from a meaningful network due to being widely shamed or subject to hate speech or aggressive trolling, the coherence of identity risks being undone because the setting becomes toxic or a space that it is no longer a space of equitable participation. This is, undoubtedly, more marked for those for whom online communication is the most significant part of identity performativity or in times (such as during the quarantining and social distancing of the COVID-19 pandemic) when online relationality might be the only form of public and social participation experienced by a subject.

From an ethical perspective, then, the digital settings we inhabit are settings that are not only meaningful but, when experienced as sites of overwhelming hostility or adversity, risk the undoing of the subject's ability to maintain the demand for intelligibility and recognition as a subject. Digital communication settings, like any other 'space,' are sites of mutual recognition in which all users make a demand to be addressed *as a (worthy) subject*. Judith Butler's statements on ethics—based not on individual conduct but the socially grounded responsibility to recognise the other as a subject—is a valuable guide for making sense of digital hostility and its impact. As Butler notes:

> When we recognize another, or when we ask for recognition for ourselves, we are not asking for an other to see us as we are, as we already are, as we have always been, as we were constituted prior to the encounter itself. Instead, in the asking, in the petition, we have already become something new, since we are constituted by virtue of the address, a need and desire for the Other that takes place in language in the broadest sense, one without which we could not be … It is also to stake one's own being, and one's own persistence in one's own being, in the struggle for recognition.
> (Butler 2004, p. 44)

That is, to engage in an online space as an *unavoidable contemporary part of sociality* is to have exposed one's self to social relationships that are constitutive of our identities. To be exposed to unwanted adversity, hostile or hate speech, to experience the 'pile on' by a massified group seeking to marginalise, to be shamed or excluded by an adversarial group claiming to represent the social norm, makes these online settings not just sites of hostility but of *instability*. In that sense, describing an online setting or experience as toxic or violent is not because it is insulting, but because it risks disrupting the identity coherence of the user, since that identity depends on recognition *as* a subject and social participation and belonging.

If we consider digital platforms conceptually as a 'spatial' setting for the relational and collective dimensions of digital practices (Third et al. 2020, p. 167), then it is important to acknowledge how the experience of massified hostility, adversity, beratement or hate speech is active in *shaming* a subject in ways which upset identity coherence, being made to feel that one "does not belong within a certain space" (Probyn 2004, p. 334). A user may have, for example, made a naïve post about a social issue or asked a question on a forum for which the answer is widely expected to be known or may have thoughtlessly shared an amusing but insensitive meme. Or a user may have contributed a social opinion such as that J.K. Rowling's stories remain enjoyable despite the author's views on transgender subjects within a forum discussing the issue with the bad luck that the forum might at that moment be dominated by those arguing for Rowling's censorship and be scolded by very large numbers of other users. The identity-based pleasures of engagement activated through *conversation*, the *sharing* of opinions, the *exploration* of contrasting viewpoints and the *synthesising* of collective intelligence (Levy 1997; Poster 2006) are *disrupted* by hostility, marking out a subject to feel shame, humiliation, marginalisation, exclusion or lost value or worthiness as a subject (McRobbie 2020, p. 8). Here, shaming operates as "the withdrawal of the approving gaze of loving acceptance" (Munt 2007, p. 224) which can be understood here as the withdrawal of online relationality produced across digital networks through the acceptance of a right to be present or to participate socially.

To be rejected, marginalised, excluded or unexpectedly subject to adversarial speech *en masse* in a digital site of attachment and identity meaning might be said to experience a disturbance in selfhood. Such a disturbance is what Cathy Caruth (1995), in her work on the psychology of trauma, refers to as an "event's essential incomprehensibility, the force of its *affront to understanding*" (p. 154). This can be understood, for example, to occur when a user is confronted with online aggression by a large number of people such that their *sense* of relationality with that online community is broadly re-orientation as an outsider, an excluded person or person 'of shame.' That is, where sociality is conducted in online settings as much as in any other, and where both the instantaneity of communication and the permanency of its record mark the performance of subjectivity online, an instance of *massified* hostility stands in for society or social norms. This prompts the undoing of a subject's intelligibility, coherence and recognition in ways which may be damaging, violent and unhealthy.

6.6 Mass shaming and the digital mob

To understand the contemporary experience of massified online hostility as a social violence, it is helpful to consider at a deeper level the operation of the Internet 'pile-on.' A Twitter pile-on, for example, describes the online cultural formation in which very large numbers of people using a platform make disparaging remarks, hate speech or otherwise humiliate or denigrate a single user (Marsden 2017). Sometimes, it is well-meaning, such as when large numbers join a mass calling-out of unethical behaviour (Hamad 2019). In other cases, it may be either an organised or non-organised activity of racism, anti-minority abuse, disinformation campaign, harassment, threats or victimisation (Ozduzen et al. 2021). In some instances, what begins as the former converges into elements of the latter, with increasingly exaggerated claims, menacing and intimidating statements made by ever-more people to the point that the target lacks the resources to count the number of hateful remarks—to 'take stock,' as it were, of the hostility. In this sense, the experience of hostility is not that as found in cyberbullying or other kinds of individual instances of hate speech which is detected by the identification of offensive content and the identification of a cooperative small group of perpetrators. Rather, it is a *new* framework of communicative experience in which it is impossible to point to individual instances of offensive speech (as it is the mass content that is offensive). And, further, the massified group presenting hostility, shaming, humiliation, hate, call-out or demands for cancellation *en masse* are no longer countable (or accountable) as *individuals*.

I am interested here in the effect of a pile-on from the perspective of what it means for self-identity when a user is berated or shamed by an uncountably large multitude of people who, by sheer numbers, come to stand in for the wider society. It is a form of digital hostility that warrants greater attention, primarily because the vast increase in users, the increased instantaneity of communication and the frameworks by which masses can respond on platforms such as Twitter and YouTube is somewhat different from the earlier kinds of bullying that operated across pre-platform Internet settings. In the instantaneity of comment and the desire for forms of communal belonging, a phenomenon with very profound negative outcomes for both users and the quality of debate has emerged, both drawing on and reinforcing other cultural shifts such as the polarisation of political, social and cultural opinion, racism and misogyny (Ringrose 2018) and the development of the angry theatrics of populist resentment (Cover 2020a).

Despite the narrowcast framework of digital media platforms (Cover 2006), the experience and language of the pile-on stands in for and represents the public in much the same way as the figure of the 'mass' or 'mob' in a geographically limited space. This is particularly marked when the hostility occurs in very public social media spaces (e.g., Twitter) but just as meaningful in sites of attachment such as semi-private and subscription-based online forums (Thompson and Cover 2021). While it is, of course, an oversimplification and indeed an inaccuracy to pre-figure the mass group engaged in a pile-on as 'anonymous' (Kennedy 2006, p. 859), in moving from being seen merely as a 'large group' of bullies to—instead—a very large, uncountable group making less-hostile individual content (when viewing each post on its own), the full body of content takes on the *form* of the anonymous by becoming not only too many users/posts to count but representative of the sociality—the mob, mass or multitude stands in for the public or society in a dichotomy between the subject and the mutual acts of violent speech of the others, made 'other.'

In drawing on the concept of the mass or mob, it is important not to characterise the participants in digital hostility within the frame of disparagement or contempt which has traditionally been associated with the figure of the masses and mass culture (Williams 2014, p. 192). The idea of a 'mob,' for example, depicts the concept of the large group of people as "a rabble, an unruly crowd," disorderly in their amorphousness and mobility and in need of regulation and governance (Urry 2007, p. 8). While the traditional contempt for a mob, mass or multitude is both unwarranted and illogical, it is at the same time important to differentiate—as does Butler (2015, pp. 134–135)—between the idea of the surging multitude and a large crowd who are assembled *democratically* for the purposes of, say, protest. In other words, not every mass crowd, group or mob is the same: the activities or beliefs that hold together a multitude need to be at the core of assessing their democratic potential. In that context, we might sometimes understand the mass pile-on calling out a person who has acted unethically (for example, through encouraging sexual harassment of women) is an act of popular assembly on behalf of democracy. At the same time, the multitude who pile-on with hate speech towards a minority designed to harm, insult or injure that person or that minority act outside of democratic speech.

There is an argument, therefore, that some 'call-out' shaming of subjects who have acted inappropriately has value in fostering more ethical relations or generating behavioural or social change (Probyn 2005). To give an alternative example, shaming may be productive when a public figure has used black face and is 'called out' in such a way as to draw attention to historical and continuing inequities and injustices—thereby demonstrating a wider community standard and serving as an *educational tool* for others to witness some of those community norms. However, we can make an alternative argument as well (because there is no necessary right answer about pile-on behaviour yet) that notes that mass call-out behaviour online risks burying the ethical intent of positively focused justice claims beneath a digital bombardment of overwhelmingly large numbers in adversity (Hamad and Liddle 2017). Such mass behaviour may work against the ethical perspective, because it does not have the capacity to produce the kind of institutional and cultural change that is more likely to come from the hard work of non-adversarial dialogue and sustained campaigns rather than belittling an individual for their archaic views (Hamad 2019).

Additionally, a pile-on that is calling out a figure who has said the 'wrong thing' may actually put that person's well-being at risk. In that sense, it may not be fully ethical to use pile-ons as a tool for social change if they are going to harm a person, even if their views are unpalatable and horrific. In one Australian case, a gay man who held moderately right-wing views and had made some anti-drag, transphobic and homophobic remarks was subject to a Twitter pile-on which resulted in his suicide (Thompson and Cover 2021). While his views were wrong—and, perhaps, he was still at the stage of 'working out' how to navigate his own identity that incorporated right-wing politics and a gay selfhood—he was not given the opportunity to learn and, sadly, possibly lacked the resilience to see the call-outs as an opportunity to reconsider his views. Obviously, no one should be driven to their death by being publicly shamed for holding a view, even if there are instances in which those views need to be challenged. In a digital era, we do not yet have a good set of mechanisms to know when to act and when to draw a line; when to speak out and when to recognise that if we all speak out we are piling-on in a way that may be harmful.

We might also look at this complex debate from the alternative side, the side of perpetrator identity. It may be important, in this sense, to bear in mind that the individual assailants in, say, a Twitter pile-on do not necessarily *perceive* themselves as the anonymous multitude but as individual actors working separately—indeed, some may not even be aware that they are part of a pile-on but only be aware of their own post calling out someone who has said something that warrants (in their view) shaming. Others, however, might be drawn to the pile-on not because they are that interested in the content, in calling someone out or in harming or injuring a minority, but because the pile-on forms a community of belonging which is a pleasurable thing to which to belong.

In theorising how the participants in a pile-on might recognise themselves, it is thus valuable to consider how practices of identification and group belonging operate. Just as, for example, a national population is constructed through an identificatory practice that combines racist, nationalist and exclusionary speech with "the brute force of great number" (Rancière 2016, p. 102) in order to reproduce and reinforce 'norms,' online groups, forums and temporary communities based in hostility or call-out are formed in the act of adversity towards a target, producing an affective relationality built upon the identification of the outsider (one who holds an alternative or marginal view). The content that makes that user an 'outsider' or 'unworthy' is snowballed by large numbers that are called upon to experience a temporary form of belonging as an affective pleasure of subjection to the perspective, opinion and discordant articulation of the multitude (Butler 1997, p. 27).

Just as a pre-digital audience was able to engage in the pleasures of a temporary community by recognising there was a "mutual link to a common readership [that] creates a kind of community to which they see themselves as belonging" (Wenger 1998, p. 182), a group engaged in a pile-on is positioned to recognise a mutual link in the shared utterance, citing the abuse or call-out, and repeating it such that it constitutes a node of performative identity in belonging to the pile-on. Again, what we can theorise is the victim's experience of being made vulnerable to digital hostility as the potential undoing of coherent or intelligible identity resulting from exclusion, marginalisation or differentiation from the multitude—from the community that excludes them. While intelligible identity can be constituted in difference, and many minorities have regularly found forms of healthy belonging at the margins of sociality (Cover 2019), exclusion from the multitude has the effect of calling upon subjects to position themselves along a normative curve and therefore to be rendered subjects of a certain kind of normativity.

6.7 Identity and cancelled subjectivity

If the act of shaming in a pile-on is as unhealthy for the victim as I've described it above, we might consider then a second framework through which digital hostility risks the unhealthy disruption of the subject. This could be said to occur when a user is positioned by the massified group to perceive themselves as an 'ungrievable' subject. Ungrievability is a concept introduced by Judith Butler (2004; 2009) to describe those whose lives are not considered worthy of grieving if they were to be lost, hurt or injured. We usually use this concept to understand how people in one part of the world may not care about, say, those who are left starving in another part of the world—that is, those who treat it as a simple fact rather than grieve the losses that have occurred elsewhere. At stake, for Butler (2009), is the fact that such people are 'framed off' to feel that they are interpreted in society as less worthy than, say, one's neighbours or members of one's own community or one's own family.

Of course, not everyone who is positioned as ungrievable sees themselves as ungrievable—as lives that would not matter if they were lost—but it becomes an interesting and useful way to think about how digital hostility disrupts identity if a hate speech, adversarial behaviour, pile-ons and bullying victimise a user because they are perceived as not mattering if they are forced out of an online community, forced off a platform or 'cancelled.' Are they victims of digital hostility because their absence would not be considered a loss, because we would not grieve their disappearance or their non-existence in our digital spaces?

An ungrievable subject, then, is a person or user considered by (some) others as not worthy of social norms of respectful, responsible or 'interested' discourse or being listened to (Dreher 2009) or worthy of belonging within a zone of public debate (Kirby 2015). Feeling that one's life is ungrievable (that it does not matter to others if it is harmed or lost) has been related to the breakdown of identity, to the expression of poor mental health and to several instances of suicidality, including in online contexts (Thompson and Cover 2021). This framework is therefore one which describes how online hate speech, pile-ons and other forms of mass hostility position subjects as inconsistent, undeserving, marginalised or non-belonging. These are felt as a result of the form of hate, insult or belligerence that has entered contemporary Western culture as a *populist* norm of communicative engagement (Ostiguy 2017), particularly online since 2016 with the instantaneity of politicised anti-minority hate, harassment, threats and insult (Nagle 2017, p. 10). Although insult itself is usually precluded from the kinds of regulation, legislation and policy that restricts certain types of speech, I would argue that in the context of the massification of insult—rather than the individual insulting remark—that a user can be positioned as a non-belonging outsider and thereby an ungrievable subject.

Insult, as a form of verbal aggression or violence, works upon the subject by shaping "the relation one has to others and to the world and thereby to shape the personality, the subjectivity, the very being of the individual in question" (Eribon 2004, p. 15). As a kind of act of speech or content, the insult that utilises recognisable hate speech serves as a "verdict" or judgement that both reduces the subject to that injurious statement (p. 17). As a form of online violence in which the insult is produced by the multitude rather than an identifiable individual or group, it positions the subject as unworthy of a liveable life that is, today, conditioned by participation in online communication. In that context, when someone calls me a 'fag' online, it is insulting and hurtful but I can argue against that person and restore my dignity and sense of self-worth. When a thousand people call me a fag, or ten thousand people tweet that LGBTQ people should be put to death, then we are in a different register of hate speech, one where the insult is now harmful because it *appears* and *feels* like the user is being judged by the whole of a society (even if 10,000 is not really that many—but who is counting? Who can count?).

To participate in online communication is in some ways to be vulnerable from the beginning to being positioned as an ungrievable subject for a mistake, an idea, an unthinking utterance or an unpopular view within a networked space. Increased online visibility and social presence is, as others have argued, at the cost of a heightened degree of vulnerability (Duffy and Hund 2019). Recognising vulnerability can be a key element in fostering ethical relationships of non-violence and mutual care in a social space. That, however, involves acknowledging the mechanisms, practices, norms and behaviours that prevent *some* people (or users) being recognised as vulnerable and therefore worthy of ethical relations (Butler 2009). In addressing an ethics of non-violence, Butler focused on national, racial and ethnic distinctions by analysing the ways in which members of one nation will grieve for lost members of that nation (during war for example), but that those who are lost from the other side are not recognised as human or worthy of such grieving (Butler 2009, pp. 22–23). We can extend that into digital culture by thinking about who is grieved and not grieved when forced from a digital space they have 'inhabited' and been effectively 'cancelled.'

To think about hostility in terms of 'cancel culture' requires acknowledging that it *might* sometimes be a part of digital hostility, although not necessarily quite the same as trolling, pile-ons or cyberbullying based in minority hatred. Nevertheless, it provides a good example of how removal of an 'ungrievable' person may be unethical. Cancel culture has been defined by Eve Ng (2020) as

> the withdrawal of any kind of support (viewership, social media follows, purchases of products endorsed by the person, etc.) for those who are assessed to have said or done something unacceptable or highly problematic, generally from a social justice perspective especially alert to sexism, heterosexism, homophobia, racism, bullying, and related issues.
>
> (p. 623)

It can often be enacted through pile-ons or regular beratement or insult that makes it impossible for that person to participate on a platform, in an online forum or more widely in public life. It may result in removal or banning from a platform if enough people call for it, or it might simply become too difficult ever to contribute online without being abused after a cancellation. Ng draws attention to the example of a musician who was called out and cancelled after it was publicly shared online that, while in high school, she had posted a laughing emoji in response to an instance in which a third party had been cyberbullied. Cancel culture is rooted in an expectation that a subject is politically and socially *unflawed*—one particular framing of the acceptable subject online. When an aspect of that user's past, whether a crime, a thoughtless act or a careless mistake that can be construed as politically incorrect (etc.) occurs, the frame by which that subject was considered a subject 'of worth' is dropped in favour of a frame by which that subject is deemed ungrievable—able to be cancelled, with calls for their eradication from social life.

Although cancel culture is problematic and complex, and emerges from a confluence of contemporary social changes, it is a problem of digital hostility because it occurs in contexts beyond aggressor/victim dichotomies but in ways that may be unethical if they do not allow a user to explain, to apologise, to beg social forgiveness, to correct a mistake or to be treated as worthy of hearing our response. To think about cancel culture, then, we might do something different from considering 'positive' and 'negative' forms of mass online shaming and instead focus on the idea of the 'mass.' Where a user's identity has been altered from *member of an online community* to *cancelled*, we witness the potential for identity disruption in ways which may be harmful for their sense of liveability and resilience and, as I have indicated, result in suicidality in some extreme cases of exclusion, forced isolation and a felt sense of being eradicated from the cohabitation of online communities (Cover 2020b). In this case, the pile-on, mass complaints or mob humiliation that calls for the subject to be cancelled is one which is experienced not through public engagement and discourse towards a *judgement*; rather, it is to be considered *prejudicial*. This is because regardless of the time each person might take posting an item of hate speech, the pile-on is received and perceived in instantaneity: the realisation that one is no longer welcome in what is perceived as 'society.'

Instantaneity "exposes the temporal incompatibility of Twitter with our conventional definitions of what is news, what separates fact from opinion, and subjectivity from objectivity" (Papacharissi 2015, p. 44). In much the same way, such instantaneity there or on other platforms exposes the problematic framework through which identity is constructed in the context of fast-changing discourses, online storytelling, ways of being and online belonging. Further, the instantaneousness of online communication has been identified as a key factor in hostile online behaviour and the dissemination of hate speech (Brown 2018). When hostile speech comes into the equation, what we see is the *reconfiguration* of the victim who is positioned to recognise themselves as ungrievable or unworthy of continuing in that space. It is therefore not the instance of the hate speech *content* that is of concern; rather it is the felt experience of instantaneity in opening one's Twitter feed and finding that hundreds of users have piled-on with a call for removal. The user is thereby positioned to perceive themselves as not having been worth retaining, keeping, part of the community.

While, of course, many users will have the social resilience, supportive networks, sense of significance or sophisticated ways of apprehending hostility, vulnerability is not democratically or equitably shared among all users, and some will be more vulnerable to the dissolutional effects of hostility than others. An ethics that recognises the violence of the multitude (even when individual instances of hostile content are mild or fall short of regulatory definitions of offence) and the impact of massified hostility on the user's sense of worth (as a grievable subject) is not, of course, in itself a remedy to digital hostility. Rather, as with all poststructuralist ethics (Ferrarese 2011, p. 11), it is the starting point, motivation, goal and grounding by which regulatory, interventional, pedagogical and support solutions need to be developed if they are to be more than simple interventions with (and penalisation of) individuals.

6.8 Conclusion

If digital hostility is to be understood as a matter of an encroaching norm in digital culture rather than instances of individual 'bad behaviour' or occasional 'insulting content,' and if we remember that identity is performed in the relational space of online belonging, then we have two things to think about for the future of digital communication:

1. how adversarial behaviour and hate speech emerge from a range of complex social factors and, therefore, how to design global and local interventions that address those factors rather than protect freedom of expression or find ways to restrict online content and activity; and,
2. how to develop an ethical approach that is attentive to the harms hostile behaviour does to a user's identity when they are victimised or made vulnerable in online settings.

To seek a remedy for digital hostility in everyday online settings is not, of course, to call for the shutting down of online debate or spaces in which ideas are strongly contested. Rather, it means looking for how we can ensure the digital ecology remains a 'safe' space without saying it is 'safe' for everyone to say whatever comes into their minds.

To say this is not just to invoke a nostalgic idea of the early Internet as a sophisticated site for liberal engagement, knowledge sharing and collective intelligence, since that is both a different era and a different Internet. Rather, it is to say that if we are to protect the digital ecology as a space in which identities are performed, we may need to consider setting obligations on *all* users firstly to recognise how some speech (e.g., hate speech) and some online activities (e.g., joining in on a pile-on) might be violent and harmful and, secondly, to find ways not to do violence to identities themselves by recognising that everyone online is in some ways vulnerable, and our vulnerability is what we share among each other from the very beginning (Butler 2004).

In some respects, this may mean that the future of digital communication as a site for identity warrants a better form of 'digital citizenship.' Digital citizenship is a concept increasingly used in education to encourage users to develop the skills and knowledge to use digital media safely and respectfully (McCosker et al. 2016; Black et al. 2022). Digital citizenship provides an analytic lens to understand 'the social, political, economic and environmental consequences of technologies in everyday life' and to 'build alternative and emancipatory technological practices' (Emejulu and McGregor 2019). Understanding that a safe online experience is paramount to good social participation, well-being and a stable digital economy (Brevini 2020), we need to work together to reconceptualise the interface between cultural identity (as a user), hostility (as an emergent communicative norm) and how ethical participation in online spaces supports well-being to protect us all from our inherent vulnerability to harm online.

Key points

- Digital hostility, hate speech and adversity are increasing problems, and early statistics are showing that it is widespread with large numbers of people experiencing hate speech, trolling and aggressive online behaviour.
- Digital hostility creates new forms of 'digital divide' for those routinely subject to it, particularly among women and racial minorities.

- Just as identities are formed and sustained in online settings and across platforms, digital hostility and the feeling of having to withdraw from those settings and platforms can destabilise a sense of identity (in addition to well-being and liveability).
- Cancellation, shaming, pile-ons and other behaviour that may be well-meaning when grounded in social justice claims might also victimise a person whose views ought to change or whom one is trying to educate—using forms of digital hostility for benevolent purposes may harm others.

References

Attewell, P., Suazo-Garcia, B. and Battle, J., 2003. Computers and young children: social benefit or social problem? *Social Forces*, 82 (1), 277–296.

Bartlett, A., Clarke, K. and Cover R., 2019. *Flirting in the Era of #MeToo: Negotiating Intimacy*. London: Palgrave.

Banet-Weiser, S. and Miltner, K.M., 2016. # MasculinitySoFragile: culture, structure, and networked misogyny. *Feminist Media Studies*, 16 (1), 171–174.

Bauman, S., Toomey, R.B. and Walker, J.L., 2013. Associations among bullying, cyberbullying, and suicide in high school students. *Journal of Adolescence*, 36 (2), 341–350. https://doi.org/10.1016/j.adolescence.2012.12.001

Baym, N.K., Zhang, Y.B., Kunkel, A., Ledbetter, A. and Lin, M., 2007. Relational quality and media use in interpersonal relationships. *New Media & Society*, 9 (5), 735–752.

Beckett, J., 2017. The media dangerously misuses the word 'trolling.' *The Conversation*, 3 July. Available from: https://theconversation.com/the-media-dangerously-misuses-the-word-trolling-79999#:~:text=The%20word%20%E2%80%9Ctrolling%E2%80%9D%20has%20become,on%20how%20to%20protect%20yourself [Accessed 2 April 2022].

Berners-Lee, T., 2019. *30 Years On, What's Next #ForTheWeb*? Available from: https://webfoundation.org/2019/03/web-birthday-30/ [Accessed 2 April 2022].

Bilewicz, M. and Soral, W., 2020. Hate speech epidemic: the dynamic effects of derogatory language on intergroup relations and political radicalization. *Advances in Political Psychology*, 41 (1), 3–33.

Black, R., Walsh, L., Waite, C., Collin, P., Third, A. and Idriss, S., 2022. In their own words: 41 stories of young people's digital citizenship. *Learning, Media and Technology*. DOI: 10.1080/17439884.2022.2044848

boyd, d., 2008. Why youth (heart) social network sites: the role of networked publics in teenage social life. *In*: D. Buckingham, ed. *Youth, Identity, and Digital Media*. Cambridge, MA: MIT Press, 119–142.

Boyd-Barrett, O., 1995. Conceptualizing the 'public sphere.' *In*: O. Boyd-Barrett and C. Newbold, eds. *Approaches to Media: A Reader*. London: Arnold, 230–234.

Brevini, B., 2020. *Amazon: Understanding a Global Communication Giant*. London and New York: Routledge.

Brown, A., 2017. What is hate speech? *Law & Philosophy*, 36 (4), 419–468.

Brown, A., 2018. What is so special about online (as compared to offline) hate speech? *Ethnicities*, 18 (3), 297–326.

Bruns, A., 2019. *Are Filter Bubbles Real?* London: Polity.

Burgess, J. and Baym, N., 2020. *Twitter: A Biography*. New York: New York University Press.

Burnap, P. and Williams M.L., 2015. Cyber hate speech on twitter: an application of machine classification and statistical modeling for policy and decision making. *Policy & Internet*, 7 (2), 223–242.

Butler, J., 1990. *Gender Trouble: Feminism and the Subversion of Identity*. London & New York: Routledge.

Butler, J., 1993. *Bodies That Matter: On the Discursive Limits of 'Sex.'* London & New York: Routledge.

Butler, J., 1997. *The Psychic Life of Power: Theories in Subjection*. Stanford, CA: Stanford University Press.

Butler, J., 2004. *Precarious Life*. London: Verso.

Butler, J., 2009. *Frames of War: When is Life Grievable?* London and New York: Verso.

Butler, J., 2015. *Notes Toward a Performative Theory of Assembly*. Cambridge, Mass. and London: Harvard University Press.

Caruth, C., 1995. Recapturing the past. *In:* C. Caruth, ed. *Trauma: Explorations in Memory*. Baltimore, MD: Johns Hopkins University Press, 151–157.

Chalmers, C., Campbell, M., Spears, B., Butler, D., Cross, D., Slee, P. and Kift S., 2016. School policies on bullying and cyberbullying: perspectives across three Australian states. *Educational Research,* 58 (1), 91–109.

Christchurch Call, 2019. *Christchurch Call to Eliminate Violent and Terrorist Content*. Available from: www.christchurchcall.com [Accessed 3 April 2022].

Cleland, J., 2017. Online racial hate speech. *In:* E. Martellozzo and E.A. Jane, eds. *Cybercrime and its Victims*. London: Routledge, 131–147.

Cohen, D.S. and Connon, K., 2015. Strikethrough (fatality): the origins of online stalking of abortion providers. *Slate,* 21 May. Available from: https://slate.com/news-and-politics/2015/05/neal-horsley-of-nuremberg-files-died-true-threats-case-reconsidered-by-supreme-court-in-elonis.html [Accessed 1 June 2022].

Cover, R., 2006. Audience inter/active: interactive media, narrative control and reconceiving audience history. *New Media & Society,* 8 (1), 213–232.

Cover, R., 2012. Performing and undoing identity online: social networking, identity theories and the incompatibility of online profiles and friendship regimes. *Convergence,* 18 (2), 177–193.

Cover, R., 2016. *Digital Identities: Creating and Communicating the Online Self*. London: Elsevier.

Cover, R., 2019. *Emergent Identities: New Sexualities, Gender and Relationships in a Digital Era*. London & New York: Routledge.

Cover, R., 2020a. Vulnerability and the discourse of 'forgotten people': populism, population and cultural change. *Continuum: Journal of Media & Cultural Studies,* 34 (5), 749–762.

Cover, R., 2020b. Subjective connectivity: rethinking loneliness, isolation and belonging in discourses of minority youth suicide. *Social Epistemology,* 34 (6), 566–576.

Cover, R., 2022. Digital hostility: contemporary crisis, disrupted belonging and self-care practices. *Media International Australia,* 184 (1), 79–91.

Daniels, J., 2009. *Cyber Racism: White Supremacy Online and the New Attack on Civil Rights*. Landham, MD: Rowman & Littlefield.

Davis, M., 2021. The online anti-public sphere. *European Journal of Cultural Studies,* 24 (1), 143–159.

Dekker, S., 2006. *The Field Guide to Understanding Human Error*. London: Ashgate.

Dreher, T., 2009. Listening across difference: media and multiculturalism beyond the politics of voice. *Continuum: Journal of Media & Cultural Studies,* 23 (4), 445–458.

Duffy, B.E. and Hund, E., 2019. Gendered visibility on social media: Navigating Instagram's authenticity bind. *International Journal of Communication,* 13 (2019), 4983–5002.

Emejulu, A. and McGregor, C., 2019. Towards a radical digital citizenship in digital education. *Critical Studies in Education,* 60 (1), 131–147.

Eribon, D., 2004. *Insult and the Gay Self,* M. Lucey, trans. Durham, NC & London: Duke University Press.

eSafety Commissioner, 2020. *Online Hate Speech*. Available from: www.esafety.gov.au/sites/default/files/2020-01/Hate%20speech-Report.pdf [Accessed 1 April 2022].

Ferrarese, E., 2011. Judith Butler's 'not particularly postmodern insight' of recognition. *Philosophy & Social Criticism,* 37 (7), 759–773.

Fielitz, M. and Marcks, H., 2019. *Digital Fascism: Challenges for the Open Society in Times of Social Media*. Berkeley Center for Right-Wing Studies Working Paper Series. Available from: https://escholarship.org/uc/item/87w5c5gp [Accessed 28 July 2021].

Flew, T., 2021. *Regulating Platforms*. Cambridge: Polity.

Friedman, R.S. and Deek, F.P., 2003. Innovation and education in the digital age: reconciling the roles of pedagogy, technology, and the business of learning. *IEEE Transactions on Engineering Management,* 50 (4), 403–412.

Gillespie T., 2018. *Custodians of the Internet: Platforms, Content Moderation, and the Hidden Decisions that Shape Social Media*. New Haven, CT: Yale University Press.

Golbeck, J., ed., 2018. *Online Harassment*. Gewerbestrasse: Springer.

Gorman, G., 2019. *Troll Hunting: Inside the World of Online Hate and its Human Fallout*. Melbourne: Hardie Grant.

Green, L., 2008. Is it meaningless to talk about 'the Internet'? *Australian Journal of Communication*, 35 (3), 1–14.

Hamad, R., 2019. Internet pile-ons are no substitute for real life change. *Get Up! Colour Code*. Available from: www.colourcode.org.au/ [Accessed 21 September 2020].

Hamad, R. and Liddle, C., 2017. Intersectionality? Not while feminists participate in pile-ons. *The Guardian*, 11 October. Available from: www.theguardian.com/commentisfree/2017/oct/11/intersectionality-not-while-feminists-participate-in-pile-ons [Accessed 1 June 2022].

Haslop, C., O'Rourke, F. and Southern, R., 2021. #NoSnowflakes: the toleration of harassment and an emergent gender-related digital divide, in a UK student online culture. *Convergence: The International Journal of Research into New Media Technologies*, 27 (5), 1418–1438.

Hegarty, J., Bostock, S. and Collins, D., 2000. Staff development in information technology for special needs: a new, distance-learning course. *British Journal of Educational Technology*, 31 (3), 199–212.

Hinduja, S. and Patchin, J.W., 2010. Bullying, cyberbullying, and suicide. *Archives of Suicide Research*, 14 (3), 206–221.

Jane, E.A., 2015. Flaming? What flaming? The pitfalls and potentials of researching online hostility. *Ethics and Information Technology*, 17 (1), 65–87.

Jane, E.A., 2017. *Misogyny Online: A Short (and Brutish) History*. London: Sage.

Kennedy, H., 2006. Beyond anonymity, or future directions for internet identity research. *New Media & Society*, 8 (6), 859–876.

KhosraviNik, M. and Esposito, E., 2018. Online hate, digital discourse and critique: exploring digitally-mediated discursive practices of gender-based hostility. *Lodz Papers in Pragmatics*, 14 (1), 45–68.

Kirby, V., 2015. Transgression: normativity's self-inversion. *Differences: A Journal of Feminist Cultural Studies*, 26 (1), 96–116.

Lévy, P., 1997. *Collective Intelligence: Mankind's Emerging World in Cyberspace*. New York: Plenum.

Lewis, R., Rowe, M. and Wiper, C., 2017. Online abuse of feminists as an emerging form of violence against women and girls. *British Journal of Criminology*, 57 (6), 1462–1481.

Light, B., 2014. *Disconnecting with Social Networking Sites*. London: Palgrave.

Livingstone, S., 2008. Taking risk opportunities in youthful content creation: teenagers' use of social networking sites for intimacy, privacy and self-expression. *New Media & Society*, 10 (3), 393–411.

Lumsden, K. and Morgan, H., 2017. Media framing of trolling and online abuse: silencing strategies, symbolic violence, and victim blaming. *Feminist Media Studies*, 17 (6), 926–940.

Marsden, M., 2017. In defence of the internet 'pile on.' *Sydney Morning Herald*, 22 June. Available from: www.smh.com.au/lifestyle/in-defence-of-the-internet-pile-on-20170621-gwvh2z.html [Accessed 23 June 2017].

Marwick, E. and Lewis, R., 2017. *Media Manipulation and Disinformation Online*. Data & Society Research Institute. Available from: https://datasociety.net/wp-content/uploads/2017/05/DataAndSociety_MediaManipulationAndDisinformationOnline-1.pdf [Accessed 31 May 2022].

McCosker, A., Vivienne, S. and Johns, A., eds., 2016. *Negotiating Digital Citizenship: Control, Contest and Culture*. London: Rowman & Littlefield.

McMahon, C., 2014. Why we need a new theory of cyberbullying. *SSRN Electronic Journal* Available from: https://papers.ssrn.com/sol3/papers.cfm?abstract_id=2531796 [Accessed 12 January 2020].

McRobbie, A., 2020. *Feminism and the Policies of Resilience: Essays on Gender, Media and the End of Welfare*. Cambridge: Polity.

Munn, L., 2019. Alt-right pipeline: individual journeys to extremism online. *First Monday,* 24 (6). DOI: 10.5210/fm.v24i6.10108.

Munt, S., 2007. *Queer Attachments: The Cultural Politics of Shame.* Aldershot: Ashgate.

Murthy, D. and Sharma, S., 2018. Visualizing YouTube's comment space: online hostility as a networked phenomena. *New Media & Society,* 21 (1), 191–213.

Nagle, A., 2017. *Kill all Normies: The Online Culture Wars from Tumblr and 4chan to the Alt-Right and Trump.* Alresford: Zero Books.

Ng, E., 2020. No grand pronouncements here …: reflections on cancel culture and digital media participation. *Television & New Media,* 21 (6), 621–627.

Olweus, D. and Limber, S.P., 2018. Some problems with cyberbullying research. *Current Opinion in Psychology,* 19 (Feb), 139–143.

Ordoñez, M.A.M. and Nekmat, E., 2019. 'Tipping point' in the SoS? Minority-supportive opinion climate proportion and perceived hostility in uncivil online discussion. *New Media & Society,* 21 (11–12), 2483–2504.

Ostiguy, P., 2017. Populism: a socio-cultural approach. *In:* C.R. Kaltwasser, P. Taggart, P. Ochoa Espejo and P. Ostiguy, eds, *The Oxford Handbook of Populism.* Oxford: Oxford University Press. Online edition. DOI: 10.1093/oxfordhb/9780198803560.013.3

Ozduzen, O., Korkut, U. and Ozduzen, C., 2021. 'Refugees are not welcome': digital racism, online placemaking and the evolving categorization of Syrians in Turkey. *New Media & Society,* 23 (11), 3349–3369.

Papacharissi, Z., 2015. *Affective Publics: Sentiment, Technology, and Politics.* Oxford: Oxford University Press.

Park, S., 2017. *Digital Capital.* London: Palgrave.

Peebles, E., 2014. Cyberbullying: hiding behind the screen. *Paediatrics & Child Health,* 19 (10), 527–528.

Phillips, W., 2015. *This is Why We Can't Have Nice Things: The Relationship Between Online Trolling and Mainstream Culture.* Cambridge, MA: MIT Press.

Poster, M., 2006. *Information Please: Culture and Politics in the Age of Digital Machines.* Durham, NC: Duke University Press.

Probyn, E., 2004. Everyday shame. *Cultural Studies,* 18 (2/3), 328–349.

Probyn, E., 2005. *Blush: Faces of Shame.* Minneapolis: University of Minnesota Press.

Rancière, J., 2016. The populism that is not to be found. *In:* A. Badiou, P. Bourdieu, J. Butler, G. Didi-Huberman, S. Khiari and J. Rancière, eds. *What Is a People?* New York: Columbia University Press, 101–105.

Ringrose, J., 2018. Digital feminist pedagogy and post-truth misogyny. *Teaching in Higher Education,* 23 (5), 647–656.

Roberts, S.T., 2019. *Behind the Screen: Content Moderation in the Shadows of Social Media,* New Haven, CT: Yale University Press.

Seymour, R., 2019. *The Twittering Machine.* London: Verso.

Smith, P.K. Mahdavi, J., Carvalho, M., Fisher, S., Russell, S. and Tippett, N., 2008. Cyberbullying: its nature and impact in secondary school pupils. *The Journal of Child Psychology and Psychiatry,* 49 (4), 376–385.

Suzor, N., 2019. *Lawless: The Secret Rules that Govern our Digital Lives.* Cambridge: Cambridge University Press.

Third, A., Collin, P., Walsh, L. and Black, R., 2020. *Young People in Digital Society: Control Shift,* London: Palgrave.

Thompson, J.D. and Cover, R., 2021. Digital hostility, internet pile-ons, and shaming: a case study. *Convergence: The International Journal of Research into New Media Technologies.* Online first. DOI: 10.1177/13548565211030461.

Tran, C.H., 2021. Stream(Age) queens: zoom-bombs, glitter bombs & other doctoral fairy tales. *Communication, Culture and Critique,* 14 (2), 356–360.

Urry, J., 2007. *Mobilities.* Cambridge: Polity.

Waldek, L., Droogan, J. and Lumby, C., 2021. *Feeling terrified? The emotions of online violent extremism.* Cambridge: Cambridge University Press.

Wenger, E., 1998. *Communities of Practice: Learning, Meaning, and Identity.* Cambridge: Cambridge University Press.

Williams, R., 2014. *Keywords: A Vocabulary of Culture and Society.* London: Fourth Estate.

7 Agencies
Algorithms, choices and artificial decision-making

7.1 Introduction

Since the early 2010s, there has been some considerable 'alarmism' in public debate about the role played by what is sometimes referred to as "algorithmic culture" or "social media algorithms" (Hristova et al. 2021, pp. 2–3). Algorithms themselves are complex frameworks for computerised calculations that drive various feeds, manage how artificial decisions are made by computers without human intervention and sometimes on our behalf and make available and unavailable various knowledges that frame how we think about ourselves and how we enact and shape our identities. However, how algorithms are *perceived* and *talked about* in contemporary culture perhaps has an even bigger impact on how we make sense of ourselves in relation to digital technologies. Public concerns about hidden algorithms, the collection of our usage statistics as part of 'big data,' the role of machine learning and artificial decision-making in shaping what content is encountered in an overcrowded information ecology have, in some ways, become the most heated area of debate about digital technology in everyday lives over the past decade (Light 2014, pp. 35–36).

If we want to understand the role of algorithmic culture and the increasing dominance of sophisticated calculation used in artificial decision-making in digital settings, and how it may participate in shaping contemporary identity practices, behaviours and knowledge, then we need to be careful not to see algorithms as something *in themselves* that are harmful, external to culture or an imposition on everyday life. In some ways, of course, algorithms are very useful. They cut the time-cost of human labour to make calculations—for example, the time it takes to curate an online newspaper's positioning of news articles in a 24-hour news cycle. This previously required the constant attention of an editor who, relying on their own experience as well as their bias, had to make relatively objective decisions about which items of news were more newsworthy than the next. While this is still the practice among many online news sites, algorithms have been deployed to help because they automate that process by very quickly and round-the-clock being able to assess and calculate how one news story is becoming more significant than others around the world (Svensson 2022, p. 119). The upside is that it frees up journalists and editors to spend more time on their traditional work. The downside is that the pre-programmed biases in that algorithmic process may prefer certain 'kinds' of news stories more than others and unwittingly feed into making a news item more popular. If the interface does not allow regular human intervention, it also means losing the value of 'instinct' and 'gut feeling' of an editor that has been developed through experience in order to 'sense' which stories are going to be more important than others. Here, the

DOI: 10.4324/9781003296652-7

algorithm itself is not at fault—rather, as Jakob Svensson (2022) points out, systems that see the algorithm's recommendations as *superior* to that of the human editor are more alarming, particularly given the role of news outlets in shaping public attitudes.

At a more personal level, the calculative power of algorithms to make content recommendations is also a time-saver, doing work on our own behalf. For example, streaming service Netflix uses algorithms that attempt to determine from my viewing habits what kinds of content I would like to watch and thereby make recommendations to me that hold my attention and require me to maintain a subscription (Lobato 2019). That is actually quite valuable to me, because there is so much content on Netflix— alongside so many other streaming services—that it is too labour-intensive for me to scroll through all titles, read the descriptions and make a decision on how I would like to be entertained on my Saturday afternoon when it is raining. At the same time, of course, there is a sacrifice: what is recommended might be limiting me to content that is similar to the content I have watched before. So part of the anxiety over algorithms in our everyday life is not so much that they are controlling our choices, but that there has been a substantial shift in how we are *presented* with choices—the TV Guide listing the day's shows that I remember from my childhood, or scanning the tape covers in a video hire store, are distant but fondly remembered experiences in a world that sometimes feels overloaded with media content.

At the same time, of course, I am not depending only on the algorithm to make those recommendations for me: no one lives in a Netflix bubble, we access information about entertainment content in a vast variety of ways, whether that is news on new releases, tracking an actor's filmography on imdb.com, stumbling across recommendations from friends on Facebook and so on. And then, from a slightly different perspective, I might find the algorithm offensive: if perhaps I watched a few LGBTQ+ themed items on Netflix, I might find myself profiled by a pre-programmed algorithm as a queer man who *only* watched LGBTQ+ content—not just a narrowing of my choices but a perception of *who I am* in a way that links a sexual identity with stereotypes of media and entertainment taste. Someone else might be grateful that an algorithm has made a calculation to recommend some content based on viewing patterns. And someone else again might be put at risk by what that algorithm might appear to reveal about taste, interest or a viewing history.

In other words, to understand the anxiety over algorithms and the extent to which they may be shaping our identities by curtailing our agency to make fully informed choices warrants us stepping back, looking at the context in which they operate and understanding how the public reaction to algorithms is sometimes conditioned by moral panics over emergent technologies. If we do that, we are in a better position to make sense of what role is played by algorithms in shaping our identities, our sense of who we are and how we are shaped by information we did not always choose and knowledge frameworks over which we have reduced capacity to access.

To do so, I would like to start by presenting a reaction to the 2020 Netflix documentary *The Social Dilemma* which gained substantial popularity after its international release and increased the alarmism over the role of algorithms and artificial decision-making in social media. While the documentary was not the first major public discussion about algorithmic culture, it was notable for leading to considerable public upset about the perceived role major platform corporations play in shaping knowledge and behaviour. This is followed by breaking down some of the ways we can make sense of algorithms in everyday life and as a *part* of the digital culture that both emanates from and participates in constituting identity. Three factors are important for identity in the context of algorithms: the role poor or unthinking modelling used by algorithms can play in embedding identity inequalities; the ways in which algorithms participate in the making available and unavailable of discourses and knowledges that are used in the construction of identity; and, finally, questions of agency and choice, particularly in terms of understanding what (if anything) we can even consider agency, whether or not we do really make choices ourselves in the first place, and if algorithmic culture is doing something to further enable or curtail any sense of agency over our identities, knowledge and behaviour.

7.2 The Social Dilemma

The Netflix documentary, *The Social Dilemma* (directed by Jeff Orlowski), was released worldwide in September 2020 during the first year of the COVID-19 pandemic when many people around the world were following social distancing and lockdown measures and thus paying more attention to screens in their homes. Concerns about the role played by platforms in COVID-19 disinformation and denial were significant (Cover et al. 2022), and much of the world was watching the lead-up to the presidential election in the United States of America with widespread news coverage concerned about platform polarisation. The documentary interviews several former key players in Silicon Valley digital enterprises, almost all expressing concern about the business models of social networking platforms, the role of algorithms in intensifying engagement, the perception of digital addiction by young people to their platform feeds and the extent to which social media is changing individual and community identities.

Interviews were interspersed with dramatisations focused on a single family—a mother (Barbara Gehring), her son Ben (Skyler Gisondo) and her two daughters Cassandra and Isla (Kara Hayward and Sophia Hammons), as well as three characters representing social media artificial intelligence (AI) by anthropomorphising AI as human beings surveiling and prompting for teenager Ben's attention. Broadly well received by commentators and reviewers, the documentary was also criticised for scapegoating digital industries for more complex social problems (Facebook 2020), for its reliance on old tropes of technology harming society (Malhotra 2020) and for its intense dramatisation of danger, social change and technological harm (Newton 2020).

From a more scholarly perspective, the documentary needs to be criticised for what is known as its technological determinism. *Technological determinism* is a view that understands society as being singularly shaped by media technologies, often in a way which perceives technology as being somehow external to culture, an accidental invention, introduced and changing how and why we do things, think, create, perceive ourselves and our identities. It is often juxtaposed with *cultural approaches to technology* that, instead, recognise that technological developments are always actively sought out as a response to a genuine cultural need. For example, while popular accounts like to see television as being the clever invention of John Logie Baird, the reality from a cultural perspective is that a massive investment of knowledge, time, infrastructure and human labour went into the development of television to meet the cultural demand for moving images to be accessible in the private home during a time in the twentieth century in which the domestic space was playing a greater role as a space of social engagement (Williams 1990).

In the same way, the use of algorithms in social media platforms and artificial decision-making is not something that was invented in a basement laboratory for a Silicon Valley corporation. Rather, the need for faster computing processes to take on some of the increasing labour of a digitised communication setting was already at play in culture. An active investment in research and development was underway in many parts of the world, building on existing knowledges and producing various tools for calculating outcomes based on the processing of very large sets of statistics or 'big data.' Technological development and social practices are always *mutually* shaping each other, rather than one determining another (Livingstone 2008, p. 396), and this means we need to acknowledge how algorithmic culture is shaped by existing social needs, rather than *only* see cultural change as brought about by algorithmic culture.

However, by positioning algorithms as technologically determining our everyday culture and lives, the *Social Dilemma* participates in what many technological-determinist perspectives have done about past communication technologies: created *moral panic*. Moral panics work by selecting a person, group, episode or artefact and labelling it as a threat to dominant values or practices (Cohen 2011). Indeed, new communication technologies have often been the subject of moral panic, including the proliferation of digital games which were seen to be addictive and produce violence (Cover 2004; 2007) or social media which has been seen to have an 'undisciplining' effect on users (Walsh 2020). And this is precisely what *The Social Dilemma* does, through its generation of anxiety that algorithms used by major platforms are insidious, controlling and threatening to stability. The moral panic is underscored in the film by the dramatic use of music, the emphatic conviction of its very select group of interviewees, the dramatisation of family breakdown resulting from algorithms, children becoming uncontrollable or addicted to their smartphones (in one case, the daughter smashing a locked box in front of her family in belligerent disobedience of her mother to regain her confiscated phone) and, perhaps most importantly, a singular set of simple statements with no genuine debate, dissent or complexification of the issues.

The documentary, however, does make six points which are interesting assessments of contemporary algorithmic culture—if a little too simplistic—that are worth unpacking. I would like to address them in this order: concerns about the profit motivation of platforms using algorithms, that algorithms are deliberately used to change behaviour, that algorithms increase the 'addictiveness' of digital media, that they are deployed in surveillance of platform users, that algorithms are responsible for the social and political polarisation experienced over the past decade and that algorithmic culture is generating unhealthy habits among young people by encouraging them to seek social approval online.

7.2.1 Algorithms used to increase advertising revenue

The first point is the observation that algorithms are used to generate, maximise and sustain user *attention* in order to expose users to a greater number of online advertisements. This is, of course, a verifiable experience of algorithms used to manage feeds. For example, while I find some algorithm-based feeds to be useful because they save me some time, it is true that the *purpose* of the algorithm is not to altruistically help me but to create profit by showing to advertisers that users are spending a certain amount of time, thereby enabling the platform to sell advertising space at the maximum price. Unfortunately, *The Social Dilemma* decries this as if it were something new, insidious and a matter for social anxiety. The tendency to decry practices that seek to maximise attention in order to increase revenue is made throughout the documentary without ever once noting that this has been the practice of print newspapers and commercial radio and television across much of the previous century.

The alarmist tones in which we hear that our attention itself is the product to be on-sold to advertisers are misplaced, since we have been living with that particular contemporary capitalist model of media for generations. Indeed, anyone who studied media in the 1990s (or before, or since) will be familiar with that discourse: television, radio and newspapers were never free—rather, these enterprises invested in the making of entertainment and the provision of news and other information in order to *purchase our time* which was then sold to advertisers. So a television network would do anything it could to maximise our viewing, often by investing in content that kept us watching (soap operas, reality television shows, re-runs of high-profile popular films being the standards). What is different in the era of social networking is that platforms use algorithms to curate feeds of information, content and posts that keep us scrolling, and keep us coming back. Yet the alarmism at play is perhaps overblown, since the strategy is not different from those used by earlier media forms, only that it is more automated and more personally targeted based on data gathered about what we have viewed already.

7.2.2 Algorithms changing behaviour

The second concern raised by *The Social Dilemma* is that the algorithm-derived feed of content is designed to produce a gradual, barely perceptible change in user behaviour. "Changing what you do, how you think, who you are." This is where the question of platform algorithms becomes interesting for thinking about identity. The idea put forward in the documentary is that this is a case of surveillance capitalism: using big data gathered from users to determine not just how successful advertising on the platform has been but gradually adapting the algorithm so that it constantly improves its targeting and therefore increases its success rate of achieving its goals.

Again, not different from other media forms that rely on advertising, whereby ongoing research and development into advertising results in persistent adjustments. What occurs in the case of platform algorithms targeting advertising to users is an adjustment that is not gradual and happening over months or years but something which is happening at a much faster pace. For example, a magazine that is read primarily by East Asian migrants in Europe may find its advertisers adjust the imagery or language used in regular advertisements to be more appealing to an identity group, although this, of course, often relies on assumptions, reductions and stereotypical beliefs. In the context of algorithm adjustment for targeted advertising, however, what we witness is not something different but a further stage in the historical and cultural basis of algorithmic frameworks: that is, that they emerge not because they are something new foisted upon society but because they are an improvement (from the advertisers' perspective, anyway) in targeting. Persistent adjustments can now be honed to the individual level, ensuring the 'right' advertisements are going to the 'right' user based on identity assumptions that have been gathered from, say, viewing habits. How we value this should not necessarily be different from the frameworks by which we value (or hate) advertisements more broadly.

7.2.3 Digital addiction

The third issue raised by the documentary is the idea that algorithms are designed to produce addictive behaviour. As with many anecdotal accounts, the evidence given is the increased amount of time of people—especially younger people—find themselves using their smartphones and other devices in favour of more 'social' or 'face-to-face' behaviours. While it is true that some people exhibit compulsive behaviours in relation to social media and other applications accessed on digital devices, the attempt to assimilate digital activities with a chemical 'drug' is, as I have discussed elsewhere, a misunderstanding that attempts to equate addiction to an external chemical substance and persistent behaviours caused by an attraction that does not involve an external substance producing an excess of body sensations. That is, only a chemical drug introduced to the body can cause an overload of dopamine and endorphins that, once damaging the body's receptors, require repeated action to feel happy, content or at peace (Cover 2004). There is nothing *inherent* about digital cultural practices, using digital platforms, or the deployment of algorithmically controlled feeds that is *in itself* addictive. Rather, if we find that people have compulsive behaviours in relation to digital technologies, then we need to look more widely at the social processes at play to understand them.

Perhaps the biggest misunderstanding about digital addiction is based in the assumption that once addicted, a person has somehow become *asocial*. Rather, what we need to recognise is that engaging with social media for most people is in fact highly social: it is a compulsion to engage in social behaviour, rather than a distraction from a social life. Finally, we might also ask if a person who is compulsively reading books—a form of media that is no longer subject to moral panic—would we say they are addicted? Or just a bookworm? In other words, it is too simple to say that algorithmically controlled feeds are *causing* people to become addicted.

7.2.4 Surveillance

One of my concerns about the documentary is the dramatised component related to surveillance. The documentary represents social networks' capture of user data and prompting of attention through anthropomorphising the algorithm—that is, representing the algorithm and its calculations as if human beings are watching teenager Ben. The three men are purported to represent platform advancement AI goals of Engagement, Growth and Advertising. The film regularly cuts to the three figures talking together as they try new things to catch Ben's attention: they bemoan the fact that he has not been online for some time and react by sending prompts and alerts. Later, they are pleased when Ben begins to be more engaged, to communicate more often with a girl in his class and then to start viewing politically polarised content that, after more surveillance, is fed to him even more regularly.

It is, of course, true that platforms capture data on use, preferences, likes, what content is viewed and so on in order to provide more targeted content and retain user attention, and it is also true that many platforms use a variety of prompts if we are not engaged. However, we should not necessarily equate this with the kind of personal, invasive and manipulative surveillance that is shown in the footage. The behind-the-scenes platform applications that use algorithms to track engagement and calculate responses are *not* a group of sociopathic human beings. It is substantially more complex and also far more mundane than that—dramatising this aspect of contemporary digital communication to look like deliberate manipulation in a form that most people would recognise as invasive or creepy (like a man watching us from outside the window) and representing this to appear as if they are sociopathic to the extent of deliberately feeding disinformation designed to cause violence or family breakdown, distracts from the *genuine issues* and reasons why a user is engaging with particular kinds of content.

Admittedly, it is not necessarily fully ethical if our viewing and engagement data is collected and held without us being aware—and particularly not if that data is shared with third parties without consent. That is, there is a substantial difference between a human-directed surveillance that makes judgements about us individually and personally and the collection of data that is used to recognise trends. The real ethical issue emerges in cases when that individual data is hacked, leaked or sold on to third parties, as occurred in the Cambridge Analytica scandal in which Facebook data was collected without consent for the purposes of third-party political advertising. In this case, *The Social Dilemma* was correct to point to the ethical issues over the surveillance but was incorrect to dramatise it as if it occurs in the form of manipulative personal surveillance of individuals by human beings making behind-the-scenes judgements and decisions about an individualised subject.

7.2.5 Polarisation

In the final half of *The Social Dilemma,* the documentary turns to the question of politics and political polarisation. Four years after the shock 2016 election of Donald Trump to the United States of America Presidency, the polarisation of American political debate, the ongoing drama of the social rifts caused by Brexit in the United Kingdom and the election of right-wing populist leaders around the world who cultivated highly partisan, cult-like followings, questions about polarisation remained significant. During the drama components of the documentary, Ben is shown to have slumped into a depression about his failure to connect with a young woman and been subsequently manipulated by careful planning by the three AI sociopaths who have slowly, carefully and strategically been feeding him conspiracy theory stories that drive him to participate in a politically motivated riot at which he and his sister are injured.

The documentary presents substantial alarmism over the generation of filter bubbles and echo chambers that polarise political views—but how realistic is the anxiety over this? Echo chambers and filter bubbles, as Axel Bruns (2019) has demonstrated, are indeed possible, but the anxieties about them are only warranted if a user were *only* getting *all* their information and communication from those settings. Bruns' research indicates that not only is this broadly improbable but not backed up by actual evidence that people (like Ben) have been forced through algorithmically managed feeds to only engage with narrow information in an echo chamber or filter bubble. Indeed, as Bruns shows, this kind of moral panic over algorithms ignores the decades of genuine research that has documented the beneficial aspects of engaging with social media and other forms of online community for expanding the field of information and knowledge and for fostering engagement in debates that have multiple perspectives. As he notes (p. 13), we should be wary of the ulterior motives of those who generate scepticism over social media *per se* on the basis of claims about social media as the source of polarisation without looking to the wider cultural factors that have generated polarised views—factors which might include socioeconomic disenfranchisement, the rhetoric of political operatives and populist movements and forms of clustering that precede and pre-exist the algorithms that might be feeding us content on the basis of calculated preferences.

It is also important to shy away from ideas that a feed that has begun to favour harmful or inappropriate content such as political extremism or misogyny is the *only* encounter a user has with knowledge frameworks. Indeed, the documentary's dramatisation itself undid its own logic by showing Ben participating in other communication forms away from his smartphone: conversations with his mother and his sister, conversations with friends at school, classroom activities. With the exception of rare, extreme cases in which a very isolated, self-isolating and obsessive person might be engaging only with one media channel and a fixation on one topic of information—as often see among conspiracy theory adherents (Fassin 2021)—most people engage with a *matrix* of information, media, communication and knowledge sources rather than finding themselves unwittingly stuck in filter bubbles and echo chambers caused by algorithmic preferencing of content.

As Barbara Creed (2003) has aptly shown, people draw on that matrix of communication and thereby relate to new information in complex, diverse ways—a change in population knowledge about a topic occurs gradually across a population, not through individual encounters with a feed (p. 9). This means, then, there is a ground for some concern about the corpus of polarising, extremist views as they occur across media matrices over a longer period of time, and it is important to pay attention to how automated processes within algorithmic culture might play a role in those slow shifts. It does not, however, mean that individuals exposed to a feed are not assessing that content in the context of their wider knowledge frameworks and thereby rejecting extreme opinions.

7.2.6 Algorithms and social approval

The sixth concern: That algorithms are used to share posts in such a way that it encourages social approval, such as Instagram likes. This is where we might want to express some concern—not about algorithms themselves but about the wider culture in which algorithms, platform use and the relationship between social media and identity discussed in Chapter 1 are at play. *The Social Dilemma* argued that the practice of receiving 'likes' and 'upvotes' on social media posts is a form of 'dosing' that encourages unhealthy behaviours and the desperate need for being 'liked' online. Images are shown of a young girl trying out different filters on an Instagram image to maximise the attention shown to her and to please, amuse or attract others. We are told "we get rewarded in these short-term signals—hearts, likes, thumbs-up—and we conflate that with value and we conflate it with truth." It may be a bit simplistic to talk about a "we" as if all users are the same, have the same needs and are as uncritical of the practices as the character in the dramatisation.

There is, of course, a genuine concern about how social approval delivered in this way might shape and normalise our practices and perception of ourselves. This is perhaps particularly worrying if we are used to receiving, say, 50 likes in the first two hours for most of our posts, but on one particularly day, due to the way the algorithm is working, our post is simply not feeding to others in the same way, and suddenly, there are only two likes after six hours. Do we feel ignored? Do we feel like we are suddenly unpopular? Do we feel that a selfie has made us look ugly and do we feel ugly as a result? Over the longer term, what do we change to increase the number of likes? Do we do our hair differently or try to take different kinds of images to restore our online popularity? Again, these kinds of questions will, of course, be relevant to some users who may have developed very deep attachments to the curation of their online profiles and the appreciation those profiles bring. However, that is not an attachment that is *caused* by social media, no matter how much some are trying to suggest that algorithmically managed feeds are enticing people into constantly checking for updates.

The question we might ask, then, is whether social approval delivered digitally is different from *other* kinds of social approval received in other settings as an ordinary part of being a social creature conditioned by practices of belonging and social participation. In other words, we have already been conditioned to seek social approval long before social media was a part of anyone's lives. For example, taking time to choose an outfit that will gain the approval of friends at a party. Working hard on each essay to get the envy of our classmates when we're delivered with a High Distinction each time. Doing our hair so superbly, we get approving glances from strangers in the street. Choosing a sports car to get the looks of jealousy that give us a sense of achievement. All of these are part of a much wider *continuum* of seeking social approval that *includes* the likes a post or image might get on social media. We therefore need to be careful to remember that the ways in which we are encouraged to conform with norms (or push those normative boundaries) and therefore shape our actions and identities are not exclusive to digital communication. Social media is just one setting in which this is done, and the power of social media is much less pervasive—what *The Social Dilemma* excluded from that discussion was the extent to which many people actively and consciously *resist* social practices of normativisation or approval-gathering, that people navigate normalisation processes in much more complex ways and that a very large number of people on the planet are broadly disinterested in the opinions of others about their appearance. That is, we are more diverse, resistant and intelligent than the documentary represents us—which is as technological dupes of algorithms.

At stake in much of *The Social Dilemma* is the question of agency—the ability to make informed and independent choices and exercise some sense of control over how we are represented, how we represent ourselves, the information and entertainment we choose to engage with and how we articulate our identities. The broad claim in the documentary is that algorithms are responsible for curtailing our agency: Ben does not choose to get involved in polarised political protest but is 'directed' to it through a feed; we are told that users do not make choices about checking their feeds but are encouraged through algorithms to become addicted; it is suggested that behaviours and choices are governed by social media's interest in increasing advertising revenue. While it is true that certain practices, events and ways of living have changed alongside the introduction of algorithmic culture into our everyday lives, it remains a fact that we are not, after all, completely duped by social media interests but that algorithms for a part of a much more complex cultural arrangement in which our identities, choices and behaviours are regulated, shaped and understood. There is therefore a lot more to unpack and would be unwise to fall into the limited intellectual trap of the techno-pessimism of the documentary.

7.3 Algorithms, everyday life and everyday inequalities

If we are to make an informed understanding of the role of algorithms in the production of our identities, we need to undertake a less alarmist approach than found in *The Social Dilemma* and other moral panic writing and instead assess algorithms as a part of contemporary digital culture, make sense of how they work, how they govern what is made available and unavailable and what that does for a sense of agency over our identities.

Algorithms are procedural abstractions that define how a computer system makes various calculations, based on inputs drawn from patterns of existing behaviour, whether our own or that of other users collected as 'big data.' They rely on *models* that are built on presumptions or extrapolations of existing relations between entities in the system: for example, models that suggest users of a particular category who are within a particular age range and have identified in a particular way *tend* to prefer news content about a particular topic. Such models, as Shrisha Rao (2021) has noted, are like all other models: imperfect representations of reality that may, on the one hand, approximate knowledge more-or-less well but, on the other hand, may lead to consequences when they are built on errors or incorrect assumptions that lead to false conclusions about a user (p. 21).

Despite the known limitations of algorithms, and the slightly problematic use of machine learning for their constant improvement by remodelling based on new patterns drawn from big data, we are very literally surrounded by algorithmic culture. For example, most home automation devices and ambient intelligence deploy algorithms to learn patterns and make predictions (de Vries 2010, pp. 77–78). The integration of sensors and microprocessors into everyday devices that are part of the 'Internet of Things' (networked home devices) use algorithms to predict patterns of behaviour such as if one is sensed as being at home on weekdays at 6 pm, the air conditioning will increase the ambient temperature. If that person has tended to have a shower at 7 pm on Mondays to Thursdays, the algorithm may begin recommending putting the under-floor heating in the bathroom on at 6.30 pm in preparation for that shower, but switch the coffee machine off already knowing that this inhabitant never makes a coffee after 7 pm.

As a model of behaviour, such an algorithm is obviously imprecise—it does not have a mechanism for accounting for the *imprecision* of human behaviour. For example, that user might be held up in traffic one day (although the ambient sensors will know they are not at home and not activate the processes they have learned). However, a better example is that this user may come home and simply not 'feel like' having a shower that evening. Or be unwell and go straight to bed. Or have slept poorly and, tired, decide to have a coffee despite never having done so. This is all to say that the modelling of human behaviour at an individual level is very imprecise, because most of us are not driven by such strict routines, and the software driving such processes is not as sophisticated as, say, a housemate who can make a better assessment based on a look, a comment or even how one is breathing as they walk in the door. That is, AI is not quite that intelligent.

On the other hand, if that algorithm draws on big data to make wider predictions, it may find it is more accurate at predicting the everyday needs of everyday human beings—that more people are likely to turn their heating up on a colder evening and so will manage that based on a model extrapolated from that data. Or that on the day of an election more users who have accessed a percentage of political news are happy to be interrupted with a feed of data about news coverage of that election, making an assumption that those who have not accessed such news will be disinterested in alerts of that nature.

These are all very benign descriptions of very simple instances of algorithmic culture. Where it becomes more complex or when algorithmically based decisions are made without full knowledge is where the everyday deployment of algorithms may be more problematic. This is the case when algorithms base preference data on factors that are less easy to account for, of which we have no knowledge, or when the modelling is corrupt or has become biased due to data choices that influenced an algorithm's machine learning. For example, companies which use algorithms to help sort and prefer job applications may be making poor decisions. If an algorithm had 'worked out' based on big data that more people who wear red clothing in a profile photograph uploaded to an application website were more likely to work longer hours in an executive position, and if a willingness to work longer hours was a preference indicated by the hiring company, the algorithm may preference or more highly rank the applications of only those who wear red in their uploaded image. And that may occur without anyone actually realising this contributed to the ranking. (This is, of course, an absurd example but demonstrates the potential for algorithmic culture to be used in ways in which the 'solution' and 'convenience' may be counterproductive or discriminatory.)

More importantly, it means that the wider 'gut feelings' of those with experience hiring and who would otherwise have to read every application to rank them is removed from the process of hiring. That is to talk about red shirts, but what if the algorithm drew on biased data that made that calculation based on race or gender? It may reinforce and exacerbate existing inequalities in hiring practices, even if using a ranking algorithm was undertaken to avoid the personal bias of human beings. As a form of AI, it lacks many of the aspects that go into human intelligence, such as those gut feelings, empathy, social considerations, ethics and so on.

This is where we might consider algorithm culture to cause more alarm than we saw in *The Social Dilemma*. There, the moral panic was focused on what algorithms feed us and what data they collect, but did not reference how existing inequalities shape those algorithmic practices, nor how their reproduction of inequalities and bias shape opportunities related to identities—a much slower, subtle influence on everyday life. The question of bias has been raised by a number of writers and scholars concerned about how models used to build algorithmic decision-making may be based on problematic assumptions that exacerbate inequalities or unethical treatment. While there has been much work on promoting digital inclusivity, algorithmically managed processes based on biases may be undoing or reinscribing inequalities (Third et al. 2020, p. 168). Thao Phan and Scott Wark (2021) have argued that despite some industry assumptions that algorithms overcome implicit human biases, they are regularly deployed in ways which allow racial difference and exclusion to be exacerbated, playing a hidden role in the shaping of social inequalities. They point to one use in the United States where proxy indicators were deployed by algorithms, such as language use, interests and locational data to assign users into categories of "ethnic affinities" which were then used to determine some people as "foreign for the purposes of state surveillance" (p. 3).

Similarly, algorithms used in facial recognition and image management have been noted for their inherent racism, including both earlier ones that automatically tagged African Americans as non-human animals (Noble 2018, p. 6) and those which are based on other kind of modelling to erase particular ethnic and racial identities from databases, such as stock image search engines that needed intervention to include non-white people against labels for various jobs or positions (Mellentin and Schmidt 2022, p. 58), or those that based the labels on existing poorly modelled data drawn from online searches.

These are just some of the ways in which algorithms have been noted for deepening inequalities, although there are many other examples compiled by scholars (e.g., Hristova et al. 2021). These are not just a matter of exclusion from being adequately represented or the reliance on narrow stereotypes to model and categorise people, both of which are very old problems. Rather, it is a matter of how the knowledge frameworks that are built on these algorithms are embedded as cultural knowledge because not all users may be critically assessing what is provided in a feed or search or other use of algorithms in everyday life. This is where we see algorithmic culture have an impact on identities, because it not only furthers stereotypes and exclusions but may be responsible for influencing certain assumptions and behaviours in relationships between people who unwittingly make their own decisions based on decisions they have witnessed made by algorithms.

7.4 Available and unavailable knowledges

A second way in which algorithms may be implicated in identity practices in ways which are problematic relates to the making available and unavailable of certain kinds of knowledge. This is not the same as the filter bubble and echo chamber political polarisations described above—although often a target of alarmist writing, evidence indicates that it is not algorithms driving polarisation but a wider range of cultural factors. Rather, here, I am interested in what knowledge frameworks become hidden, unavailable or less available as a result of algorithms based on popularities.

Discourses or 'ways of speaking and thinking' play an important role in identity formation, because they make available the codes of behaviour and practice that are performed reiteratively to shape our identities. Unconscious alignment of our identities and behaviours with dominant discourses makes us feel authentic and coherent as subjects (Hall 1995), and this is because such discourses are the setting that communicates the norms, categories and signifiers we are "compelled to cite or repeat or mime" in the constitution of identity (Butler 1993, p. 220). Discourses exclude particular ways of thinking or speaking about a subject, often under the influence of institutions and expertise that, over time, set up limitations on thinking (Mills 1997, pp. 57–58). For example, discourses about education usually limit the 'discussion' to styles of teaching (experts) and styles of learning (students) and may have competitive views but dominant discourses of education tend to exclude discussion of, perhaps, less hierarchical practices of learning that work outside the dyad of teacher/student or equalise the participants in the learning process.

An important consideration, of course, is that while we often talk about dominant or hegemonic discourses, very few discourses are so dominant that there are no existing alternatives. For example, while there are dominant discourses of sexuality that usually assume people will be either heterosexual or LGBTQ+ and that these are innate or genetically programmed identities in which the gender of the object of attraction is seen as the main determinant, there are alternative and emergent discourses that suggest there may be hundreds of possible ways of thinking about sexual identity and that have encouraged the proliferation of new identities labels—terms such as sapiosexual, meaning attraction to intelligent people regardless of their gender (Cover 2019). These emerging or alternative discourses circulate and are communicated, but they may be more difficult for the average person to find. This is why I often use the terms 'available and unavailable discourses' to describe how, say, a younger person might have less access to certain ways of speaking and thinking than those which are most popular.

The advent of digital communication was a major change in the availability of alternative and less-available discourses, because it permitted the circulation of knowledges that were not necessarily those used by authorised institutions such as medicine, family, religion and primary and secondary education. While we can never assume that a person is going to take the time to search for alternatives or unavailable discourses if they do not yet know they exist, the possibilities for creative exploration and for social media to share and exchange knowledge has had a powerful impact on the emergence of new identity practices. Where we might be concerned, then, about algorithmic culture is how it can be used to curtail that exploration by providing the most 'obvious' knowledges based on popularity that re-normalises in the face of the diversification of identities we have seen over the past two decades.

Bruns (2019) notes that several social media algorithms encourage what he refers to as "unconstrained majority rule, where only already popular accounts and content can ever cut through to a wider audience" effectively silencing minority voices in public debate and excluding more "nuanced and diverse perspectives" (p. 5). This is perhaps where I am most concerned about the operation of algorithms in the making available and unavailable of discourses and knowledge frameworks. Majoritarian or popular perspectives are not always synonymous with dominant discourses, as we have seen in the proliferation of COVID denialism and anti-vaccination discourses which are certainly not a part of the dominant, authorised and institutional discourses of population health and medicine (Cover et al. 2022). However, in some settings, they became remarkably significant and very 'available' because they were popularly accessed by a wide group of people, reinvigorating older calls for investigating just how algorithms were gatekeeping information and whether or not human intervention in more traditional gatekeeping (such as used by newspaper editors for centuries) was necessary to combat misinformation (Morozov 2013, pp. 141–142).

An issue with the use of majoritarian or popular results by algorithms to 'make available' only discourses which are widely accessed by others is that it participates in new practices of normalisation. Often considered regimentary and constraining on the potentialities of identity diversity, normalisation does not mean making everyone the same or encouraging everyone to behave in the same way by suggesting some behaviours are normal while others are abnormal. Rather, in a large society, we see 'distributional curves' at play in which there are a range of normative behaviours and identities are considered broadly normal, and others are more-or-less normal—one can be varied in their identity from the norm but only up to a point (Foucault 2007). In other words, normalising discourses that primarily share the majority perspective do not necessarily curtail diversity and diverse identity practices, but they help establish a norm by using what is 'common' or 'popular' as the centre point of a normative curve, allowing for debate and variance but calling upon users to plot their identities in relation to how close or distant they are to the norm.

One of the remedies to the 'making unavailable' of diverse discourses has been put forward by Mark Andrejevic (2020) who argued for a return to some of the original ideas articulated in the mid-1990s by industry figures such as Bill Gates—that news feeds could be sought, sorted and curated on an individual basis by software 'bots' operating for individuals on their individual devices according to individual tastes and preferences (p. 28). While such curation may be limited to the tastes and preferences of users in much the way Netflix algorithms seem to align with existing viewing patterns, they would at least be customisable and adjustable by the users themselves, making available a wider array of discourses and alternative knowledges. What occurred instead of such a technological framework for automated news-gathering, however, was the centralisation of the practice in algorithms which also serve the advertising and marketing priorities of platforms. Further development of those which allow users a greater agency in what is curated for them would be one potential way to curtail the shutting down of alternative discourses through popularity and majoritarian practices and, therefore, increase the range of discourses made available through which a wider range of identities, performativities and ways of participating socially can emerge.

7.5 Algorithms, identity and agency

The third and final concern for identity practices in relation to algorithms involves returning to the question of agency that was raised in *The Social Dilemma*. Ultimately,

The Social Dilemma tries to show platforms as destroying aspects of the culture through which our identities are derived, suggesting that this occurs through a curtailment of our everyday agency to make informed decisions about our own lives. The suggestion that algorithmic culture does so results in harm to the dramatised people shown in the documentary: the family who fall apart due to excessive social media use, the young girl who falls into depression, the young man who has been overexposed to polarised information and joins a violent political rally where he is injured. Unfortunately, this approach to agency was not only alarmist but misunderstood what agency means in terms of identity.

Yes, real-world behaviours are manipulated as I have discussed above—bias and inequalities, the making available and unavailable of certain knowledges and algorithms are implicated in these in ways which possibly open questions over how much agency we have today to choose practices, knowledges and ways of thinking on our own. However, the documentary tended to focus on what scholars often refer to as an individualised, liberal-humanist perspective on agency: the idea that every individual has freedom of choice over all aspects of selfhood, behaviour, attitude and speech. As culturally produced subjects whose identities and practices are built on the fact we are constituted in interdependency in a society at all stages of our lives (Butler 2020, p. 51), and no one has ever had true and complete agency over their identity, subjectivity and selfhood, whether before algorithmic culture or after. This is not to suggest that there is no agency or free will at all. Rather, it is to point to the fact that any agency we do have is not completely untethered from society but is perceived and exercised within spaces of norms, available discourses, social surveillance and political constraint (Berlant 2007, p. 758).

This is to suggest that there have always been social forces that condition us into particular behaviours and practices of identity, often in ways which serve dominant institutions—for example, the assumption that there is no agency except to have a paying job and that jobs themselves are 'normative' does not prevent people from dropping out of the labour force, but it does prevent many of us at certain points in our life from thinking about a life without work, from coming up with alternative ways to live a good life (even when we complain about our jobs). Obviously, such a perspective serves the needs of employers, big businesses and those who benefit most from economic exchange. This is the form in which agency is constraining and conditions us to practice identities in particular ways that may foreclose on others. Today, by making certain knowledges available and others unavailable, algorithms participate in this shaping of agency and identity.

Where *The Social Dilemma* got agency wrong, then, is in representing platforms as deliberately manipulating people as if there was no agency, such as the agency to disconnect (Light 2014). By attempting to suggest that there is deliberate curtailment of agency, the documentary framed the question in terms of *control* rather than *shaping* and represented this as if we have all had total and complete sovereign agency over ourselves and our actions in pre-algorithmic culture days.

7.6 Conclusion

The use of algorithms by platforms, social media and in home devices and other artificial decision-making applications has been the source of anxiety and alarmism not for the reasons given in *The Social Dilemma* and other popular and techno-pessimistic moral panic. Rather, they cause social anxiety because, arguably, they operate behind the scenes in ways that are beyond ordinary human visibility, scrutiny and personal investigation (Phan and Wark 2021). Algorithms do indeed play a role in shaping our identities, agency and the knowledges we are able to access. However, many of the practices deployed are no different from the other problematic forms of shaping that have been undertaken by institutions and those with vested interests in encouraging patterns of behaviour, such as marketers, advertisers and those selling goods and services.

As algorithms become even more embedded in our everyday lives, we will continue to see ways in which they shape identity and agency. However, one of the key elements that will be at fault if they become constraining our everyday lives will be the adoption of algorithms as the technological solution to everything. That is, the use of algorithmic culture to solve problems such as the labour time of sorting; the assessment of who is or is not a criminal based on a range of measured patterns, norms and profiling biases; their use in various assessments of risk rather than relying on human judgement; and the value of experience in such judgements are all problems of *human* decision-making, rather than a problem of artificial decision-making.

In other words, by handing over decision-making to algorithms to solve such problems (because it's not as if algorithms invaded us and enslaved us), we fall into the trap of technological solutionism because the tasks of human management of large amounts of data and the scope of many social problems of distribution are too great to handle without handing over some of the labour to machines. This is helpful when it is about labour-saving, but more problematic when human intervention is removed from the picture altogether and personal or democratic participation is excluded as too costly (Morozov 2013; Milan 2020). The implications, then, for how we perceive ourselves as identities with agency is a genuine one but calls on us to do more about the ethics and the practices of shaping the future that algorithmic culture has entailed, rather than panicking about them in wholly pessimistic tones.

Key points

- There is substantial public anxiety about the rise of algorithmic culture and artificial decision-making, although some of this is based in moral panic of the sort that has accompanied the development of new communication technologies.
- A more sophisticated and less alarmist approach involves assessing the role of algorithms in shaping practices.
- Algorithms have been implicated in exacerbating existing inequalities, particularly in terms of gender, race and minorities and usually where popular or majority data and practices have been used to design algorithmic models.
- Algorithms are implicated in making some knowledge frameworks more 'available' than others, and this has implications for how we perform identities, particularly in the context of norms and diversities.
- Concerns about the loss of human agency are only partly warranted and we need to make sense of what agency is and what are its limits before accusing algorithms and artificial decision-making systems from taking that agency away.

References

Andrejevic, M., 2020. *Automated Media*. London & New York: Routledge.
Berlant, L., 2007. Slow death (sovereignty, obesity, lateral agency). *Critical Inquiry,* 33 (4), 754–780.
Bruns, A., 2019. *Are Filter Bubbles Real?* London: Polity.
Butler, J., 1993. *Bodies That Matter: On The Discursive Limits of 'Sex.'* London & New York: Routledge.

Butler, J., 2020. *The Force of Nonviolence: An Ethico-Political Bind*. London: Verso.

Cohen, S., 2011. *Folk Devils and Moral Panics*. London: Routledge.

Cover, R., 2004. Digital addiction: the cultural production of online and video game junkies. *Media International Australia*, 113 (1), 110–123.

Cover, R., 2007. Gaming addiction: the role of narrative and play in the production of the addiction myth. *Game Studies: International Journal of Computer Game Research*, 6 (1). Available from: http://gamestudies.org/0601/articles/cover [Accessed 2 February 2022].

Cover, R., 2019. *Emergent Identities: New Sexualities, Gender and Relationships in a Digital Era*. London & New York: Routledge.

Cover, R., Haw, A. and Thompson, J.D., 2022. *Fake News in Digital Cultures: Technology, Populism and Digital Misinformation*. London: Emerald Publishing.

Creed, B., 2003. *Media Matrix: Sexing the New Reality*. St. Leonards: Allen & Unwin.

de Vries, K., 2010. Identity, profiling algorithms and a world of ambient intelligence: ethics, technology, and identity. *Ethics and Information Technology*, 12 (1), 71–85.

Facebook, 2020. *What 'The Social Dilemma' Gets Wrong*. Available from: https://about.fb.com/wp-content/uploads/2020/10/What-The-Social-Dilemma-Gets-Wrong.pdf [Accessed 2 June 2022].

Fassin, D., 2021. Of plots and men: the heuristics of conspiracy theories. *Current Anthropology*, 62 (2), 128–137.

Foucault, M., 2007. *Security, Territory, Population: Lectures at the Collège de France, 1977–78*, ed. M. Senellart, trans. G. Burchell. Hampshire: Palgrave Macmillan.

Hall, S., 1995. The whites of their eyes: racist ideologies and the media. *In:* G. Dines and J. M. Humez, eds. *Gender, Race and Class in Media: A Text-Reader*. Thousand Oaks, CA: Sage, 18–22.

Hristova, S., Hong, S. and Slack, J. D., 2021. Introduction: in the presence of algorithms. *In:* S. Hristova, S. Hong and J. D. Slack, eds. *Algorithmic Culture How Big Data and Artificial Intelligence Are Transforming Everyday Life*. Lanham, MD: Lexington Books, 1–14.

Light, B., 2014. *Disconnecting with Social Networking Sites*. London: Palgrave.

Livingstone, S., 2008. Taking risk opportunities in youthful content creation: teenagers' use of social networking sites for intimacy, privacy and self-expression. *New Media & Society*, 10 (3), 393–411.

Lobato, R., 2019. *Netflix Nations: The Geography of Digital Distribution*. New York: New York University Press.

Malhotra, P., 2020. The social dilemma fails to tackle the real issues in tech. *Slate*, 8 December. Available from: https://slate.com/technology/2020/09/social-dilemma-netflix-technology.html. [Accessed 8 December 2020].

Mellentin, J. and Schmidt, F., 2022. Surveillance, artificial intelligence and power. *In:* S. Quadflieg, K. Neuburg and S. Nestler, eds. *(Dis)Obedience in Digital Societies: Perspectives on the Power of Algorithms and Data*. Edinburgh: Transcript Verlag, 48–68.

Milan, S., 2020. Techno-solutionism and the standard human in the making of the COVID-19 pandemic. *Big Data & Society*. Available from: https://journals.sagepub.com/doi/full/10.1177/2053951720966781 [Accessed 2 July 2022].

Mills, S., 1997. *Discourse*. London & New York: Routledge.

Morozov, E., 2013. *To Save Everything, Click Here the Folly of Technological Solutionism*. New York: Public Affairs.

Newton, C., 2020. What 'The Social Dilemma' misunderstands about social networks. *The Verge*, 16 September. Available from: www.theverge.com/interface/2020/9/16/21437942/social-dilemma-netflix-review-orlowski-sarah-zhang-memo-facebook-buzzfeed [Accessed 13 June 2022].

Noble, S. U., 2018. *Algorithms of Oppression: How Search Engines Reinforce Racism*. New York: New York University Press.

Phan, T. and Wark, S., 2021. Racial formations as data formations. *Big Data & Society*. Available from: https://journals.sagepub.com/doi/full/10.1177/20539517211046377 [Accessed 12 July 2022].

Rao, S., 2021. Algorithms in society: arbitrage, bias, and culture. *In:* V. Sridhar, ed. *Data-Centric Living: Algorithms, Digitization and Regulation*. London: Routledge, 17–30.

Svensson, J., 2022. Coffee with the algorithm: imaginaries, maintenance and care in the everyday life of a news-ranking algorithm. *In:* S. Pink, M. Berg, D. Lupton and M. Ruckenstein, eds. *Everyday Automation: Experiencing and Anticipating Emerging Technologies*. London: Routledge, 114–125.

Third, A., Collin, P., Walsh, L. and Black, R., 2020. *Young People in Digital Society: Control Shift*, London: Palgrave.

Walsh, J. P., 2020. Social media and moral panics: assessing the effects of technological change on societal reaction. *International Journal of Cultural Studies*, 23 (6), 840–859.

Williams, R., 1990. The technology and the society. *In:* D, Bennett, ed. *Popular Fiction: Technology, Ideology, Production, Reading*. London: Routledge, 9–22.

8 Authenticities

TikTok and the perception of authentic identities

8.1 Introduction

New platforms emerge regularly but not many of them have the kind of public uptake that makes them capable of the popularity, profile, earnings and reach of those which dominate the space: Facebook, Instagram, WeChat, YouTube, SnapChat and Twitter. TikTok surprised many when it became one of the most popular, and it is useful to unpack some of the reasons why, what is different about it and what it does differently as a setting for identity. According to Trevor Boffone (2022), Chinese-owned TikTok has been a major game-changer in app use in the United States of America and elsewhere, not just providing an innovative alternative to existing content-sharing and social networking platforms but pushing against the older culture of platform use in ways which have engendered new practices of creativity as well as fostered controversies and political concerns. The fact that its use requires persistent scrolling to see the next item of 20- to 60-second video content has raised concerns—mostly unfounded—that it is addictive and that it is encouraging very short attention spans among users (Zhang 2018; Su 2020).

As with all new platforms, the cultural practices around its use—including how it facilitates representation and identity performativity—develops over time, meaning TikTok is new enough that unlike the alarmist and negative claims, we cannot yet have a full grasp not just of what it is capable of but how people are using it. However, its early use presents an interesting case study for understanding the relationship between identity and platform use from the perspective of *authenticity*. TikTok was widely hailed for providing opportunities for representing the self with more authentic, unfiltered and unsophisticated content creation, often in contrast to platforms such as Instagram which have become better known as sites of curation of self-image (Hutchinson 2021).

A Nielsen study commissioned in 2020 by TikTok observed that three-quarters of TikTok users found the platform more appealing than other platforms as they felt more comfortable being "authentic," genuine and unfiltered (Cohen 2020). Certainly, the viral dance trends in which untalented, everyday users of TikTok distributed footage of themselves dancing badly but joyfully to their favourite music (Guillaume 2021) is a good example of the way in which the platform has been used in very different ways from the more filtered and curated setting of many earlier platforms—a sense that people were expressing their 'authentic selves' online in a way that would ordinarily be subject to criticism or remain unpopular on other platforms.

While it would be difficult to argue that older platforms are always 'fake' and that TikTok users have opportunities to be 'real,' what we see in the public proclamation of

DOI: 10.4324/9781003296652-8

TikTok as a return to less-curated identity content is that the platform is perceived to provide a setting to fulfil a cultural need that was seemingly no longer being achieved in other spaces. To unpack some of the implications, I will start with a discussion of TikTok in the context of the wider digital culture of constantly emerging platforms to answer the question as to why this particular platform became popular while many similar other platforms do not. I will then discuss how authenticity can be understood theoretically in the context of identity before ending with a discussion as to some of the ways in which a 'curated authenticity' and 'feelgood' framework that has made many users' content viral online is potentially harming others.

8.2 TikTok in a culture of platform renewal

In this section, I would like to address three aspects of TikTok's recent emergence: firstly, how it has been understood as an innovative platform that changes or further develops practices that are familiar to us over the past two decades; secondly the way in which new platforms have an appeal in generational terms as older ones become more associated with older users; and thirdly, the ways in which gratifications and unexpected uses—or attainment—operate to create platform appeal. Together, these three elements have been at least partly responsible for the unexpected attractiveness of TikTok to new users.

8.2.1 TikTok and platform innovation

TikTok launched in China under the name Douyin in September 2016 and was released for international operating systems iOS and Android in 2017. Subsequent to the acquisition of Musical.ly which had been popular with younger teenagers, TikTok grew in notoriety and reached two billion downloads in 2020 during the first year of the COVID-19 pandemic (Carman 2020). It was initially notable for its very simple editing features, the short length of its videos (approximately 20–60 seconds) and for its capacity to allow video content to be produced with existing music—an extension of the popular form of remix in which extant or new audio and video are juxtaposed by everyday users, fans and content creators to present new texts with meanings different from but linked with the original audio or its lyrics (Cover 2013).

Despite its popularity, it has been implicated in a number of controversies. The most serious among them is, perhaps, the attempted ban in the United States by the Trump Administration. In 2020, President Trump signed an executive order banning the downloading of the TikTok app if the United States wing of its business was not sold by the Chinese company ByteDance to a third party, ostensibly on the basis that ByteDance was collecting and viewing US user data. Following a lawsuit by TikTok, a court temporarily suspended the ban order while the new Biden Administration revoked it. Nevertheless, concerns about the harvesting of US user data have remained into mid-2022 (Fung 2022).

Other controversies have included attempted bans in several middle-eastern countries as well as the arrest of users for the production of content which was considered in those jurisdictions to be obscene (Agence France-Presse in Cairo 2020), its use for the distribution of fake news and disinformation, including in relation to COVID-19 and vaccination (Cover et al. 2022), and the cultural appropriation of black TikTok users' content by white influencers who were better able to monetise that content (Moftah and Lorenz 2022).

While the controversies relate to individual content and to TikTok's ownership and data-gathering practices, the platform arguably invoked responses because it had innovated around platform frameworks that had become familiar within digital culture. The capacity to scroll content rather than select, the short length of the videos and the appeal to a new generation of users of video content that seemed to have less 'purpose' and was perhaps more 'playful' than, say, YouTube content prompted a reaction from many who read that innovativeness as problematic or 'alien' to normative digital culture.

8.2.2 The 'big sibling' platform syndrome

Despite the controversial response from more conservative journalists and writers, TikTok was also hailed as an innovation that benefited specifically younger people. Trevor Boffone (2021) described TikTok as a setting used explicitly by teens today "to self-fashion identity, form supportive digital communities, and exert agency" (p. 6). Here, TikTok is expressly differentiated from older platforms which are represented as a constraint on opportunities for younger people to employ control over self-representation and to innovate with new identity practices. What is it, however, to associate a platform for a generation? How does TikTok become associated with younger people while Facebook, for example, 'travels up' the lifecycle in association with their older siblings and parents? What does this do for identity practices online?

TikTok has been regarded as being synonymous with the cultural practices, identities and tastes of 'Generation Z' or the post-millennial generation, particularly in the United States of America (Boffone 2022). I use the term 'big sibling' platform syndrome to describe a pattern we have seen in relation to the uptake of other social media services: those which trend and become popular often do so among the younger siblings or children of those using other platforms as a way of differentiating. Part of Facebook's appeal to younger users was, anecdotally, a way of differentiating from MySpace used by those who were several years older (and therefore not as cool). In some respects, this relates to generational differences, whereby an age group undertakes certain identity practices, preferences and tastes as a form of cultural belonging to that generation and in marked differentiation from older groups (Wyn and Woodman 2006). Understanding identity from generational perspectives involves making sense of how a generational group take on particular practices as 'their own' and utilise these across life, in contrast to more transitional understandings of young people who see particular tastes and practices as a normative 'phase.'

For example, while some might argue that younger people choose TikTok due to its entertainment value but will eventually be spending more time using LinkedIn as employed adults (a transitional perspective), others might argue that TikTok can be identified as a post-millennial platform because part of the appeal was its differentiation from the more familiar Instagram, YouTube and Facebook which were already identified as involving practices 'belonging' to older generational groupings. This is not to say that TikTok is exclusively used by younger people, but that it is associated with a different, emerging cultural taste that is identified with younger people—obviously, it is widely used by those from a wide variety of ages, class demarcations, social identities and communities.

8.2.3 Uses, gratifications and attainment

This is also not to suggest that TikTok was developed *intentionally* to appeal to a particular cultural taste or social generation. Rather, understanding its use involves thinking about it from what is called a 'uses and gratifications' perspective—how those who take up a technology, application or platform shape the uses and the cultural values such that participating on it becomes an act of identity affiliation with a generation. Uses and gratifications theory is usually juxtaposed to technological-determinist approaches which, incorrectly, assume that a new technology has been foisted upon society and changes that society. From a uses and gratifications perspective, a more appropriate analysis understands everyday users as active agents in *how* they take up, utilise, select, interpret and engage with media and communication technologies to serve particular needs (Blumler and Katz 1974).

TikTok is an excellent example of uses and gratifications at play, and how users' own desires for particular practices of identification, representation and content creation shape the wider content trends on a platform. For example, in addition to TikTok being utilised by users to fulfil a need for communicating their everyday existence—in many cases during the era of lockdowns and social distancing that marked the first couple of years of the COVID-19 pandemic—and the desire to communicate unsophisticated, playful and meaningless content, we have also seen it become popular as a setting for other people doing things for which it was never intended. For example: health and well-being 'explainers' by practitioners showing real footage of everyday medical and dental work, professional research scientists making short videos that explain a scientific concept and so on. In other words, while TikTok is just another video-sharing platform, its uptake has been driven by what *gratifies* the uploader, generating a new aesthetics of posting that focuses more on everyday life.

From a different angle, J. Mitchell Vaterlaus and Madison Winter (2021) used a uses and gratifications approach to study not those who use the platform for content creation and distribution but those who only view it, finding that there has been a widespread preference particularly in China to engage with the content passively for the purposes of escapism. Just as the choices made about content creation and self-representation are an act of identity, so too is passively viewing. The researchers found that there were two themes across how and why users engage with TikTok videos: as a valued leisure activity and for the purposes of social connection. The latter, in particular, flies in the face of those who have found the platform to be controversial, addictive, isolating or building bad concentration habits among users. What is key here is that *all* communication—including that experienced in isolation—is a form of social connection, whether reading a book that was written centuries ago or watching content that was uploaded in the past ten minutes. In looking not to what the platform does to society (a technological-determinist approach) nor what are the reasons that encouraged its development to respond to social needs (a cultural approach), the researchers' interest in uses and gratifications reveals to us that users engage with the videos due to a deeply desired need for social connection that was not being met through other applications. Given the 'big sibling' factors, this may imply that a younger social generation *utilises* TikTok to fulfil a need that worked for other generations across other social media and face-to-face forms—a possibility we would need to research for a longer period to fully understand.

In their book about webcamming, Daniel Miller and Jolynna Sinanan (2014) developed a theory of 'attainment' to help understand how a new technology does more than simply facilitate a sociocultural condition that "people already knew they wanted." Attainment is not deemed to be the same as achieving or fulfilling a personal need but a framework through which the new, the emergent and the novel become the taken-for-granted condition of everyday life (pp. 11–12). At the same time, attainment does not imply a wholesale change to some previous state or ideal but suggests that a new technology *both* fulfils a cultural need among a group while *also* stimulating new aspirations and needs that were not previously thinkable. In this way, TikTok might be theorised as gratifying a need experienced by some (to find social connection), gratifying different needs among others (professionals wanting to engage in a pedagogical way with a wider community) and providing new aspirations to those who did not previously experience these needs (finding that scrolling through videos provides them with a sense of the world they did not know they lacked or desired).

8.3 Authenticity and representation

TikTok has been widely described as a platform that contrasts with the professionalisation among dominant users of earlier platforms—especially YouTube and Instagram—and much of this has to do with how celebrities and influencers have utilised the affordances of those platforms while bringing to it a variety of professionalised techniques to curate a persona, images and self-presentation that is seen to be artificial and unrepresentative of everyday life. This is not, of course, a surprise given that many social media influencers treat the representation of selfhood as a form of content creation that crosses labour, self-promotion, marketing and acting (Abidin and Cover 2018), and that the success and monetisation of content production by those influencers has encouraged others to produce their content using similar filtration of imagery, careful selection and curated promotion.

One of the reasons why TikTok has been described as a game-changer in the social media space (Boffone 2022) is because it competes favourable against the growing professionalisation of content production among those who dominated spaces such as Instagram and YouTube. Substantial media commentary argued that TikTok was the space for 'authenticity' among users who represented themselves in amateurish, fun, non-professionalised and unsophisticated ways. I would suggest there is some need to distance ourselves from the idea that this was such a drastic change—older platforms such as YouTube were very much regarded in the same way: as a space for the production and distribution of 'amateur' content. Jean Burgess and Joshua Green (2009) critiqued the use of a professional/amateur distinction regarding YouTube, suggesting that interactive media was a setting that opened the exploration of that distinction. The problem with attempting to label some platforms as overly professionalised and others as authentic, amateur or everyday is that professional video production in film and television is incorrectly used by critics of social media as the *benchmark* of recognisable professional content. Rather, Burgess and Green noted that the "interpersonal, playful, and identity-forming practices" (p. 24) witnessed in the early years of YouTube could be better described as *vernacular*—part of the "the wide range of everyday creative practices (from scrapbooking to family photography to the storytelling that forms part of casual chat) practiced outside the cultural value systems of either high culture or commercial creative practice" (p. 55).

In this respect, YouTube content represented itself initially as more genuine or authentic because it reflected on the everydayness that is much less a part of professional contemporary film and television: content about the lived experiences of families, vlogging about feelings and relationships and playing with creative forms rather than adopting recognised genres and standards. Content that articulated the 'identity' of the vlogger as an authentic, genuine and 'real' self was seen as the hallmark of YouTube in its first decade of production. Much of what dominates YouTube in the 2020s, however, has become more systematised and professionalised, with major influencers among the most popular content creators, a recognition of the capacity to monetise content creation, the use by YouTubers of professional camera crews, third-party audiovisual editing and the strong representation in that space from major television networks and film services. That is, what we might call a more professionalised space.

We might use the same language to describe what is happening a generation later with TikTok—a space in which a more authentic-seeming representation emerged in contrast to YouTube, with even shorter videos than the ten minutes of the early YouTube years and the use of less-sophisticated albeit powerful tools such as phone cameras and in-built app editing. If TikTok is a space, then, to discuss the representation of a more authentic sense of identity than found among the dominant content in the more professionalised space of older platforms, it is important to address what authenticity might mean, what the claims about TikTok's authenticity signify for contemporary identity and selfhood and how some of the most recent trends are indicative of what might be expected to happen to TikTok in the future.

8.3.1 What is authenticity?

The idea of authenticity and 'authentic identities' is much older than TikTok, as well as YouTube and other platforms and settings that were initially describing everyday content in this way. Authenticity is valorised and valued in contemporary culture and serves as a commodity that draws the attention of everyday viewers and users for a few reasons. Firstly, identities (or people) represented as 'authentic' are those which are coherent, intelligible and recognisable without logical gaps, anomalies, slippages or complexities while maintaining a groundedness in everyday realities. Politicians, public figures and celebrities are regularly assessed on authenticity: holding a policy belief (such as carbon pollution reduction) but not expressing that in everyday life (such as using a private plane) is seen as a breach of authenticity, even if a logic argument for this inconsistency can be given (such as the use of a private jet to enhance security so as better to fight climate change). At a deeper level, more complex identity experiences (such as mixed-race identities) have often been dismissed as somehow inauthentic, leaving large numbers of people perceived as lesser humans because they are unable to represent themselves through a 'singular' truth of identity (Radhakrishnan 1996, p. 162).

What I have sometimes referred to as a 'cult of authenticity' (e.g., Cover 2019) governs many aspects of the contemporary production of the performative self. This is a subject or identity who is culturally compelled to respond to the social demand for coherence, intelligibility and recognisability in order to participate in and belong to the wider society. Authenticity is a very important aspect of this requirement for coherence, for without authenticity, the subject is open to the accusation of falsehood or being a 'phony' and therefore of being perceived as schizophrenic, abject, inhuman or untrustworthy. It is, of course, the case that the language that constructs the categories of identities authentic identity (such as sex, gender, bodies and sexuality), in addition to the language used to describe and represent oneself through online storytelling, is by no means stable but change, develop and react to the "making available" of alternative languages and discourses—all of which allow certain kinds of fluidity and change in identity. In that context, there is no actual, *genuine* authenticity of identity. Rather, we are all from the beginning doomed to perform our identities against the possibility that coherence and intelligibility will fail—so we act to shore up our identities by performing in ways that *appear* authentic to ourselves and others; a sort of 'true to oneself' motif and an embrace of everyday experience as somehow more real than representation.

This practice of authenticity is a very old part of contemporary culture that emerged in Enlightenment and liberal-humanist approaches to the unified, individualist perception of identity emanating from an inner reality or self. Although this is sometimes questioned through more postmodern concepts of identity fluidity, spectacle, simulacra and the unreality of real life, the demand for coherence and authenticity remains a core aspect in how we 'belong' to society. Such approaches to identity clearly also play a role not in TikTok content necessarily but in why TikTok has been valorisation as a setting for the expression of that inner, lived authenticity.

'Real' authenticity is always something which escapes us, since the self is only knowable through the discourses and languages available to make sense of identity (Foucault 1980, p. 118). Indeed, there is a danger in attempting to invoke an idea of authenticity in which some identity practices are seen to be more authentic than others. For example, suggesting that TikTok content is superior (rather than just different) to content in more professionalised media settings is unhelpful. The distinction poses dangers when it is used as a mechanism for disavowing the lived experience of, say, Instagram influencers, just because the material is presented in a more professionalised, curated or filtered way. Indeed, such content may well be just as meaningful, felt and representative as a user doing a silly, playful dance to a cheesy popular song on TikTok. What is far more useful, then, is understanding TikTok content not as being more authentic but as adopting a particular mode or genre of communication—an aesthetics of authenticity that is recognisable because it values the ordinary, individual lived experience and encourages the representation of ordinariness over the hyperreality, simulation and professionalisation expressed in other settings.

8.3.2 TikTok as 'authentic' aesthetic

Is TikTok therefore more 'authentic' than other platforms that pre-exist it? I would like to suggest an alternative to this question: does the genre of content that emerged on TikTok, at least initially, represent not authenticity but what I am calling an 'authenticity aesthetic.' To ask this is to avoid trying to assess whether or not some content is more authentic, more real or more everyday than other content. Boffone (2022) suggests that part of the attraction involved in the way TikTok has been taken up is a cultural practice of revealing even more of the self in unfiltered and unchecked ways than we found with earlier platforms:

> teenage TikTokers routinely upload videos in which they give tours of their houses, vlog about their everyday routines, including their specific locations, and detail where they go to school, who they are dating, where they go to church, you name it. TikTok, then, is incredibly unfiltered and extremely public. This unfiltered, public social media activity lends itself to the vulnerability of being silly, honest, and real— elements that are part of the aesthetic and attraction for TikTok.
>
> (p. 6)

This is not to fall into the older, pessimistic trap of suggesting young people are putting themselves at risk by revealing 'too much' of themselves online (Third et al. 2020). Rather, it is part of the ongoing cultural evolution of digital communication in which we reveal material in contexts of: normative practices of self-representation, perceptions of revelations about embodied life as communicative acts, and our understandings of revelation as an identity practice itself.

In other words, TikTok is no more authentic in its design, use or practice than any other platform, given what is already discussed above about the impossibility of authenticity. Rather, it is just as much curated content about the self as any other platform. What is different is that the aesthetic of its use is much more like early YouTube: marked by everydayness, casualness, unedited uploads, play, creativity and representing the banal and mundane, such as dancing around in one's pyjamas in the living room.

An aesthetic of authenticity is usually a pointer to *entertainment value*, even for content that has an information or knowledge-sharing basis (seeking and accessing dry knowledge can, of course, be very entertaining, and entertainment does not have to be banal or funny in every instance). That is, the aesthetic of authenticity is grounded in the idea that content-making and what it represents is *fun*. One key aspect of entertainment—or having fun—is that it is often understood as an act of cultural communion or sharing and that, in the act of sharing entertainment, it creates a community by having a common element among that group (McKee 2016, pp. 13, 22). TikTok content we feel is entertaining, playful, comedic or produces sensational emotions is *more likely* to be shared. Unlike 'high art' or formal informational texts such as traditionally taught online classes that are more regularly consumed alone (Storey 1993), the value of the material is found in the act of sharing. We already know that comedic material is now recognised as being more likely to be shared and on-forwarded (Albury 2019), and, indeed, TikTok increases the authenticity of the shared aesthetic by demonstrating to us just how much others have already accessed that material such that our viewing is never in a fabricated creator–text–audience relationship but is grounded in the fact that we are among many others taking pleasure in viewing that content. In that sense, TikTok's interface adds to the affordances of an aesthetic of authenticity because it not only fosters the greater reach of everyday 'fun' texts that seem to represent a certain kind of identity authenticity of its creators but enables viewers to engage with the text in a way that highlights the authenticity of being part of a sharing community.

8.3.3 Celebrity culture and professionalisation

There is an opportunity here to consider not just how TikTok represents itself as a setting for authentic identity expressions but also how quickly the adoption of an emergent platform by celebrities and influencers can change and adapt the culture. When the sudden popularity of TikTok swept Western countries, it quickly incorporated two frameworks of celebrity, professional production and influencers: (1) those professional content producers who sought a new opportunity to reach a wider audience using a platform that had a very substantial new popularity and (2) those who became popular enough on TikTok alone to be able to adopt a more professionalised framework of engagement, becoming celebrities themselves and monetising the content that was originally produced for pleasure and engagement.

This has followed a familiar pattern. Crystal Abidin (2018) has written extensively about the practices of Internet celebrity, including the development of influencers. Celebrity culture that emerges in traditional media settings (film, television, magazines) and that which emerges in online settings (Facebook, YouTube, Twitter, memes and influencers) have always overlapped and woven into each other (p. 14), including the uptake of digital platforms to extend notoriety and reach by those whose celebrity was forged in other settings. For example, actor George Takei, who was a public figure since performing in *Star Trek* in the late 1960s reinvigorated and expanded his public following after he began posting content across several social media platforms. Former politicians who traditionally were limited to television interviews and giving speeches on a global speaking circuit gain new followings and expanded celebrification on Twitter years after they have left office.

It is therefore no surprise that TikTok very quickly became a site adopted by those who had become celebrities in other settings, including earlier social media. To give just one example, Troye Sivan gained celebrity for his amateur singing on YouTube, before crossing over into professional acting and singing subsequent to gaining a recording contract with EMI Records and a handful of film acting roles. Part of Sivan's appeal was, arguably, an authenticity to his public persona developed by not limiting his YouTube presence to his singing but providing personal accounts of life, romantic interests, family, LGBTQ+ politics and the everydayness of Troye Sivan "being himself" at home (Abidin and Cover 2018). Despite his increasing professional work, commercially released albums and film and television roles, Sivan maintained an ongoing social media presence and began posting on TikTok in January 2018. These were initially short clips from his music videos. Three months later, he began posting within the more 'authentic' aesthetic, with very short clips noting his experience of anxiety, backgrounders on exploring the different layers or stems in electronic copies of his songs, casually trying on clothes in his bedroom and showing his side-by-side reaction face to other people's TikTok content. Ostensibly, TikTok afforded for Sivan a return to the behind-the-scenes and backend persona with which his career began on YouTube, providing a platform in which to present short clips that *both* promote his professional work and engage users with more personal material—albeit, as with all TikTok content falling into the authenticity aesthetic, equally curated.

At the same time, and not unlike earlier platforms, TikTok afforded an opportunity for some everyday users to *become* celebrities, including cases of people leaving paid employment to concentrate full time on content creation for TikTok. Similar to the earlier YouTube experience of Sivan or Liza Koshy, this involved a combination of popular appeal (making content viral) and an investment of labour (sustaining a regular supply of content that holds interest). What has been different, however, on TikTok is the capacity of the site to enable viral interest in content that is relatively diverse but underpinned by the authenticity aesthetic and the representation of identities grounded in 'having fun.' For example, Melbourne-based TikTok user and primary schoolteacher Caleb Finn began uploading content to TikTok in 2018 performing what was described in the framework of the authenticity aesthetic as "goofing around," which included drawn-on freckles, some dancing, some slapstick comic behaviour, dressing up as popular culture figures and snippets of his home life with his girlfriend and, later, newborn child. By 2021, he had 10 million followers internationally, was noted as the fifth most-followed Australian account and was required to leave his job teaching as his popularity was becoming a risk to the students once his fans started coming into the school to find and meet him (Dexter 2021).

What made his content so popular? According to journalist Rachael Dexter (2021), it was a combination of his childish, playful behaviour, popular culture references and an avant-garde transition experimentations using quite sophisticated camera and editing tricks. While this is true, what grounds Caleb Finn's corpus of TikTok content is the representation of play and fun as 'authentic components' of identity, liveability and self-representation—regardless, of course, of what his 'real' life might be like or the labour involved in producing these very short instances of playfulness. Being a spectator of playful fun is, according to Alan McKee (2016), a long-recognised cultural practice of entertainment, marked by silliness of sombre reflection, and disguising worthiness, value and virtue in favour of "pleasure without purpose" (pp. 26, 29). In McKee's assessment, entertainment works best historically when it is short and fast, rather than protracted, weighty and philosophical, as we see in the shortening over the twentieth century of popular songs, television episodes, YouTube content (p. 22) and now the even shorter TikTok upload.

TikTok's platform and genre provided, therefore, a perfect fit for Caleb Finn's work to have entertainment value: purposeless, goofy and disguising the labour and sophistication of the art form and editing. The scrolling capability that takes casual users from clip to clip Caleb Finn's content stands out as—arguably—more entertaining than others. And through disguising its sophisticated and careful construction while including material from his personal life, regular shots of his family, his child and his home, the aesthetic of authenticity is taken to a greater level, encouraging a connection with something that at least appears 'real,' even if we know from the beginning that it is not. In other words, Caleb Finn gains celebrity through a careful cultivation of a persona that is pure entertainment on a platform designed precisely to take advantage of contemporary cultural shifts in what 'works' as entertainment. Finally, the framework here encourages the adoption of a celebrity identity performed not through the content but through the extra-curricular activities he now pursues as a full-time content creator: monetising content through sponsorship, attending film openings, wearing clothes provided by avant-garde designers and other behaviours and activities that are widely recognised as the performance of contemporary celebrity. Whether that remains *balanced* with authenticity or if the authentic persona is obscured by celebrity behaviour—as has occurred for many other influencers on earlier platforms (Abidin 2018)—obviously remains to be seen. We can, perhaps, envision TikTok as having an ephemeral appeal, becoming more professionalised over time and seeing authentic amateur content crowded out by more professional and celebrity-driven users.

8.4 TikTok authenticity and the inconvenience of other people

Although TikTok was widely framed as a space for authentic identity representation (with all the conceptual problems that idea brings about the value and reality of authenticity), and while much of the public focus on the platform has shifted very quickly to consider how some users have become celebrities on TikTok while some existing influencers have adopted TikTok as a platform to extend their following, one element that intersects those two is how people attempting to generate popularity have recorded various activities designed to *present themselves as authentic* in ways which are potentially harmful to bystanders. This opens questions about how attempting to align content with an 'authenticity aesthetic' might actually undo authenticity and everyday ethics.

One very notable case has been the use of TikTok by professionals. TikTok has afforded ordinary, everyday users an opportunity at celebrity, particularly once their content begins trending. This has often been because they provide amusing, entertaining or informative content in ways not experienced in other settings. However, those who have innovated at the interface of entertainment and information have drawn attention and cultivated substantial followings, including particularly scientists such as Darrion Nguyễn, who goes by lab_shenanigans on TikTok. The account has over half a million followers and over

16 million content likes. Nguyễn became notable for providing content that crossed a range of types: dancing in the laboratory, humour involving other scientists in everyday lab settings and providing content that described advances in inclusivity for scientists who represent minority backgrounds—all alongside short clips showing experiments and the everyday labour of a research scientist (Bender 2020). Here we have a good example of the crossover between information and entertainment that performs a certain kind of authenticity described above, which is particularly valuable in a field (the applied sciences) that has been rejected by elements of populism in the era of COVID—biochemistry.

However, other professionals working in the cosmetic surgery field have come under marked criticism for their behaviour when entertainment (for others) includes mocking or a perceived lack of care (for patients). For example, cosmetic surgeon Daniel Aronov became an international TikTok celebrity after posting regular content that crossed between informing on cosmetic surgery practices, showing cosmetic operations on video and dancing during the performance of surgery. With 13 million followers, he was among the most viewed internationally of those on TikTok providing content that drew on their professional setting. Aronov was banned by the Australian Health Practitioner Agency (AHPRA), which regulates the work of cosmetic surgeons, after the agency became aware that he was recording clips during surgical procedures, mocking anaesthetised patients, showing removed body fat and the bodies of patients without their consent or knowledge, dancing with his staff during the conduct of surgery and prioritising recording over safety and hygiene (Ferguson and Day 2021; Marshall 2021).

Aronov is not just an example of someone who recorded and shared footage that raised questions about his practice. Rather, he is an example of a TikTok user who presented content within the authenticity aesthetic—in this case, the authentic setting of actual cosmetic surgery combined with the everyday play of entertainment and humour. However, that content utilised patients as part of generating authenticity in ways which would not meet ethical standards if it occurred in other media settings such as film, television news or any format that ordinarily requests participant consent. This presents a problem for the way in which the *culture* of TikTok has cultivated and promoted the authenticity aesthetic as part of the self-identity of its content producers. A sense of authenticity acknowledges that events occur in front of bystanders, and this is one aspect that differentiates TikTok from, say, vlogging practices which more traditionally have involved a talking head to a camera with a tasteful background and only consenting others in the room.

In other contexts, attempts at pushing the authenticity aesthetic through recording apparent acts of kindness using non-consenting bystanders has resulted in criticism and public anger. In one case, a young male TikTok creator posted a video of himself giving a bunch of flowers to an elderly woman sitting alone in a café. The exchange used a recognisable pranking tactic: he asked the woman to hold the flowers while he put on his jacket and then quickly said "have a nice day" and ran off, leaving the confused recipient welling in tears over what at first looked like a generous act of random kindness. The video gained 57 million views after going viral and being further distributed by a tabloid website. The recipient, however, later told a news service that she felt humiliated by someone she thought might be making a lot of money out of a viral video that, therefore, was not indeed an act of random kindness but a cynical use of her reaction. Rightly, she felt that such a video was patronising on the basis of the assumption that an older woman sitting alone was lonely and unloved (Chwasta 2022).

Similar videos that have contributed to this problematic trend of utilising bystanders include the case of TikTok user Rustam Raziev who gained a following from content in which he carefully selects a person at a supermarket pay station and steps in with his card at the moment of payment to pay for their groceries, often with the statement "This is from my heart." In many cases, the recipient of this generosity is a person who looks dishevelled, from a lower socioeconomic background, possibly living close to the poverty line. However, the generation of following and the monetisation of content failed in Raziev's case after one recipient complained to newspapers that he felt traumatised by the unwanted public attention online when people assumed he was a "beggar" and overseas family members contacted the recipient to ask if he was in financial trouble (Vincent 2022).

What we witness here are cases of making a *gain* (financial, monetised content, notoriety and/or followers) through what is sometimes referred to as 'virtue signalling.' Virtue signalling is a term often used to denounce behaviour that is designed to show good character and increase social acceptability but that otherwise is insincere and inauthentic. In the case of gifts of flowers or shopping payments that are conducted not because the content creator is performing a 'good deed' anonymously but because it generates content, likes, praise, followers and thus monetisation of content can be seen to fall into the same practice of insincerity. Those who virtue signal in online settings are contributing to a public persona or online identity that seeks to represent the self as authentic and socially engaged, but given the context of the recording and distribution of such acts is actually contrived and manipulative (Levy 2021). It is particularly notable that much of this content and the commentary from viewers focuses on the reaction from the recipient of this contrived generosity—surprise, happiness, relief or shock—in ways which dehumanise, stereotype or objectify the recipient by making them the focus of content.

Whether discussing a cosmetic surgeon recording their patients during procedures without consent or content creators recording the reactions of contrived acts of generosity in public settings, the effect of public outrage and the accusation of virtue signalling does two things. Firstly, it undoes the curation of authentic identity by instantly generating a public reading position that sees the identity (professional surgeon; generous figure) as explicitly inauthentic. This results in the breakdown of identity in the way described in Chapters 1 and 2 through the accusation of incoherence and unintelligibility. That is, that how they represent themselves does not *align* with their perceived identity, motivation, self-perception and behaviour. Secondly, while such videos might have mass appeal to TikTok followers who gain a sensation from viewing the entertaining or emotional aspects of the content, they broadly disrupt the public perception of TikTok as a setting for authentic, 'real' and 'everyday' content and instead begins to reveal the platform as available for the generation of contrived content—similar to other platforms but in this case attempting to use an authenticity aesthetic for hits.

8.5 Conclusion

In trying to make sense of the relationship between TikTok as an emerging, highly popular platform and the practices of identity in digital communication settings, it is important to bear in mind one of the points described above: no identity is truly authentic because authenticity always fails in the construction of identity, whether in pre-digital or post-digital times. Rather, in some contexts, identities are performed through what I have described as an aesthetic of authenticity, using behaviours, representations, contexts and alignments that make a particular practice of self-identity appear to be authentic, real, grounded, everyday, non-constructed or non-contrived.

TikTok has afforded and enabled such seemingly authentic performances in ways which points not just to how TikTok's culture of content creation is oriented towards the simple and everyday but to how users found a way to gratify or fulfil a deep-seated cultural desire for simple, everyday storytelling that was entertaining, grounded and represented a particular kind of reality. This groundedness had existed on other earlier platforms (such as YouTube's genre of vlogging) but has often been sidelined on those platforms in favour of more professionalised, curated, cultivated and sophisticated content which—not quite rightly—has been seen as somehow 'less authentic.'

Given some of the developments we have seen in TikTok such as the growth of celebrity culture, the professionalisation of video production and the way bystanders have been cynically used by content creators, it is unclear if TikTok will remain a setting marked by an authenticity aesthetic or go the same way as other platforms. At this stage, it is definitely a case of 'watch this space…'

Key points

- TikTok has widely been regarded as a platform providing opportunities for more authentic identity representation. However, since real authenticity is 'unknowable' to ourselves, we might regard it as a platform culture based on an 'authenticity aesthetic.'
- The authenticity aesthetic provides codes of practice for content that is grounded in identity, everydayness, fun, entertainment and silliness. This is just as legitimate a form as any professional content.
- The attempt to align content with an authenticity aesthetic has had both positive and negative consequences. Negative consequences include the use of bystanders without consent and virtue signalling, thereby undoing authenticity claims.

References

Abidin, C., 2018. *Internet Celebrity: Understanding Fame Online*. London: Emerald.

Abidin, C. and Cover, R., 2018. Gay, famous and working hard on YouTube: influencers, queer microcelebrity publics, and discursive activism. *In*: P. Aggleton, R. Cover, D. Leahy, D. Marshall, M. L. Rasmussen, eds. *Youth, Sexuality and Sexual Citizenship*. London and New York: Routledge, 217–231.

Agence France-Presse in Cairo, 2020. Egypt jails women for two years over TikTok videos. *The Guardian*, 28 July. Available from: www.theguardian.com/world/2020/jul/27/egypt-jails-women-for-two-years-over-tiktok-videos [Accessed 18 July 2022].

Albury, K., 2019. 'Recognition of competition' versus Will to App: rethinking digital engagement in Australian youth sexual health promotion policy and practice. *Media International Australia*, 171 (1), 38–50.

Bender, M., 2020. Meet Darrion Nguyen, the Bill Nye of millennials. *Inverse*, 2 September. Available from: www.inverse.com/science/meet-darrion-nguyen-the-bill-nye-of-millennials [Accessed 12 June 2022].

Blumler, J. G. and Katz, E., 1974. *The Uses of Mass Communications: Current Perspectives on Gratifications Research*. London: Sage.

Boffone, T., 2021. *Renegades: Digital Dance Cultures from Dubsmash to TikTok*. New York: Oxford University Press.

Boffone, T., 2022. Introduction: the rise of TikTok in US culture. *In*: T. Boffone, ed. *TikTok Cultures in the United States*. London & New York: Routledge, 1–13.

Burgess, J. and Green, J., 2009. *YouTube: Online Video and Participatory Culture*. Cambridge: Polity.

Carman, A., 2020. TikTok reaches 2 billion downloads. *The Verge*, 29 April. Available from: www.theverge.com/2020/4/29/21241788/tiktok-app-download-numbers-update-2-billion-users [Accessed 20 July 2022].

Chwasta, M., 2022. Melbourne woman featured in viral TikTok video without consent says she feels 'dehumanised.' *ABC News*, 14 July. Available from: www.abc.net.au/news/2022-07-14/tiktok-video-maree-melbourne-flowers/101228418?utm_medium=social&utm_content=sf25 8454571&ut%E2%80%A6 [Accessed 14 July 2022].

Cohen, D., 2020. Nielsen study commissioned by TikTok examines community, authenticity, positivity. *AdWeek*, 5 October. Available from: www.adweek.com/programmatic/nielsen-study-commissioned-by-tiktok-examines-community-authenticity-positivity/ [Accessed 20 July 2022].

Cover, R., 2013. Reading the remix: methods for researching and analysing the interactive textuality of remix. *M-C: Journal of Media and Culture*, 16 (4). Available from: https://journal.media-culture.org.au/index.php/mcjournal/article/view/686 [Accessed 20 June 2022].

Cover, R., 2019. *Emergent Identities: New Sexualities, Gender and Relationships in a Digital Era*. London & New York: Routledge.

Cover, R., Haw, A. and Thompson, J. D., 2022. *Fake News in Digital Cultures: Technology, Populism and Digital Misinformation*. London: Emerald Publishing.

Dexter, R., 2021. School teacher to online influencer: introducing Melbourne's TikTok megastars. *The Age*, 30 May. Available from: www.theage.com.au/national/victoria/school-teacher-to-onl ine-influencer-introducing-melbourne-s-tiktok-megastars-20210527-p57vpq.html [Accessed 21 June 2022].

Ferguson, A. and Day, L., 2021. TikTok star Dr Daniel Aronov banned by regulator from performing cosmetic surgery. *ABC News*, 29 November. Available from: www.abc.net.au/news/2021-11-29/tiktok-celebrity-cosmetic-surgeon-daniel-aronov-banned/100659694 [Accessed 14 June 2022].

Foucault, M., 1980. *Power/Knowledge: Selected Interviews & Other Writings 1972–1977*, ed. C. Gordon, trans. C. Gordon et al. New York: Pantheon.

Fung, B., 2022. FCC Commissioner calls on Apple and Google to remove TikTok from their app stores. *CNN Business*, 29 June. Available from: https://edition.cnn.com/2022/06/29/tech/fcc-google-apple-tiktok-block/index.html [Accessed 22 July 2022].

Guillaume, J., 2021. More to TikTok than viral dance trends—and these Aussies are proving it. *Sydney Morning Herald*, 20 June. Available from: www.smh.com.au/culture/tv-and-radio/more-to-tiktok-than-viral-dance-trends-and-these-aussies-are-proving-it-20210618-p5825q.html [Accessed 22 July 2022].

Hutchinson, A., 2021. TikTok shares new insights into why people use the app, and how it celebrates authenticity. *Social Media Today*, 20 October. Available from: www.socialmediatoday.com/news/tiktok-shares-new-insights-into-why-people-use-the-app-and-how-it-celebrat/608617/ [Accessed 22 July 2022].

Levy, N., 2021. Virtue signalling is virtuous. *Synthese*, 198, 9545–9562. Available from: https://link.springer.com/article/10.1007/s11229-020-02653-9 [Accessed 21 July 2022].

Marshall, S., 2021. TikTok plastic surgeon banned from performing cosmetic procedures. *A Current Affair*, November. Available from: https://9now.nine.com.au/a-current-affair/dr-daniel-aro nov-banned-plastic-surgeon/f64e173d-c338-4a93-a9d7-bc76394c57be [Accessed 9 July 2022].

McKee, A., 2016. *Fun! What Entertainment Tells Us About Living a Good Life*. London: Palgrave Macmillan.

Miller, D. and Sinanan, J., 2014. *Webcam*. London: Polity.

Moftah, L. and Lorenz, T., 2022. Chasing TikTok Dreams in the 'New Black Hollywood.' *New York Times*, 27 January. Available from: www.nytimes.com/article/who-gets-to-be-an-influencer.html [Accessed 22 July 2022].

Radhakrishnan, R., 1996. *Diasporic Mediations: Between Home and Location*. Minneapolis: University of Minnesota Press.

Storey, J., 1993. *An Introduction to Cultural Theory and Popular Culture*. New York: Harvester Wheatsheaf.

Su, X., 2020. The trouble With TikTok's global rise. *The News Lens*, 8 May. Available from: https://international.thenewslens.com/article/134846 [Accessed 18 July 2022].

Third, A., Collin, P., Walsh, L. and Black, R., 2020. *Young People in Digital Society: Control Shift*. London: Palgrave.

Vaterlaus, J. M. and Winter, M., 2021. TikTok: an exploratory study of young adults' uses and gratifications. *The Social Science Journal*. Available from: https://doi.org/10.1080/03623319.2021.1969882 [Accessed 29 July 2022].

Vincent, P., 2022. TikTok star's 'random act of kindness' spectacularly backfires as shopper is left 'traumatised' when he pays for his groceries at the supermarket: 'I'm not a beggar.' *Daily Mail*, 23 July. Available from: www.dailymail.co.uk/news/article-11041551/Afghan-asylum-seeker-traumatised-TikTok-star-Rustam-Raziev-pays-groceries-viral-video.html [Accessed 24 July 2022].

Wyn, J. and Woodman, D., 2006. Generation, youth and social change in Australia. *Journal of Youth Studies*, 9 (5), 495–514.

Zhang, K., 2018. 'I risked my life, please like!' mobile app TikTok has Hong Kong children craving acceptance—and some are going to dangerous extremes. *South China Morning Post*, 19 May. Available from: www.scmp.com/news/hong-kong/community/article/2146904/i-risked-my-life-please-mobile-app-tik-tok-has-hong-kong [Accessed 18 July 2022].

9 Futures

The self in development

9.1 Introduction

In this brief conclusion, I would like to work through what we have learned about the fast-developing framework of digital communication and the ways in which it enables, constrains and facilitates practices of identity.

I would then like to discuss some of the new predicted developments in what is sometimes referred to as the 'metaverse,' an artificial scape that combines the tangible objects with visual and aural intangibilities that are computer generated, and in which we are expected to see the development of artificial companions that rely on algorithmic culture to develop responsive relationships with users. What might it mean for identity when we develop relationships with purely digital objects that mimic pets, children, friends, companions and others?

9.2 Digital communication and identity

Whenever we discuss identity we have to begin with the premise that whatever identity is, its truth or reality is unknowable. We only have knowledge frameworks and practices of storytelling available to us to make it sensible and understandable. With that in mind, any of the theories of identity, whether liberal, psychological, psychoanalytic, Marxist or poststructuralist, are simply theories, ways of knowing or what I like to call different 'lenses' that allow us to see ourselves, our belonging, our ways of relating to each other and our society in different forms or registers. With that in mind, poststructuralist theories of identity have, I argue, provided the most useful because they acknowledge that even though we may go through life feeling like we have an identity and that we know ourselves, they are most sophisticated at explaining why, without trying to provide an all-encompassing truth of identity.

By understanding identity not as a form or substance but as a set of non-voluntary, reiterative *performances* that respond to the cultural demands of being a coherent, intelligible subject, communication is put at the very centre of identity. That is, no performative identity makes sense unless it is expressed, articulated and communicated. At the same time, no framework of storytelling that gives us the knowledge to know what *is* a coherent and intelligible identity happens without some form of communication. In a media- and digitally saturated contemporary culture, we cannot discount the fact that the setting in which knowledge-gathering and identity performance occurs not only includes digital communication but is increasingly dominated by it.

DOI: 10.4324/9781003296652-9

In Chapter 2, I outlined some of the ways in which factors of contemporary digital communication such as *interactivity* have presented a very substantial shift in how we acquire and understand knowledge (because we now interact, edit, remix and adapt those knowledge texts) and how we perform online (because we have a complex array of social media profiles through which to perform, alongside the interactions from others on those identity performances, such as tagging, commenting and conversing). What that means is that the 'labour' of performing a coherent identity is substantially more intensive and more difficult than it was previously, and this may be one of the reasons why we see anxieties over the question 'who am I?' becoming more substantial in everyday life.

One of the problems of understanding the relationship between digital communication and identity has been the fact that there is a tendency to disavow the role of the body. This, as I explained in Chapter 3, is the result of older discourses of cyberculture and the Internet that aligned the body with 'real' and the mind with 'virtual.' There, I pointed to the fact that the separation between mind and body is philosophically outdated but continues to have purchase in contemporary thinking. However, once we look at examples as to how we *use* digital communication (through devices that interact with our body) and once we *see* what is digitally communicated today (endless representations of the body in different forms, whether selfies or avatars), we have to understand the body as very central to that relationship between selfhood and digital worlds—indeed, it is *all* about the body. That fact, of course, opens significant questions around representation, differences, stereotypes and accessibility, and we need to acknowledge that the freedom of identity expression online is not enjoyed universally or equitably from the perspective of bodies and their abilities.

Chapter 4 allowed us to think deeper about the representation of bodies in the context of new developments in digital culture. The deepfake has enabled significant creative shifts by providing the tools to make very realistic representations of people that look like recordings but are actually placing the face and voice on a recording of someone else. More advanced than photoshopping, this has real implications for the embodiment of identities. While the technology allows films to 'resurrect' dead actors and organisations to make it look like a real person was giving a speech when they simply recorded a voice, it also opens the possibility of identity fraud, misrepresentation and disinformation. And this opens serious questions for identity.

Making sense of bodies and identity also means locating our digital communication practices in place and concepts of space. Chapter 5 worked through some of the competing notions of place and space, particularly globalisation (which has long been associated with the Internet), the local (where obviously our engagement with devices occurs) and the national (which is represented in different ways but which also is involved in regulatory practices that are sometimes thought to be 're-nationalising' digital communication through legal measures that will make online experiences differ in different nation-states). How we navigate the global, local and national facets of identity has therefore become more complex due to regulatory measures.

Another way in which our digital identities are made more complex is in light of the massive increase in online hate speech and digital hostility (cyberbullying, trolling, pile-ons, doxxing and so on). While we need to be careful not to blame digital communication for hostility, polarisation and adversarial behaviours, they have certainly found a home online in ways which have, for some, created a very toxic environment. Chapter 6 considered some of the ways in which that toxicity is about identities and other ways in which experiencing online toxicity, shaming, callouts and cancellation play a role in destabilising identity and making lives less liveable.

Exploring another set of new digital developments, Chapter 7 took to task some of the moral panic, alarmism and techno-pessimism that dominates public discussions about algorithms. While we do not want to make good-versus-bad judgements, it is necessary to consider how algorithms present both opportunities and challenges for an important element in identity: sense of agency. By shaping what knowledge is accessed and by undertaking tasks on our behalf whether managing home devices or driving decision-making in the workplace, we need to consider how algorithms foster changes to the frameworks by which we perform identities and gain knowledges to make identities intelligible.

TikTok was widely hailed as a new setting for genuine, authentic identity performances, although Chapter 8 disagreed with that sentiment, arguing instead that TikTok is marked by what I have called an 'authenticity aesthetic.' This has had positive implications (bringing everydayness further into content creation in contrast to the more professionalised content found in older platforms today) and implications for ethics (particularly where users have drawn in non-consenting bystanders in order to increase their own performance of an authentic identity). TikTok is a great example of yet another new development in digital communication that is shifting some of the frameworks of identity, although we do not yet know quite how that will look in the future.

9.3 The metaverse and beyond

To end this book, I would like to make a few brief remarks about some near-future developments in digital culture that, arguably, will impinge or change how we think about identities. Trying to predict future developments in digital communication and its role in identity practices is not an easy task. We often need to rely on science fiction and speculative writing to get a sense of where technologies are going and how they may form part of the 'future.' This is not because science fiction writers, filmmakers and fans develop ideas that are later taken up as technologies. Rather, because these genres of thinking and writing often reflect the cultural desires, demands and imaginings which are already at play, providing stories which not only use imaginative futures to reflect on our current socio-political and cultural experiences but inform us how those actively foreseen technologies might 'fit' within culture, identity and society of the near future (Cover 2011). For example, *Star Trek's* handheld communicator from the 1960s can be said not only to predict but also to reflect the advent in the late 1970s and 1980s of the mobile phone. The touchscreen tablets that were used in the 1980s series *Star Trek: The Next Generation* clearly reflect the development that was going into iPads, tablets and touchscreen laptops as well as smartphones, and that series communicator device worn on the uniform reflects the cultural desires for wearable technology controlled without the presence of a smartphone that are becoming commonplace today.

These are just a few examples of how the very ideas of technologies are actively part of cultural representation, understanding that if a technology was truly alien and therefore truly changing cultural processes of communication, it would be unthinkable even in the most speculative of science fiction. That is not to say that technologies do not have unforeseen uses and gratifications that come from particularly innovative uses, only that they should not be seen as being the *source* of change. Whether that is a change to cultural and communication practices or if it is changes to how we think about ourselves, those changes are always emergent from within cultural processes, and communication technologies are *part of those processes.*

9.3.1 The metaverse

One area of technological development that has been getting some considerable journalistic coverage is the metaverse. Building on existing practices of virtual reality (VR) and augmented reality (AR), the metaverse has been defined as a post-reality universe that merges our multisensory bodily spaces with virtual enhancement (Mystakidis 2022). It is understood to provide a framework for interacting simultaneously with our physical spaces and digital artefacts, such as using glasses and other sensory devices to redecorate our living room, bring the image of a person into our space when we converse online, add to our sensory repertoire by providing digitised and simulated smell and increase a sense of digital immersion without the restrictions of geographic surrounds. For example, the metaverse may enable us to attend a digital party and 'feel like' we are realistically interacting with our friends without leaving home. Or it can enable an archaeology student to feel and sense what it is like to be on a real dig without going to the site.

One prediction circulating in popular discourse about the metaverse is the idea that algorithmic culture is now well adapted to help the metaverse provide us with digital offspring within the next 50 years. According to Catriona Campbell (2022), virtual children who can be designed, grow up and age in normative time, learn from us, talk to us, play with us and be cuddled could be experienced using tools that are increasingly available, from algorithms and machine learning that adapt the growth and learning of a child across a lifecycle, gloves and other wearable technology that mimic the sensation of hugging or holding a child and wearable audiovisual aids that allow that child to be seen, heard and engaged with in our homes or public settings. While the idea of artificial children created and run by computer networks that manage their interaction and their growth may seem slightly horrifying, part of Cambell's argument in favour of digital children is that would allow people to *experience* caring for a child over a lengthy period of time without contributing to an already overpopulated world (Ough and Nanu 2022).

Indeed, while we are culturally positioned by a long-standing assumption that population growth is broadly good, religiously sanctioned or a benefit to the well-being and economic growth of various nation-states (Cover 2020), and while it is true that there has been a counter-argument that presents alarm over the rapid growth of the global population of human beings and what that might mean for environmental change, common access to resources and general liveability (Ehrlich 1968), there has not been until now been much consideration as to how to provide alternatives to those who deeply desire raising and caring for children. Any parent knows that their identity is shaped by their relationship with their offspring. What will happen, then, if and when we begin relating to digital children? Is it merely a simulation that leaves our identities static? Or will we be constituted in a relationship with the simulacra of a child—a child who is an improvement on the real? Can we love a digital child?

Again, elements of this thinking have appeared in recent science fiction in similar forms: the technologically speculative television series *Black Mirror* has represented the idea of an algorithmically generated boyfriend to replace a young woman's deceased fiancé. In that series, a cloud-based programme used machine learning based on inputs from her dead partner's social media to generate a personality that, at first, could communicate with her by textual messages and, once it had learned the young man's voice, could then speak to her on the phone, mimicking the 'real' that she had lost. Eventually, a robotic device was able to be built and sold to her that looked and acted (more or less) like her deceased partner, providing her with the experience of touch, being held and a sexual life. The series explored the identity crisis that such virtuality creates—a sense of well-being, a problematic psychological disavowal or postponement of grieving, the potential for others to condemn her for her 'fake' relationship and questions about what might be an ethical relationship with a non-human mimicking a deceased 'real' person in the near future.

There may, to some, appear to be a certain kind of selfishness in wanting a digital child to whom an attachment is not built on risk (the risk they are harmed, the risk we may outlive a child, the risk they do not love us back). However, the same technology may be valuable in allowing people to manage grieving a lost loved one, to manage loneliness in old age, to be assisted in infirmity in a way that realistically mimics genuine care or to enhance our interactions the next time a pandemic forces us into seclusion and isolation.

Our identities are always formed and constituted in relation to others—no one on the planet is so fully alone that we do not perform our identities in interdependency with others (Butler 2020). However, we might ask here what it would mean if our identities are constituted in relationalities with non-human metaverse families, friends, children, pets and carers that were fully generated within algorithmic culture and reliant on machine learning and artificial intelligence systems? Are these relationships real? Are we in a loving relationship because the experience of a virtual lover might so closely mimic the realities of domestic partnership? Just as people cared for and loved Tamagotchi devices in the 1990s, are we engaged in care and affection for virtual others? There are a lot of questions to ask, and no answers that can be given in advance. The only thing we know is that this will have built on the existing intersection of digital culture and identity practices that has been covered in this book, taking many of these to a new level while overturning some aspects that are no longer needed.

References

Butler, J., 2020. *The Force of Nonviolence: An Ethico-Political Bind*. London: Verso.

Campbell, C., 2022. *AI By Design: A Plan for Living with Artificial Intelligence*. London & New York: Routledge.

Cover, R., 2011. Generating the self: the biopolitics of security and selfhood in Star Trek: The Next Generation. *Science Fiction Film & Television*, 4 (2), 205–224.

Cover, R., 2020. *Population, Mobility and Belonging: Understanding Population Concepts in Media, Culture and Society*. London & New York: Routledge.

Ehrlich, P. R., 1968. *The Population Bomb*. New York: Ballantine.

Mystakidis, S., 2022. Metaverse. *Encyclopedia*, 2 (1), 486–497.

Ough, T. and Nanu, M., 2022. Digital offspring will replace human babies, says AI expert. *The Age*, 31 May. Available from: www.theage.com.au/world/europe/digital-offspring-will-replace-human-babies-says-ai-expert-20220531-p5apsb.html [Accessed 31 May 2022].

Index

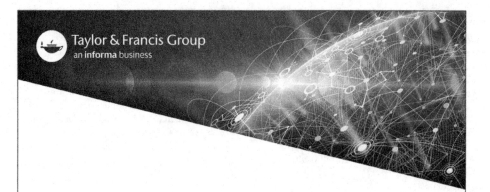